I0815711

ENGLISH
FOR EVERYONE
LIBRO DE EJERCICIOS
NIVEL 4 AVANZADO

AUDIO GRATUITO
www.dkefe.com

Autora

Claire Hart es autora independiente de textos para el aprendizaje del inglés. Ha publicado una gran variedad de materiales y ha creado distintos cursos en línea. Es profesora de inglés en la Universidad de Ciencias Aplicadas de Neu-Ulm, en Alemania.

Consultor del curso

Tim Bowen ha enseñado inglés y ha formado profesores en más de 30 países en todo el mundo. Es coautor de libros sobre la enseñanza de la pronunciación y sobre la metodología de la enseñanza de idiomas, y autor de numerosos libros para profesores de inglés. Actualmente se dedica a la escritura de materiales, la edición y la traducción. Es miembro del Chartered Institute of Linguists.

Consultora lingüística

La profesora **Susan Barduhn** cuenta con una gran experiencia en la enseñanza del inglés y la formación de profesores. Como autora ha participado en numerosas publicaciones. Además de dirigir cursos de inglés en cuatro continentes, ha sido presidenta de la Asociación Internacional de Profesores de Inglés como Lengua Extranjera y asesora del British Council y del Departamento de Estado de Estados Unidos. Actualmente es profesora de la School for International Training en Vermont, Estados Unidos.

ENGLISH FOR EVERYONE

LIBRO DE EJERCICIOS

NIVEL 4 AVANZADO

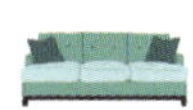

SEGUNDA EDICIÓN
Edición sénior Ankita Awasthi Tröger
Edición Beth Blakemore
Edición de arte Amy Child
Edición ejecutiva Carine Tracanelli
Edición ejecutiva de arte Anna Hall
Edición de producción Gillian Reid
Control de producción sénior Poppy David
Diseño de cubierta sénior Surabhi Wadhwa-Gandhi
Dirección de desarrollo de diseño de cubierta Sophia MTT
Dirección editorial Andrew Macintyre
Dirección de arte Karen Self
Dirección de publicaciones Jonathan Metcalf

DK INDIA
Coordinación sénior de cubiertas Priyanka Sharma Saddi
Diseño de maquetación Rakesh Kumar

PRIMERA EDICIÓN
Asistencia editorial Jessica Cawthra, Sarah Edwards
Ilustración Edwood Burn, Denise Joos, Michael Parkin, Jemma Westing
Producción de audio Liz Hammond
Edición ejecutiva Daniel Mills
Edición ejecutiva de arte Anna Hall
Dirección de proyecto Christine Stroyan
Producción, preproducción Luca Frassinetti
Producción Mary Slater
Diseño de cubierta Natalie Godwin
Edición de cubierta Claire Gell
Dirección de desarrollo de diseño de cubierta Sophia MTT
Dirección editorial Andrew Macintyre
Dirección de arte Karen Self
Dirección de publicaciones Jonathan Metcalf

DK INDIA
Edición sénior Vineetha Mokkil, Anita Kakar
Edición sénior de arte Chhaya Sajwan
Edición del proyecto Antara Moitra
Edición Agnibesh Das, Nisha Shaw, Seetha Natesh
Edición de arte Namita, Heena Sharma, Sukriti Sobti, Shipra Jain, Aanchal Singhal
Asistencia editorial Ira Pundeer, Ateendriya Gupta, Sneha Sunder Benjamin, Ankita Yadav
Asistencia editorial de arte Roshni Kapur, Meenal Goel, Priyansha Tuli
Ilustración Ivy Roy, Arun Pottirayil, Bharti Karakoti, Rahul Kumar
Documentación iconográfica Deepak Negi
Edición ejecutiva Pakshalika Jayaprakash
Edición ejecutiva de arte Arunesh Talapatra
Dirección de proyecto Pankaj Sharma
Dirección de preproducción Balwant Singh
Diseño de maquetación sénior Vishal Bhatia, Neeraj Bhatia
Diseño de maquetación Sachin Gupta
Diseño de cubierta Surabhi Wadhwa
Edición ejecutiva de cubiertas Saloni Singh
Diseño de maquetación sénior Harish Aggarwal

DE LA EDICIÓN EN ESPAÑOL
Servicios editoriales Tinta Simpàtica
Traducción Anna Nualart
Coordinación de proyecto Cristina Sánchez Bustamante
Dirección editorial Elsa Vicente

Publicado originalmente en Gran Bretaña en 2016, 2024 por Dorling Kindersley Limited
DK, 20 Vauxhall Bridge Road, Londres, SW1V 2SA
Parte de Penguin Random House

Copyright © 2016, 2024 Dorling Kindersley Limited
© Traducción española: 2016, 2026 Dorling Kindersley Limited
002-348945-Feb/2026

Título original: *English For Everyone. Practice Book. Level 4. Advanced*
Segunda edición: 2026

Reservados todos los derechos.
Queda prohibida, salvo excepción prevista en la ley, cualquier forma de reproducción, distribución, comunicación pública y transformación de esta obra sin la autorización escrita de los titulares de la propiedad intelectual.

ISBN: 979-8-2171-3540-0

Impreso y encuadernado en China

www.dkespañol.com

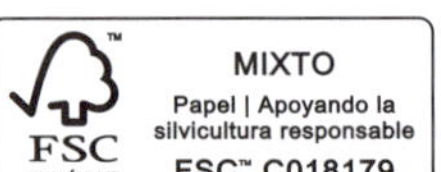

Este libro se ha impreso con papel certificado por el Forest Stewardship Council™ como parte del compromiso de DK por un futuro sostenible. Más información: **www.dk.com/uk/information/sustainability**

Contenidos

Cómo funciona el curso

English for Everyone está pensado para todas aquellas personas que quieren aprender inglés por su cuenta. Como cualquier curso de idiomas, cubre las habilidades básicas: gramática, vocabulario, pronunciación, escucha, conversación, lectura y escritura. A diferencia de otros cursos, todo ello se practica y aprende de forma enormemente visual, con el apoyo de gráficos e imágenes que te ayudarán a entender y a recordar. Los ejercicios de este volumen están pensados para consolidar lo aprendido en el libro de estudio. Sigue las unidades por orden y utiliza al máximo los audios disponibles en la web.

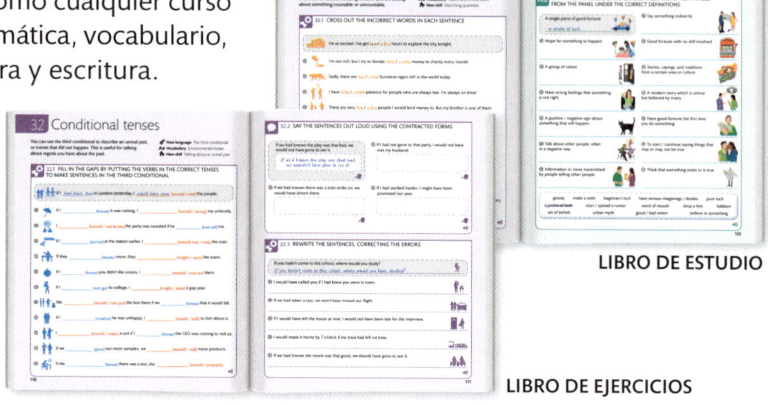

LIBRO DE ESTUDIO

LIBRO DE EJERCICIOS

Número de unidad Este libro está dividido en unidades. En cada una de ellas se practica lo aprendido en la misma unidad del libro de estudio.

Qué vas a practicar La unidad comienza con un resumen de lo que practicarás en ella.

Módulos Cada unidad se compone de distintos módulos que debes seguir por orden. Puedes tomarte un descanso tras completar cualquiera de ellos.

59 The future perfect

You can use the future perfect to talk about events that will overlap with, or finish before, another event in the future.

New language The future perfect
Aa Vocabulary Life plans
New skill Making plans and predictions

59.1 FILL IN THE GAPS BY PUTTING THE VERBS IN THE FUTURE PERFECT

By next March, I *will have bought* (buy) my own house.

1. I ______ (finish) my degree by the time I am 22.
2. You ______ (be) married for one year in a week's time.
3. We ______ (complete) all our essays by the end of June.
4. By the time I am 24, I ______ (find) a good job.
5. I think my son ______ (propose) to his girlfriend by the end of the year.
6. By the time we are 30, we ______ (have) our first child.
7. Liza ______ (move) to London by the end of the month.
8. I ______ (graduate) from college by this time next year.
9. By the time I am 25, I ______ (leave) my parents' house.
10. I ______ (make) one million dollars by the time I'm 40.
11. They ______ (start) their new business by the end of the month.

196

59.2 REWRITE THE HIGHLIGHTED PHRASES, CORRECTING THE ERRORS

will have taken

59.3 SAY THE SENTENCES OUT LOUD, FILL

Ken *will have read* (read) all his textboo

1. They ______ (choose) the bes
2. Jenny ______ (buy) a new dres
3. By the end of the year, I
4. I ______ (open) all my presents
5. By the time he starts his new job, Hans
6. We ______ (visit) 15 countries

Vocabulario Las páginas de vocabulario ponen a prueba tu memoria sobre las palabras y las expresiones clave que has aprendido en el libro de estudio.

Guía visual Imágenes y gráficos te dan pistas visuales que te ayudan a fijar en la memoria las palabras más importantes.

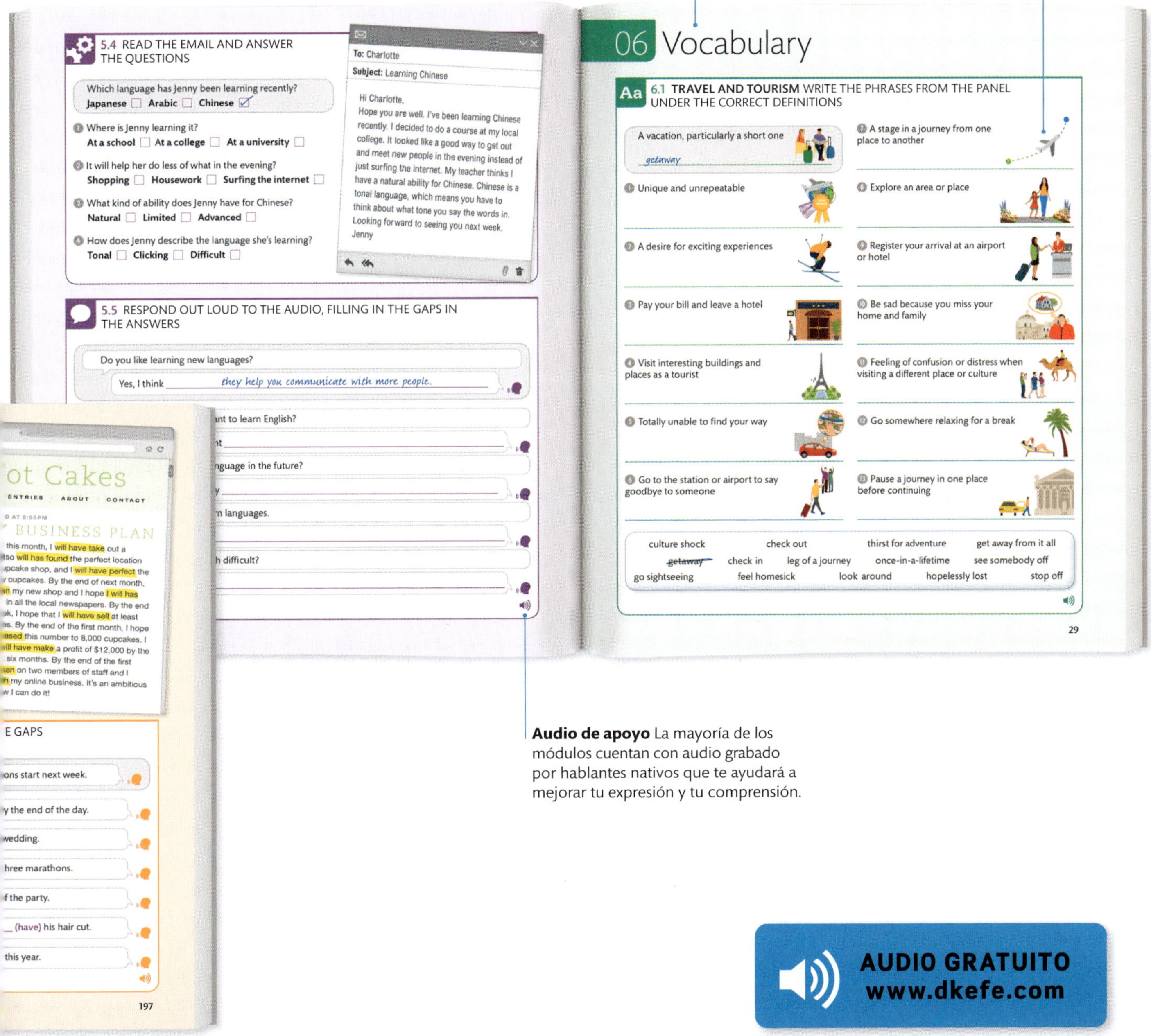

Audio de apoyo La mayoría de los módulos cuentan con audio grabado por hablantes nativos que te ayudará a mejorar tu expresión y tu comprensión.

Módulos de ejercicios

Cada ejercicio está cuidadosamente graduado para que profundices y contrastes lo que has aprendido en la unidad. Si haces los ejercicios a medida que avanzas, asimilarás y recordarás mejor los conceptos, y tu inglés será más fluido. Cada ejercicio indica con un símbolo qué habilidad vas a practicar con él.

GRAMÁTICA
Aplica las nuevas reglas en distintos contextos.

LECTURA
Analiza ejemplos del idioma en textos reales en inglés.

ESCUCHA
Comprueba tu comprensión del inglés hablado.

VOCABULARIO
Consolida tu comprensión del vocabulario clave.

CONVERSACIÓN
Compara tu dicción con los audios de muestra.

Número de módulo Cada módulo tiene su propio número, para que te sea fácil localizar las respuestas y el audio correspondiente.

Instrucciones En cada ejercicio tienes unas breves instrucciones que te dicen qué debes hacer.

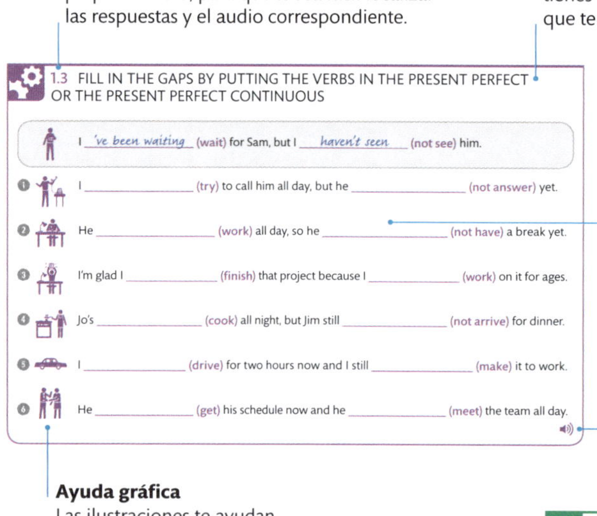

Espacio para escribir Es útil que escribas las respuestas en el libro, pues te servirán para repasar lo aprendido.

Audio de apoyo Este símbolo indica que las respuestas a los ejercicios están disponibles en grabaciones de audio. Escúchalas tras completar el ejercicio.

Ayuda gráfica
Las ilustraciones te ayudan a entender los ejercicios.

Respuesta de ejemplo
La primera respuesta ya está escrita, para que entiendas mejor el ejercicio.

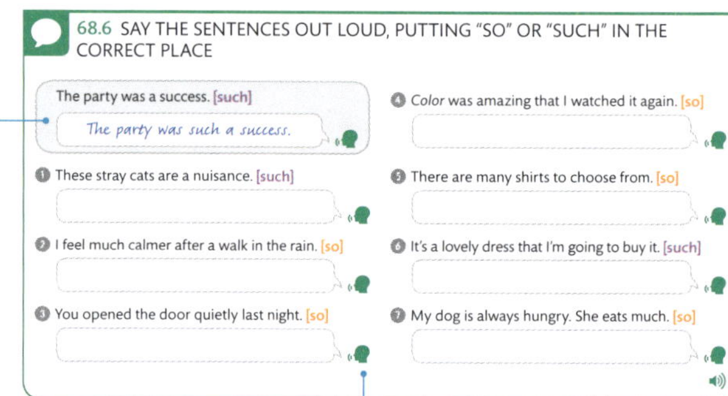

Ejercicios de escucha
Este símbolo te avisa de que debes escuchar el audio para poder responder a las preguntas.

Ejercicio de conversación
Este símbolo indica que debes decir las respuestas en voz alta y compararlas a continuación con su audio correspondiente.

Audio

English for Everyone incorpora abundantes materiales en audio. Te recomendamos que los utilices al máximo, pues te ayudarán a mejorar tu comprensión del inglés hablado y a lograr una pronunciación y un acento más naturales. Escucha cada audio tantas veces como quieras. Páusalo y vuelve atrás en los pasajes que te resulten difíciles, hasta que estés seguro de que has entendido bien lo que se dice.

EJERCICIOS DE ESCUCHA
Este símbolo indica que debes escuchar el audio a fin de poder responder las preguntas del ejercicio.

AUDIO DE APOYO
Este símbolo indica que dispones de audios adicionales que puedes escuchar tras completar el módulo.

Respuestas

Al final del libro tienes una sección con las respuestas correctas de todos los ejercicios. Consúltala al terminar cada módulo y compara tus respuestas con los ejemplos para comprobar si has entendido bien los contenidos que has estado practicando.

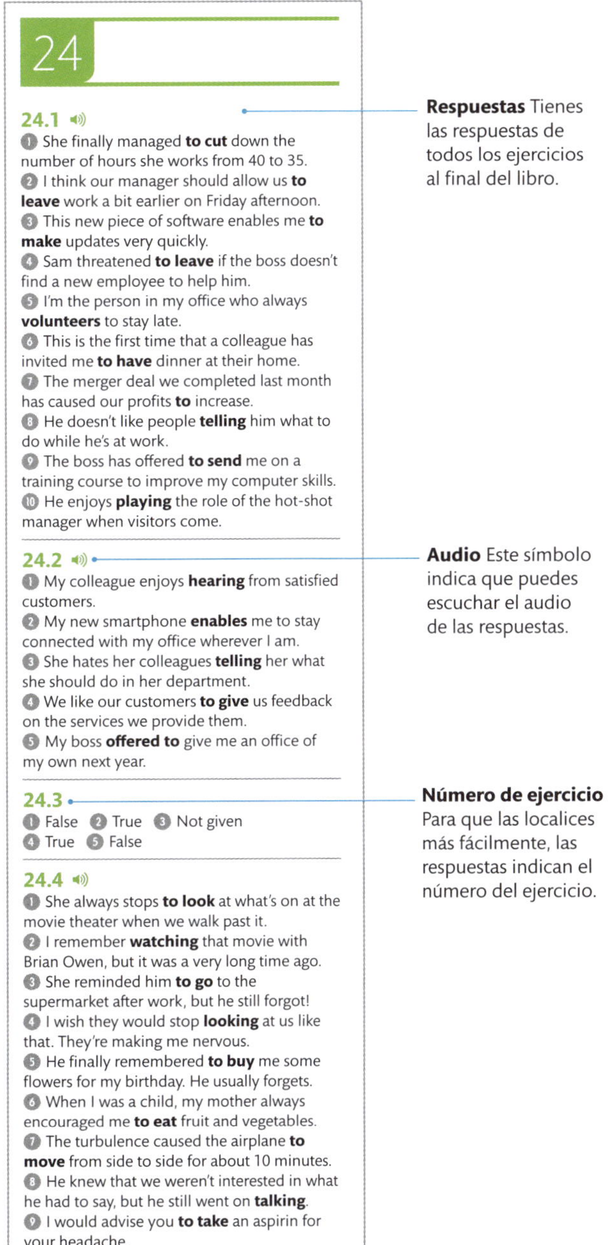

24

24.1
1. She finally managed **to cut** down the number of hours she works from 40 to 35.
2. I think our manager should allow us **to leave** work a bit earlier on Friday afternoon.
3. This new piece of software enables me **to make** updates very quickly.
4. Sam threatened **to leave** if the boss doesn't find a new employee to help him.
5. I'm the person in my office who always **volunteers** to stay late.
6. This is the first time that a colleague has invited me **to have** dinner at their home.
7. The merger deal we completed last month has caused our profits **to** increase.
8. He doesn't like people **telling** him what to do while he's at work.
9. The boss has offered **to send** me on a training course to improve my computer skills.
10. He enjoys **playing** the role of the hot-shot manager when visitors come.

24.2
1. My colleague enjoys **hearing** from satisfied customers.
2. My new smartphone **enables** me to stay connected with my office wherever I am.
3. She hates her colleagues **telling** her what she should do in her department.
4. We like our customers **to give** us feedback on the services we provide them.
5. My boss **offered to** give me an office of my own next year.

24.3
1. False 2. True 3. Not given
4. True 5. False

24.4
1. She always stops **to look** at what's on at the movie theater when we walk past it.
2. I remember **watching** that movie with Brian Owen, but it was a very long time ago.
3. She reminded him **to go** to the supermarket after work, but he still forgot!
4. I wish they would stop **looking** at us like that. They're making me nervous.
5. He finally remembered **to buy** me some flowers for my birthday. He usually forgets.
6. When I was a child, my mother always encouraged me **to eat** fruit and vegetables.
7. The turbulence caused the airplane **to move** from side to side for about 10 minutes.
8. He knew that we weren't interested in what he had to say, but he still went on **talking**.
9. I would advise you **to take** an aspirin for your headache.

01 Making conversation

Verbs have various forms in the present tense, including continuous and perfect. You need to understand these differences when making question tags.

New language Present tenses
Aa Vocabulary Meeting new people
New skill Using question tags

1.1 MARK THE SENTENCES THAT ARE CORRECT

Today is being my first day in my new job at the bank. ☐
Today is my first day in my new job at the bank. ☑

1. I'm being a sales assistant in a department store that opened recently. ☐
   I'm a sales assistant in a department store that opened recently. ☐

2. Hurry up! The bus is coming. If we miss it, we will be late for work. ☐
   Hurry up! The bus comes. If we miss it, we will be late for work. ☐

3. I'm meeting my new team leader right now to discuss plans for next year. ☐
   I meet my new team leader right now to discuss plans for next year. ☐

4. I'm getting up at 7 o'clock every day to get to the office on time. ☐
   I get up at 7 o'clock every day to get to the office on time. ☐

5. I'm always having a coffee break at 10 o'clock so I can work faster. ☐
   I always have a coffee break at 10 o'clock so I can work faster. ☐

6. Today I'm wearing a new white blouse I bought from the store near my office. ☐
   Today I wear a new white blouse I bought from the store near my office. ☐

7. She's working in the New York office at the moment, but she's planning to move to California. ☐
   She working in the New York office at the moment, but she's planning to move to California. ☐

8. I'm thinking I'm in the wrong building. Cathy lives in building number seven. ☐
   I think I'm in the wrong building. Cathy lives in building number seven. ☐

9. I'm having lunch in 30 minutes. Would you like to join me? ☐
   I have lunch in 30 minutes. Would you like to join me? ☐

10. I'm going home at 5 o'clock every day after I finish work. ☐
    I go home at 5 o'clock every day after I finish work. ☐

1.2 REWRITE THE SENTENCES, CORRECTING THE ERRORS

My boss is being a lot older than me.
My boss is a lot older than me.

1. I'm being the new member of the team.
2. He is always sits at that desk. You'll have to move!
3. The train is arriving at 7:22am every morning.
4. The bus is usually being on time, but not today.
5. I talk to my boss at the moment.
6. I work on the new project with David today.
7. We are being a very good team!
8. I'm having a meeting at 9 o'clock every day.
9. I wait for you in front of the office.

1.3 FILL IN THE GAPS BY PUTTING THE VERBS IN THE PRESENT PERFECT OR THE PRESENT PERFECT CONTINUOUS

I *'ve been waiting* **(wait)** for Sam, but I *haven't seen* **(not see)** him.

1. I ______ **(try)** to call him all day, but he ______ **(not answer)** yet.
2. He ______ **(work)** all day, so he ______ **(not have)** a break yet.
3. I'm glad I ______ **(finish)** that project because I ______ **(work)** on it for ages.
4. Jo's ______ **(cook)** all night, but Jim still ______ **(not arrive)** for dinner.
5. I ______ **(drive)** for two hours now and I still ______ **(make)** it to work.
6. He ______ **(get)** his schedule now and he ______ **(meet)** the team all day.

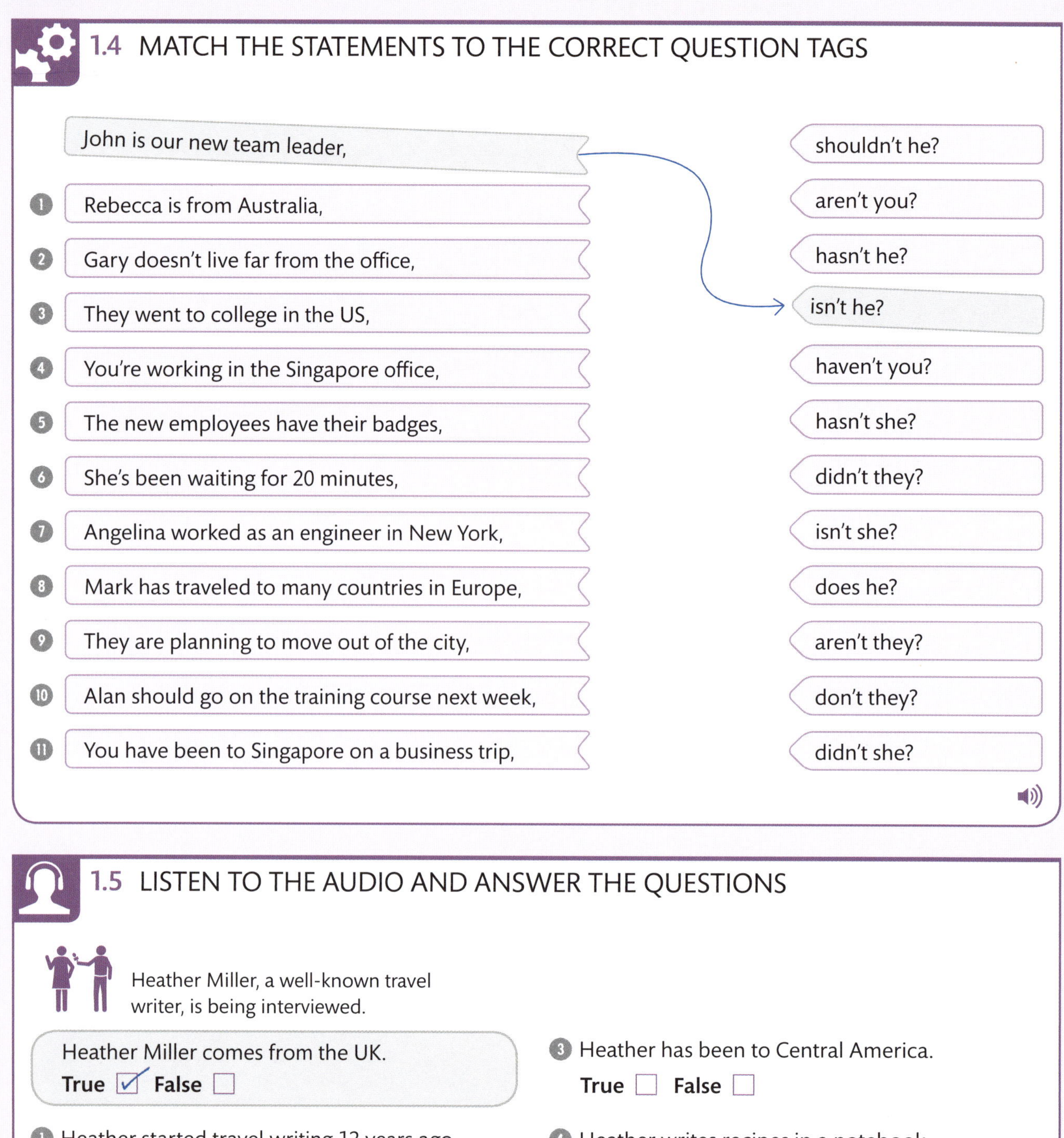

1.4 MATCH THE STATEMENTS TO THE CORRECT QUESTION TAGS

John is our new team leader, → isn't he?

1 Rebecca is from Australia,
2 Gary doesn't live far from the office,
3 They went to college in the US,
4 You're working in the Singapore office,
5 The new employees have their badges,
6 She's been waiting for 20 minutes,
7 Angelina worked as an engineer in New York,
8 Mark has traveled to many countries in Europe,
9 They are planning to move out of the city,
10 Alan should go on the training course next week,
11 You have been to Singapore on a business trip,

- shouldn't he?
- aren't you?
- hasn't he?
- isn't he?
- haven't you?
- hasn't she?
- didn't they?
- isn't she?
- does he?
- aren't they?
- don't they?
- didn't she?

1.5 LISTEN TO THE AUDIO AND ANSWER THE QUESTIONS

Heather Miller, a well-known travel writer, is being interviewed.

Heather Miller comes from the UK.
True ☑ **False** ☐

1 Heather started travel writing 12 years ago.
True ☐ **False** ☐

2 Heather has been to fewer than 20 countries.
True ☐ **False** ☐

3 Heather has been to Central America.
True ☐ **False** ☐

4 Heather writes recipes in a notebook.
True ☐ **False** ☐

5 Heather thinks scorpion soup tastes awful.
True ☐ **False** ☐

1.6 SAY THE SENTENCES OUT LOUD, ADDING THE CORRECT QUESTION TAGS

Robin should tell us when he's going to be out of the office, *shouldn't he*?

1. Maxine always takes the 7:45 train to work like Paul, ______________________?
2. Your car is parked on the road in front of the company reception, ______________________?
3. Jonathan doesn't work in the sales department anymore, ______________________?
4. She worked for one of our competitors before she started working here, ______________________?
5. Nick and Philip have visited a lot of different countries on business trips, ______________________?
6. You would like to join us for lunch in the cafeteria today, ______________________?
7. Jessica didn't go to the strategy meeting we had last Tuesday, ______________________?
8. The boss should be showing the new employees around the office, ______________________?
9. Katrina and John know each other from their days in college, ______________________?
10. He's been waiting for some time to talk to the boss about his promotion, ______________________?
11. James isn't going to be the next head of the Human Resources department, ______________________?
12. Daniel should present the results of his research to the rest of the team, ______________________?
13. You worked with Janet on the project we did in Singapore, ______________________?
14. He works from home two days a week so he can spend time with his family, ______________________?
15. Simon and Gregory are working on a prototype for the new product, ______________________?

02 Action and state verbs

Verbs that describe actions or events are known as "action" or "dynamic" verbs, whereas those that describe states are known as "state" or "stative" verbs.

New language State verbs in continuous forms
Aa Vocabulary Action and state verbs
New skill Describing states

2.1 MARK WHETHER EACH VERB DESCRIBES AN ACTION OR A STATE

I **think** we should go home now.
Action ☐ State ☑

1. The train **arrives** in 10 minutes.
   Action ☐ State ☐
2. I'll **send** her an email about it.
   Action ☐ State ☐
3. This tomato soup **tastes** delicious.
   Action ☐ State ☐
4. I **love** hiking in the mountains.
   Action ☐ State ☐
5. I **understand** exactly how you feel.
   Action ☐ State ☐
6. We're **watching** a film in the living room.
   Action ☐ State ☐
7. I **belong** to a sports club in my town.
   Action ☐ State ☐
8. They **seem** to be very open and friendly.
   Action ☐ State ☐
9. Someone's **knocking** on the door.
   Action ☐ State ☐
10. I **spoke** to my parents about it yesterday.
    Action ☐ State ☐

2.2 MARK THE SENTENCES THAT ARE CORRECT

Are you having a dictionary? ☐
Do you have a dictionary? ☑

1. She's concentrating hard at the moment. ☐
   She concentrates hard at the moment. ☐
2. I'm hating video games. They're so boring. ☐
   I hate video games. They're so boring. ☐
3. He's wanting to move to a bigger place. ☐
   He wants to move to a bigger place. ☐
4. She is seeming to be a reliable employee. ☐
   She seems to be a reliable employee. ☐
5. He's reading a science-fiction novel. ☐
   He reads a science-fiction novel. ☐
6. I'm just cooking some pasta for dinner. ☐
   I just cook some pasta for dinner. ☐
7. The package is weighing four pounds. ☐
   The package weighs four pounds. ☐
8. I'm not hearing you at all. ☐
   I can't hear you at all. ☐
9. Laura is appearing in the show this evening. ☐
   Laura appearing in the show this evening. ☐
10. What are you thinking of me? ☐
    What do you think of me? ☐

2.3 REWRITE THE SENTENCES, CORRECTING THE ERRORS

I was loving pop music when I was a teenager.
I loved pop music when I was a teenager.

1. The items that the bags are containing are heavy.
2. I'm seeing the mountains in the distance.
3. He weighs the boxes on the scales right now.
4. We were spending two hours doing our work.
5. I am believing everything you say.
6. I'm sorry, but I'm feeling that you're wrong.
7. I listened to the radio when you came in.
8. This milk is smelling bad.
9. Shaun is usually arriving at work at 8am.

2.4 SAY THE SENTENCES OUT LOUD, PUTTING THE VERBS IN THE CORRECT TENSE

We're *expecting* **(expect)** some guests for an early dinner this evening.

1. William ______ **(want)** to travel around the world when he's older.
2. I ______ **(taste)** the soup to see if it needs more salt or pepper.
3. I ______ **(see)** my dentist later this afternoon for a consultation.
4. My knees ______ **(hurt)** when I walk too far or sit for too long.
5. My colleagues ______ **(have)** lunch right now in the cafeteria.
6. Michael ______ **(be)** all shy and quiet now that you're here to visit.

03 Using collocations

Collocations are often formed of two words, but can contain more. Using them will make you a more fluent English speaker.

New language Collocations
Vocabulary Beliefs and opinions
New skill Talking about your life

3.1 FILL IN THE GAPS TO COMPLETE THE SENTENCES

All their lives Jim and Alice appeared to be *happily married*.

1. Laura ______________ straight after school, at the age of 18.
2. The difference between these two cars is ______________.
3. You've studied so much for the exam. Now all that's left is to ______________.
4. I ______________ asking you to pack the passports. Don't tell me you forgot!
5. I think it's ______________ that you'll win the lottery tonight.
6. I don't think Steffi likes me. She seems to have a ______________ of me.
7. The smell of fresh bread always ______________ of my grandma.
8. Bill made a big mistake at work and it has ______________.
9. I'm very lucky to have a ______________. We meet up every Sunday for lunch.

~~happily married~~ | clearly visible | close family | distinctly remember | do your best
extremely unlikely | low opinion | ruined his career | stirs up memories | went into business

3.2 READ THE ARTICLE AND ANSWER THE QUESTIONS

34 Global Beat

ENIGMA FOREVER

Seventy years on, the mystery of Amelia endures

Amelia Earhart, one of the first female aviators, has been missing since 1937. She was attempting a round-the-world flight when, on July 2 1937, her plane disappeared over the Pacific Ocean. Despite a huge search effort, no body or wreckage was ever found.

Opinions are divided as to what happened to Amelia. Jack Berger, an aviation expert, firmly believes that the plane ran out of fuel and crashed into the ocean, where Amelia drowned. Berger's reasonable theory is poles apart from other, more outlandish, explanations. For example, another popular belief is that Amelia ditched her plane on purpose, and went to spy on the Japanese. Even more unlikely is that she completed the round-the-world trip, but didn't want to be in the spotlight anymore, so moved to a small town in the US and changed her name.

It seems extremely unlikely that we will ever know for sure what happened to Amelia. What is not a matter of opinion however, is that Amelia was declared dead in 1939, despite no body ever being found.

A LOCKHEED VEGA SIMILAR TO THE ONE FLOWN BY AMELIA EARHART

Not many women had flown a plane in 1937.
True ☑ False ☐ Not given ☐

1. Amelia's plane disappeared over water.
True ☐ False ☐ Not given ☐

2. Amelia's plane was found.
True ☐ False ☐ Not given ☐

3. Jack Berger has written a book about Amelia.
True ☐ False ☐ Not given ☐

4. Berger's theory seems reasonable.
True ☐ False ☐ Not given ☐

5. Amelia could speak fluent Japanese.
True ☐ False ☐ Not given ☐

6. Some people believe Amelia is still alive.
True ☐ False ☐ Not given ☐

7. A woman with Amelia's name lives in the US.
True ☐ False ☐ Not given ☐

8. Experts are close to solving the mystery.
True ☐ False ☐ Not given ☐

9. Officially, Amelia has been dead since 1939.
True ☐ False ☐ Not given ☐

3.3 REWRITE THE SENTENCES, PUTTING THE WORDS IN THE CORRECT ORDER

born | small | Jenni | in | Spain. | town | in | was | a

Jenni was born in a small town in Spain.

1 while | in | was | I | met | wife | college. | my | I

2 climbing | When | was | trees. | young, | I | loved | I

3 I | After | to | moved | retired, | I | Florida.

4 in | café. | I | worked | During | summer | the | a

5 was | part-time. | I | worked | studying | I | while | abroad.

3.4 LISTEN TO THE AUDIO AND MATCH THE IMAGES OF THE EVENTS TO THE CORRECT TIME

1

2

3

23 years ago | This morning | 25 years ago | 15 years ago

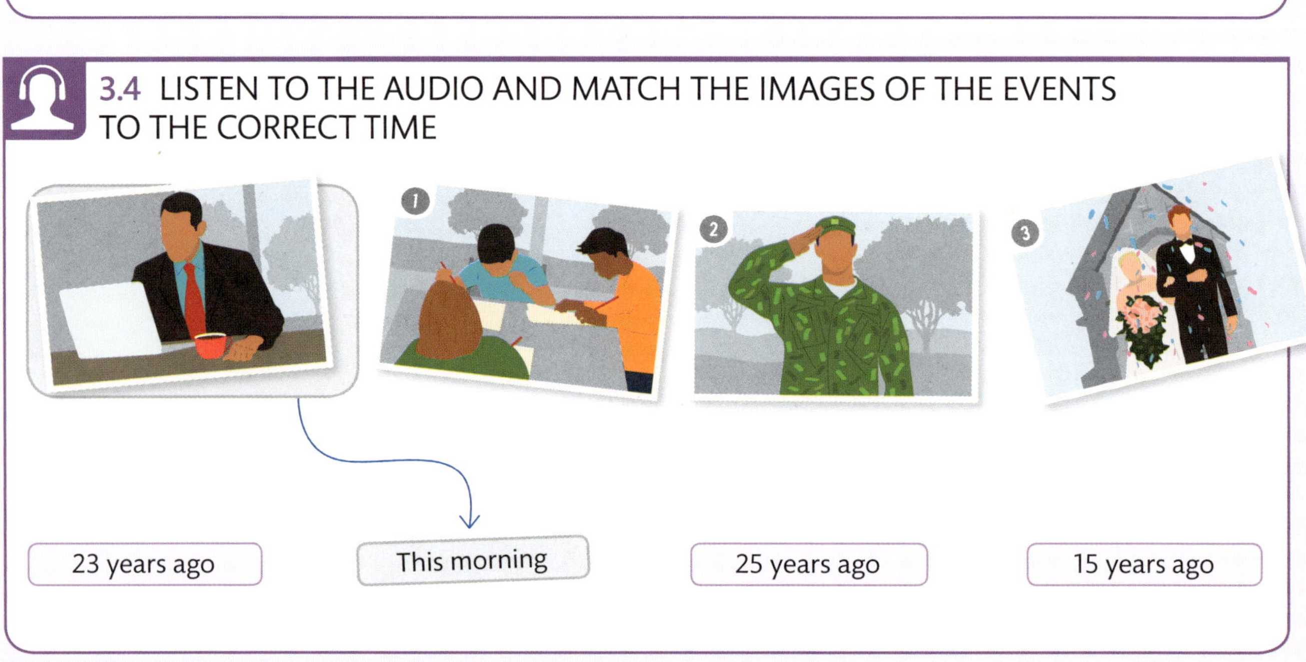

3.5 CROSS OUT THE INCORRECT WORDS IN EACH SENTENCE

I think Adrian ~~was having~~ / had an interview for a new job this afternoon / ~~every afternoon~~.

1. Stephanie has graduated / graduated from college with an honors degree last / before year.
2. Bill had been running / was running for many years when he decided / has decided to run a marathon.
3. Matthew was starting / started working at the company 33 years since / ago.
4. Leah was having / had a baby previous / last month. Her name's Sophie and she's beautiful.
5. Peter arrived / has arrived very early this / previous morning because he has an important meeting.
6. Jenny was working / worked in a bar in London when she has met / met Stephen.
7. Jenny and Stephen were getting married / got married this year on / in June 7.
8. Stuart had been living / has lived in the US since / for 10 years before he moved to the UK.
9. When they were / had been five years old, Anna and Jasmine were / have been best friends.

Aa 3.6 MATCH THE BEGINNINGS OF THE SENTENCES TO THE CORRECT ENDINGS

I firmly believe → that there is someone for everyone.

1. Whether too much sleep is bad for you
2. There is a popular belief that
3. Lionel has gone into business,
4. There's forecast to be light rain later on,
5. When I smelled that perfume, it stirred
6. The airport is still closed, so
7. I'm not sure why Rebecca has
8. The scandal over drug-taking ruined

- so take an umbrella.
- her career in athletics.
- up memories of my first love.
- that there is someone for everyone.
- it's extremely unlikely we'll fly today.
- such a low opinion of me.
- selling clothes he has designed himself.
- the number 13 is unlucky.
- is a matter of opinion.

04 Complex descriptions

When you describe something using more than one adjective, the adjectives usually have to go in a specific order. There are several categories of adjectives.

New language General and specific adjectives
Aa Vocabulary Personalities
New skill Ordering adjectives

4.1 REWRITE THE SENTENCES, CORRECTING THE ERRORS

That looks like a new interesting movie. We should go to see it.
That looks like an interesting new movie. We should go to see it.

1. She's a little intelligent girl. She always does well at school.

2. It's a old, horrible ugly car. I'm not going to buy it as I don't like it.

3. We're going on a cheap, fantastic train trip across Europe for our vacation.

4. This is such an old comfortable sweater. I love wearing it in winter.

5. Gio always wears Italian stylish clothes. He is a fashion designer in London.

6. Today we're going to present our new innovative tablet to you for the first time.

7. Don't forget to try these spicy delicious sauces, which we've created ourselves.

8. I was one of the first to ride in a high-speed unique train while I was there.

9. Sometimes a low-tech reliable product is a better option than a more hi-tech one.

Aa

4.2 FIND EIGHT OPINION ADJECTIVES IN THE GRID AND WRITE THEM UNDER THE CORRECT HEADING

U	R	I	T	T	N	A	T	E	E	I	L	F
F	E	U	N	A	D	W	S	V	L	A	P	K
L	S	Y	R	S	T	F	T	D	E	S	A	D
M	X	R	D	T	E	U	I	L	X	Z	N	L
N	O	A	S	Y	E	L	B	Z	C	P	G	O
E	B	S	S	E	T	U	G	L	Y	K	L	V
N	B	S	S	I	R	I	I	T	T	I	U	E
R	I	G	A	R	L	X	I	Y	I	T	G	L
R	D	C	O	N	F	K	I	N	D	W	M	Y
R	N	H	E	T	P	D	A	O	G	E	Y	R

GENERAL OPINION

nice

SPECIFIC OPINION

kind

4.3 FILL IN THE GAPS, PUTTING THE ADJECTIVES IN THE CORRECT ORDER

uncomfortable | wooden | horrible

It's a horrible, uncomfortable wooden chair.

old | wonderful | generous

1 My grandma is a ________, ________ ________ lady.

ugly | awful | expensive

2 I bought this ________, ________ ________ dress on the internet.

pleasant | young | friendly

3 What a ________, ________ ________ man Peter is!

stylish | beautiful | new

4 Jon's got a ________, ________ ________ car.

4.4 FILL IN THE GAPS USING THE PREFIXES IN THE PANEL

Tom was very rude and __un__ friendly toward my friends.

1. Lana's ______ honest. She hides information and never tells the truth.
2. You're so ______ considerate! Think about other people for a change!
3. It was very ______ kind of you to make your sister cry. You should apologize to her.
4. Leon always has a solution for a problem. Unfortunately, he's often ______ correct.
5. Susanne is always being rude to her parents. She's so ______ respectful.
6. Stop behaving like a five-year-old! You're so ______ mature!

in | dis | ~~un~~ | dis | in | im | un

4.5 LISTEN TO THE AUDIO AND ANSWER THE QUESTIONS

Richard and Jenni are talking about filling a job vacancy in their company.

Jenni thinks the person they choose must be...
- **blunt** ☐
- **fair-minded** ☐
- **resourceful** ☑

1. The person they choose must not be...
   - **rude** ☐
   - **inexperienced** ☐
   - **mature** ☐
2. Richard thinks Sonia is reliable, but also...
   - **lazy** ☐
   - **efficient** ☐
   - **arrogant** ☐
3. The person that Richard is considering is...
   - **Anna** ☐
   - **Esther** ☐
   - **Mary** ☐
4. Esther has been working with the company for...
   - **five years** ☐
   - **six years** ☐
   - **seven years** ☐
5. Jenni thinks Esther is...
   - **trustworthy** ☐
   - **arrogant** ☐
   - **popular** ☐

4.6 READ THE PERFORMANCE REVIEW AND ANSWER THE QUESTIONS AS FULL SENTENCES

Name: Jenson Lee
Position: Website administrator
Subject: Performance Review

Jenson joined the company just over a year ago. He appeared rather quiet to begin with, but has proved himself to be hardworking and proactive. For example, in June the company website crashed while May Wong, Jenson's boss, was on vacation. Jenson took charge of the situation and sought help from others on the team. He was incredibly organized, and thanks to his excellent planning, the website was back online within six hours. Jenson is also clearly ambitious, and he has expressed a desire to be promoted into management.

Because Jenson is so shy, some people think he is unfriendly and insensitive. We discussed this and he agreed he sometimes feels uncomfortable in social situations. We will look for training courses that will help him with this. Jenson needs to improve his social skills before he can be considered for promotion.

When Jenson first started working for the company, what was his personality like?
Jenson was very quiet when he first started working for the company.

1. How did Jenson solve the problem with the website?

2. What are Jenson's hopes for his future career?

3. Why might Jenson sometimes appear rude?

4. What solution has Jenson's company come up with to help him overcome his shyness?

5. How can Jenson improve his chances of getting promoted?

6. Would you say the review is generally positive or negative?

05 Making general statements

It is very useful to know how to start sentences with the word "it" in English. You can use "it is" at the beginning of a sentence to make a general statement about something.

New language Introductory "it"
Aa Vocabulary Talents and abilities
New skill Expressing general truths

5.1 FILL IN THE GAPS USING THE PHRASES IN THE PANEL

It is *not important that* we lost the first game. You should forget about that.

1. It's ________ some people aren't interested in learning languages.
2. It's ________ you chose that book because it's the book that I chose, too.
3. It's ________ win. What you should be focused on is doing your very best.
4. It is ________ learn English vocabulary, but it's difficult to learn the grammar.
5. It's ________ our neighbors are so understanding because we make a lot of noise!
6. When it's so cold outside, it's ________ wrap yourself up as warmly as possible.
7. It's ________ everyone has enough water to drink while we're out walking in the heat.
8. It's ________ look at your phone while you're driving. You could have an accident.
9. Joshua has been doing so badly at school that he's ________ do well in his exams.
10. It is ________ understand people when they speak English very quickly.
11. Look at those black clouds over there. I think it's ________ rain sometime soon.
12. Our train is so delayed. I think it's ________ we'll get home before midnight!
13. It's really ________ some people don't care about the environment. They should!
14. It's ________ our children do their best at school and get a good education.
15. It's ________ have all of the family here together again. I've missed everyone.

interesting that · important to · important that · not important to · essential that · difficult to · unlikely that · unlikely to · likely to · bad that · bad to · good that · good to · easy to · ~~not important that~~ · a shame that

5.2 CROSS OUT THE INCORRECT WORDS IN EACH SENTENCE

To / ~~That~~ / ~~It~~ get to the school, go straight ahead and then turn left.

1  That / To / It is unlikely that I will finish this assignment on time.

2  It's difficult that / to / it decide what to order because it all sounds delicious.

3  That / To / Them lose at this point would be very difficult after coming so far.

4  It's easy that / to / they start writing an essay, but it's not always easy to finish one!

5  It's essential that / to / they everyone follows the rules and does what they're told.

6  That / To / They read English is easy, but to write in English is more difficult.

7  It's important that / to / it choose an interesting topic to give a presentation about.

Aa 5.3 MATCH THE BEGINNINGS OF THE SENTENCES TO THE CORRECT ENDINGS

My brother surprised us with his → hidden talent for baking cakes.

1 I have a certain aptitude for

2 My friend has a complete inability

3 It seems like some people have a

4 Dr. Finn had a remarkable capacity

to plan ahead. He's always late!

navigating with a map, but I still get lost.

to memorize huge passages of text.

hidden talent for baking cakes.

natural ability to run long distances.

5.4 READ THE EMAIL AND ANSWER THE QUESTIONS

Which language has Jenny been learning recently?
Japanese ☐ **Arabic** ☐ **Chinese** ☑

1. Where is Jenny learning it?
At a school ☐ **At a college** ☐ **At a university** ☐

2. It will help her do less of what in the evening?
Shopping ☐ **Housework** ☐ **Surfing the internet** ☐

3. What kind of ability does Jenny have for Chinese?
Natural ☐ **Limited** ☐ **Advanced** ☐

4. How does Jenny describe the language she's learning?
Tonal ☐ **Clicking** ☐ **Difficult** ☐

To: Charlotte

Subject: Learning Chinese

Hi Charlotte,

Hope you are well. I've been learning Chinese recently. I decided to do a course at my local college. It looked like a good way to get out and meet new people in the evening instead of just surfing the internet. My teacher thinks I have a natural ability for Chinese. Chinese is a tonal language, which means you have to think about what tone you say the words in.

Looking forward to seeing you next week.

Jenny

5.5 RESPOND OUT LOUD TO THE AUDIO, FILLING IN THE GAPS IN THE ANSWERS

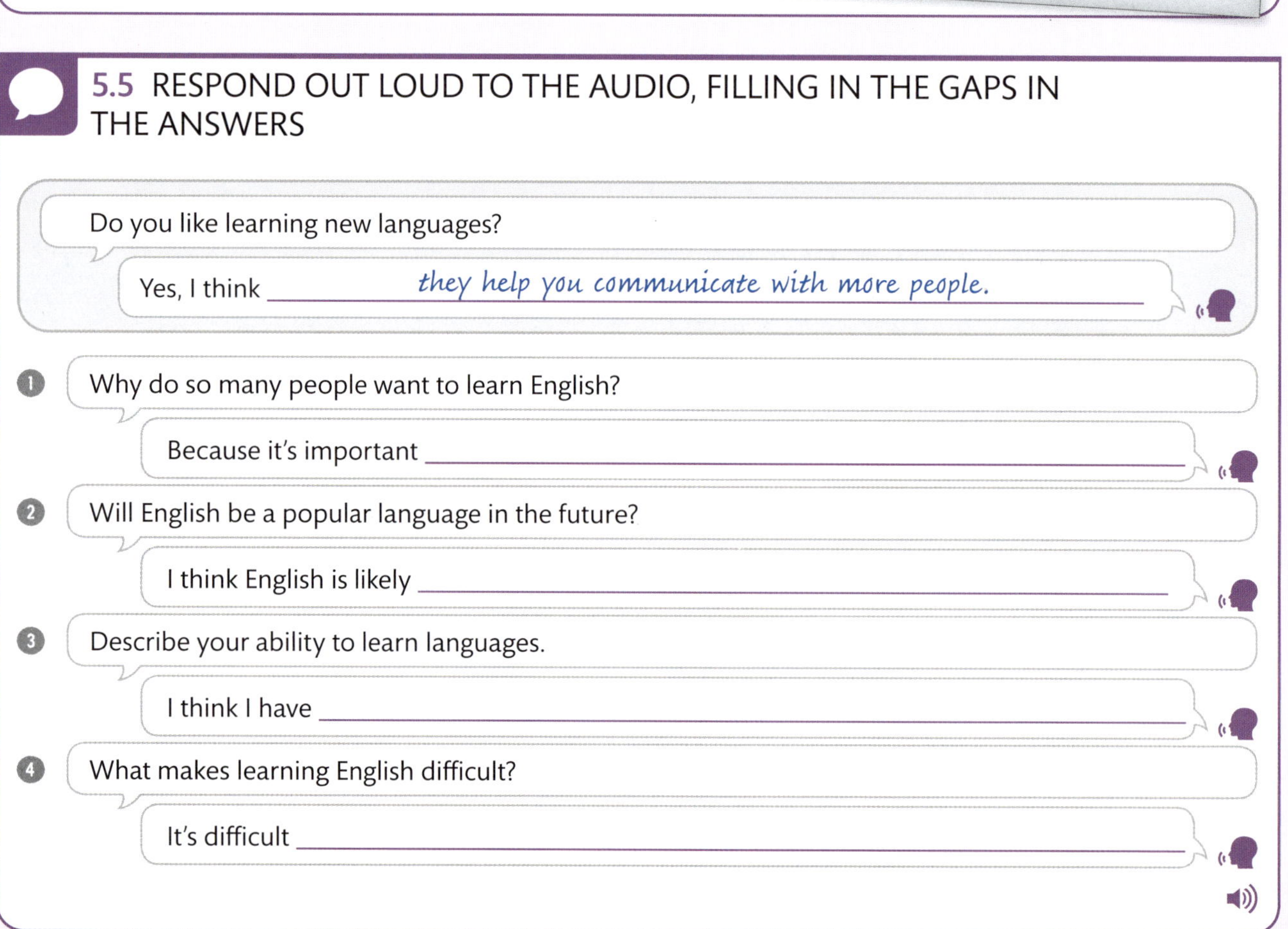

Do you like learning new languages?

Yes, I think *they help you communicate with more people.*

1. Why do so many people want to learn English?

Because it's important ____________________

2. Will English be a popular language in the future?

I think English is likely ____________________

3. Describe your ability to learn languages.

I think I have ____________________

4. What makes learning English difficult?

It's difficult ____________________

06 Vocabulary

Aa 6.1 **TRAVEL AND TOURISM** WRITE THE PHRASES FROM THE PANEL UNDER THE CORRECT DEFINITIONS

A vacation, particularly a short one

getaway

7 A stage in a journey from one place to another

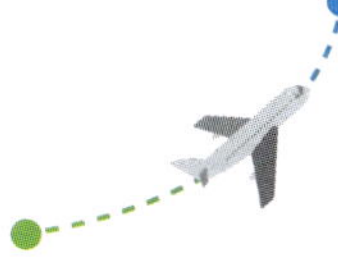

1 Unique and unrepeatable

8 Explore an area or place

2 A desire for exciting experiences

9 Register your arrival at an airport or hotel

3 Pay your bill and leave a hotel

10 Be sad because you miss your home and family

4 Visit interesting buildings and places as a tourist

11 Feeling of confusion or distress when visiting a different place or culture

5 Totally unable to find your way

12 Go somewhere relaxing for a break

6 Go to the station or airport to say goodbye to someone

13 Pause a journey in one place before continuing

culture shock | check out | thirst for adventure | get away from it all | ~~getaway~~ | check in | leg of a journey | once-in-a-lifetime | see somebody off | go sightseeing | feel homesick | look around | hopelessly lost | stop off

07 Phrasal verbs

Phrasal verbs occur in many different forms. They have two or more parts, which are sometimes separable. They are very common, especially in spoken English.

New language Phrasal verbs overview
Aa Vocabulary Travel
New skill Using complex phrasal verbs

7.1 REWRITE THE SENTENCES, PUTTING THE WORDS IN THE CORRECT ORDER

all | It | on | raining | kept | night.

It kept on raining all night.

1. get | at | I | up | 7am. | usually
2. would | in | early. | like | to | check | I
3. out | need | by | I | to | check | 9am.
4. works | two | He | hours. | out | for
5. Fridays. | We | go | always | out | on
6. up | in. | Please | go | line | here | to
7. the | Martin | showed | at | party. | up

7.2 MARK THE SENTENCES THAT ARE CORRECT

This is where you have to line up. ☑
This is where you have to lines up. ☐

1. They want to check in at the hotel. ☐
   They want to check up at the hotel. ☐
2. He keeps on complaining about his job. ☐
   He keeps complaining on about his job. ☐
3. She doesn't like getting up early. ☐
   She doesn't like getting on early. ☐
4. She works down in the morning. ☐
   She works out in the morning. ☐
5. We're going for Sheila's birthday out. ☐
   We're going out for Sheila's birthday. ☐
6. He shows up late to work yesterday. ☐
   He showed up late to work yesterday. ☐
7. Jo, please come in and join us here. ☐
   Jo, please come into and join us here. ☐
8. Tim is coming down for my birthday. ☐
   Tim is coming under for my birthday. ☐
9. Cooking is hard, but you should keep it at. ☐
   Cooking is hard, but you should keep at it. ☐
10. He always checks down early. ☐
    He always checks out early. ☐

7.3 REWRITE THE SENTENCES, SEPARATING THE PHRASAL VERBS

We seem to throw away too much food. We should buy less when we go to the supermarket.
We seem to throw too much food away. We should buy less when we go to the supermarket.

1. She really needs to clean up her desk. It's full of papers and old coffee cups.

2. The sixth grade students are putting on a show to celebrate the end of their time at this school.

3. Everyone needs to hand in their forms by Friday. Otherwise you can't go on the trip.

4. I need you to look up a few words in the dictionary for me. Can you do that?

5. I'll check out the hotels in Monte Carlo and let you know what the prices are.

7.4 REWRITE THE SENTENCES USING PRONOUNS

We're getting a new gymnasium at school. They're putting the building up this year.
We're getting a new gymnasium at school. They're putting it up this year.

1. It's not a problem. We'll come over and pick up the sofa from your place.

2. He was so angry he tore up the contract and threw the pieces around the room.

3. You should put on that pullover when you go outside. It's absolutely freezing.

4. If you cut out that coupon, you can use it to get two for the price of one at the supermarket.

7.5 SAY THE SENTENCES OUT LOUD, FILLING IN THE GAPS

TIP
Remember that when you're saying a three-part phrasal verb, you need to stress the second word.

I'm lucky that I *get along with* all of my colleagues really well.

1 He's always trying to ______ his reputation as a big spender.

2 We're ______ some really good ideas at the moment.

3 I should just ______ the things that I don't need.

4 She's so fast. I can't ______ her.

5 Melissa's great. I really ______ her.

get rid of
coming up with
live up to
keep up with
look up to
~~get along with~~

7.6 FILL IN THE GAPS BY PUTTING THE VERBS IN THE CORRECT TENSES

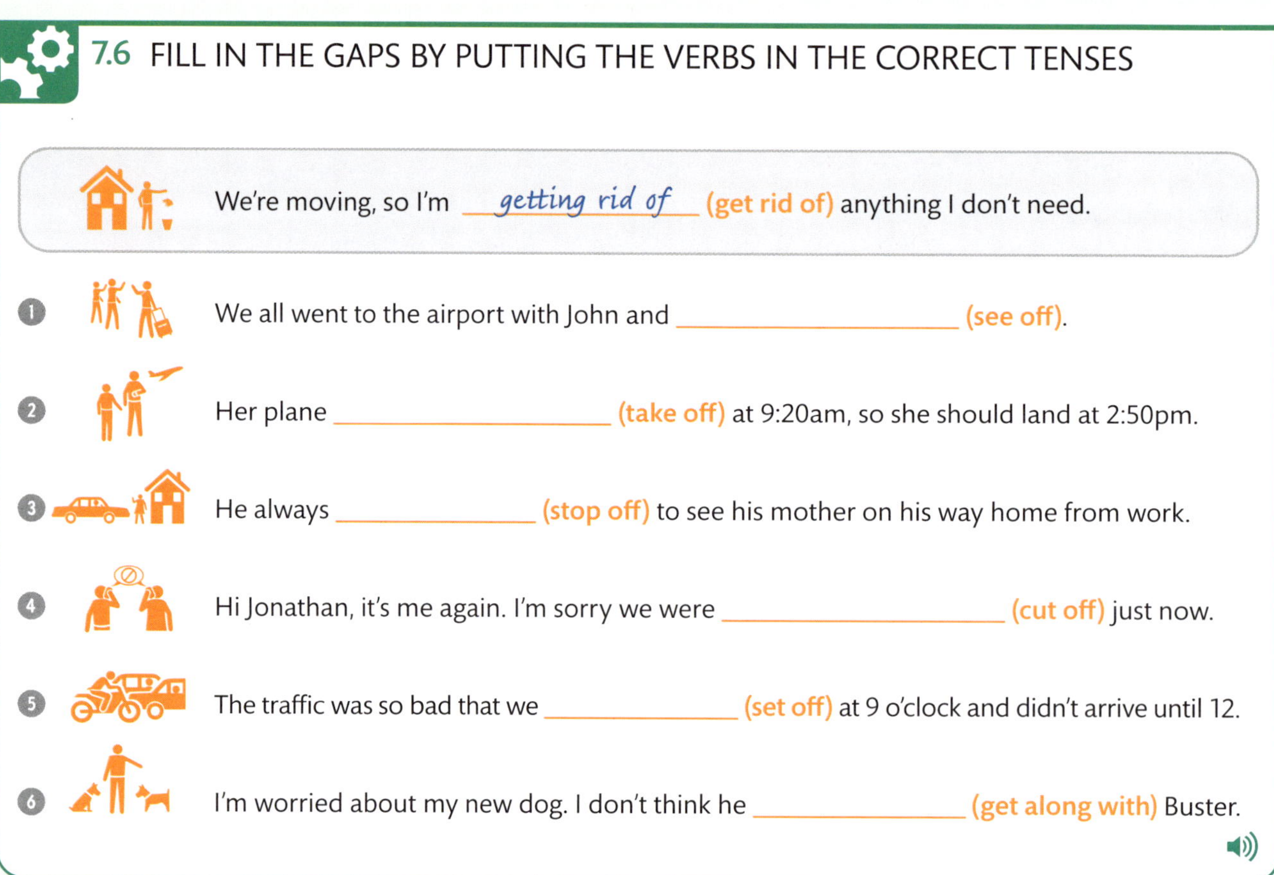

We're moving, so I'm *getting rid of* (get rid of) anything I don't need.

1 We all went to the airport with John and ______ (see off).

2 Her plane ______ (take off) at 9:20am, so she should land at 2:50pm.

3 He always ______ (stop off) to see his mother on his way home from work.

4 Hi Jonathan, it's me again. I'm sorry we were ______ (cut off) just now.

5 The traffic was so bad that we ______ (set off) at 9 o'clock and didn't arrive until 12.

6 I'm worried about my new dog. I don't think he ______ (get along with) Buster.

7.7 READ THE ARTICLE AND ANSWER THE QUESTIONS

TEAM-BUILDING UPDATE

A trip to Salzburg

How a weekend in the mountains brought a team together

Last year our boss, Robert, suggested we go on a team-building trip to help us get along with each other better. Robert said we needed to keep up with other companies and live up to our reputation as an efficient company. We set off early one morning and our plane to Salzburg took off at 8am. When we landed, someone from our hotel came to pick us up. As soon as we arrived we had to put some extra layers on because it was freezing cold.

We went climbing in the mountains and at one point, I got cut off from the others. Luckily Sebastian, our guide, called out to me and I found the group again. Sebastian said we needed to get rid of our inhibitions and just climb. At the end of the weekend, we all agreed that the trip had been enjoyable and we even came up with some ideas for a new sales campaign!

They went on the team-building trip this year.	True ☐	False ☑	Not given ☐
1 Their boss suggested the team-building trip.	True ☐	False ☐	Not given ☐
2 The aim of the trip was to improve team relationships.	True ☐	False ☐	Not given ☐
3 Other people don't see the company as being efficient.	True ☐	False ☐	Not given ☐
4 The team flew from London Heathrow airport.	True ☐	False ☐	Not given ☐
5 Their plane arrived in Salzburg at 8am.	True ☐	False ☐	Not given ☐
6 The team took the bus to the hotel in Salzburg.	True ☐	False ☐	Not given ☐
7 The team discovered they weren't dressed warmly enough.	True ☐	False ☐	Not given ☐
8 The writer lost the group and couldn't find them again.	True ☐	False ☐	Not given ☐
9 Sebastian encouraged the group to feel inhibited.	True ☐	False ☐	Not given ☐
10 The team thought of some new ideas while on the trip.	True ☐	False ☐	Not given ☐

08 Narrative tenses

When telling a story, even if you're just talking about something that happened recently, you need to use a variety of tenses so that the story can be understood easily.

New language The past perfect continuous
Aa Vocabulary Travel adjectives and idioms
New skill Talking about a variety of past actions

8.1 FILL IN THE GAPS BY PUTTING THE VERBS IN THE PAST SIMPLE OR PAST CONTINUOUS

We *decided* **(decide)** to order a bottle of wine while we *were having* **(have)** dinner.

1. I ______________ **(learn)** a lot of Japanese while I ______________ **(live)** in Japan.
2. While I ______________ **(wait)** for the train, I ______________ **(meet)** my favorite singer.
3. As we ______________ **(walk)** home last night, we ______________ **(see)** a firework display.
4. We ______________ **(stop)** at the café while we ______________ **(visit)** the castle.
5. I ______________ **(get)** off my bike a few times while I ______________ **(cycle)** to work.
6. I ______________ **(see)** a lot of cafés when I ______________ **(stroll)** around town.
7. While I ______________ **(wander)** around, I ______________ **(find)** a good bookstore.
8. She ______________ **(take)** so many pictures when she ______________ **(travel).**
9. I ______________ **(have)** problems with my car until he ________ **(help)** me.

8.2 COMPLETE THE SENTENCES USING THE PAST PERFECT, SPEAKING OUT LOUD

They **decided** to travel around the country, so they rented a car at the airport.

They rented a car at the airport because *they had decided to travel around the country.*

1. The hotel receptionist **recommended** a local restaurant to us, so we tried it.

   We tried a local restaurant because ______________________

2. I **went** in the swimming pool at the hotel and then I went in the sauna.

   I went in the sauna after I ______________________

3. A friend of ours **said** it was a good idea to rent a bike, so we did.

   We rented a bike because ______________________

4. Just after we **arrived** at the hotel, they gave us a welcome drink.

   They gave us a welcome drink just after ______________________

5. We **bought** advance tickets, so didn't have to wait in line to go into the museum.

   We didn't have to wait in line to go in because ______________________

8.3 FILL IN THE GAPS BY PUTTING THE VERBS IN THE BRACKETS INTO THE PAST PERFECT CONTINUOUS

They *had been walking* **(walk)** around Rome for two hours before they found the restaurant.

1. The Miller family ______________ **(go)** to Croatia for years before it became popular with tourists.
2. We needed to move around after we ______________ **(sit)** on the plane for 14 hours.
3. I ______________ **(wait)** for them at the airport for half an hour before they arrived.
4. Our team ______________ **(lose)** in the first half of the game, but they came back in the second.
5. She ______________ **(study)** Spanish for six months before she went to Mexico.
6. It ______________ **(rain)** for five days in a row before we had some sunshine.

8.4 FILL IN THE GAPS BY PUTTING THE VERBS IN THE PANEL IN THE CORRECT TENSE

We *had been waiting* in line for an hour before we *were able to* buy our train tickets.

1. She ______ to cycle across China, but then she ______ an accident on her bike.
2. When they ______ back home, they discovered that someone ______ their house.
3. After I ______ around Asia for six months, I ______ very happy to be back home.
4. Before I ______ to South America, I ______ tango dancing.
5. He ______ to visit the fjords because he ______ they were beautiful.

go, want, ~~be able to~~, travel, not try, get, plan, hear, feel, burgle, ~~have~~, wait

8.5 MATCH THE BEGINNINGS OF THE SENTENCES TO THE CORRECT ENDINGS

After I left home, I realized	I realized that someone had stolen my car.
1 I had written some practice answers	but they decided to go to bed early.
2 When I got back to the parking lot,	been working in the US for six months.
3 Before I started working here, I had	that I had forgotten my umbrella.
4 I had given the matter a lot of thought	before I decided to change jobs.
5 They were eating at a restaurant when	I had not been sleeping very well.
6 She wanted to go to Spain because	her parents had told her it was fantastic.
7 They had been planning to go out,	a famous author came in.
8 I was feeling extremely tired because	before the exam, so I was well prepared.

8.6 READ THE ARTICLE AND WRITE ANSWERS TO THE QUESTIONS AS FULL SENTENCES

TRUE STORIES

An unusual friendship

Two strangers became friends without even knowing each other's names

Jason works in an office in New York. One Monday morning, he looked out of the window and saw a woman working in the building across the street. To his surprise, she smiled and waved. Jason had moved to New York a few months earlier. Before that, he had been doing an internship in London, and he was certain he and the woman in the window had never met.

A few days later, Jason saw the woman again. This time she was holding up a piece of paper with the word "hi" written on it. Jason found a piece of paper and wrote "hi" back. From that day on, they sent regular messages using pieces of paper, without ever meeting face-to-face. Finally, some weeks later, the mystery woman wrote: "Do you want to meet for coffee?" Jason wrote back: "Yes, sure."

Their unusual meeting had led to a genuine friendship, which has lasted many years.

When did Jason first see the woman in the office building across the street?

Jason first saw the woman on a Monday morning.

1. How long had Jason been living in New York at the time?

2. What had Jason been doing before he moved to New York?

3. How long was it before Jason saw the woman a second time?

4. Who was the first person to start writing messages?

09 Giving advice and opinions

When you want to give advice or make recommendations, you can use a variety of modal verbs. You can vary the strength of your advice by using different modals.

New language Modals for advice and opinion
Aa Vocabulary Recommendations
New skill Giving advice and opinions

9.1 MARK ALL THE RECOMMENDATIONS

It's difficult to find a hotel in the center of Paris that isn't really expensive. ☐ 
You could try the Hôtel du Théâtre. It's quite cheap. ☑

1
When you're in Berlin, you ought to visit the television tower. ☐ 
Oh yes. I heard there are some great views from the top. ☐

2
It's so hot today, I can't believe it! ☐ 
I know! You really should take the kids down to the swimming pool. ☐

3
You might want to take a boat trip around the lake while you're here. ☐ 
That sounds like a good idea. We couldn't do that last time. ☐

4
Jonas could make a reservation. Then he'll definitely get a seat on the train. ☐ 
You're right. I'll tell him to do that. ☐

5
We could go to visit the Great Wall on our third day in Beijing. ☐ 
Yes, it's awesome. You really must do that. ☐

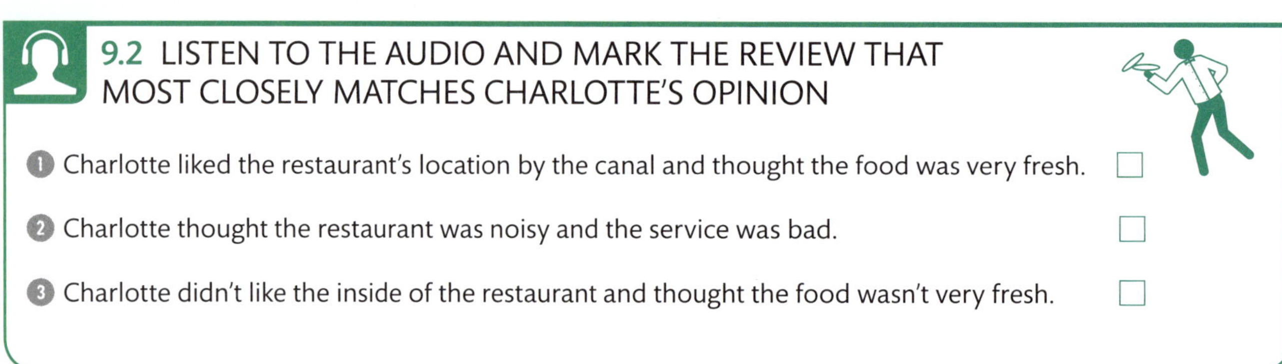

9.2 LISTEN TO THE AUDIO AND MARK THE REVIEW THAT MOST CLOSELY MATCHES CHARLOTTE'S OPINION

1 Charlotte liked the restaurant's location by the canal and thought the food was very fresh. ☐

2 Charlotte thought the restaurant was noisy and the service was bad. ☐

3 Charlotte didn't like the inside of the restaurant and thought the food wasn't very fresh. ☐

9.3 FILL IN THE GAPS WITH THE RECOMMENDATIONS FROM THE PANEL

The science museum is a lot of fun for all the family!

You really should take your kids there soon.

We can't praise our tour guide enough. She gave us such a lot of interesting information.

3 ______________________

We had some outstanding food at Lionel's restaurant!

1 ______________________

I had trouble sleeping because the sheets were very rough.

4 ______________________

The room wasn't bad, although ours was a lot smaller than some of the others.

2 ______________________

The staff at the bar had fantastic recommendations for drinks.

5 ______________________

You might want to bring a sheet!
You could ask for a larger room if this is an issue.
You really must try the cocktails.
~~You really should take your kids there soon.~~
You must ask for Irene if you go there.
You ought to try the pasta.

9.4 LISTEN TO THE AUDIO AND MARK WHETHER VICTOR LIKED OR DISLIKED EACH ACTIVITY

Like ☐ Dislike ☑

1 Like ☐ Dislike ☐

2 Like ☐ Dislike ☐

3 Like ☐ Dislike ☐

4 Like ☐ Dislike ☐

9.5 SAY THE SENTENCES OUT LOUD, CHOOSING THE CORRECT WORDS

You **should** / ~~**had better**~~ take some photographs when you get to the top of the tower.

1. You **must** / **could** put on a lot of sun cream or you'll burn.
2. You **could** / **had better** take your walking boots if you're going to go hiking while you're there.
3. The firework display will be absolutely stunning. You **would** / **must** go and see it.
4. If I were you, I **would** / **could** take the train from Paris to London instead of flying.
5. You **would** / **should** ask if they have any vacancies at the Hotel Bennetton.

9.6 READ THE EMAIL AND ANSWER THE QUESTIONS

Severine went on vacation to...
France ☐ **South Africa** ☑ **Belgium** ☐

1. Severine recommends traveling around by...
   car ☐ **bus** ☐ **plane** ☐
2. Severine recommends taking a lot of...
   cameras ☐ **photographs** ☐ **videos** ☐
3. Severine advises locking your...
   car doors ☐ **trunk** ☐ **car windows** ☐
4. Severine recommends trying a South African...
   safari ☐ **car** ☐ **dish** ☐
5. Severine wants to show Tim her...
   photographs ☐ **camera** ☐ **South African dishes** ☐

To: Tim

Subject: Our trip!

Hi Tim,

Robert and I have just come back to Belgium after our trip to South Africa! We flew from Paris to Cape Town and took a bus along the coast. If I were you, I'd rent a car when you come. You ought to take a good camera with you, so you can take lots of photos because there are animals everywhere. Some of them can be dangerous, so you'd better keep your car doors locked! The food was also great. You should try bobotie, a typical South African dish. You should come over some time so we can show you all our photos.

Best wishes,

Severine

9.7 WRITE A LETTER RECOMMENDING A TRIP USING THE PHRASES IN THE PANEL

Hi Jake!

How are you? It's been a long time since I sent you a letter, so I thought I would tell you about our family trip to Paris.

We went to	I really enjoyed the	You ought to	You'd better
If I were you, I'd	Best wishes	You must	The highlight for me was

10 Making predictions

When you talk about a future event, you might need to say how likely it is that the event will happen. There are a number of ways that you can do this.

New language Degrees of likelihood
Aa Vocabulary Idioms about time
New skill Talking about possibilities

10.1 MATCH THE BEGINNINGS OF THE SENTENCES TO THE CORRECT ENDINGS

If you get to the pool at 8am, → you'll probably find a sunbed to lie on.

1. The plane is two hours late now,
2. Sadly, the project won't be finished
3. We might have time to visit the spa
4. Ask the rep from the travel agency, as
5. He definitely won't be trying beef
6. It's unlikely that he will call, as
7. When we arrive at the airport,
8. It's very unlikely that it will rain, since

- by the end of June after all.
- because he's a vegetarian.
- I don't think he has my phone number.
- you'll probably find a sunbed to lie on.
- we will wait for you in the arrivals hall.
- so we will miss our connecting flight.
- there isn't a cloud in the sky today.
- she will probably know the answer.
- if we leave now and we hurry up.

10.2 LISTEN TO THE AUDIO AND MARK WHETHER EACH ACTIVITY IS LIKELY OR UNLIKELY TO HAPPEN

Likely ☑ Unlikely ☐

1 Likely ☐ Unlikely ☐

2 Likely ☐ Unlikely ☐

3 Likely ☐ Unlikely ☐

4 Likely ☐ Unlikely ☐

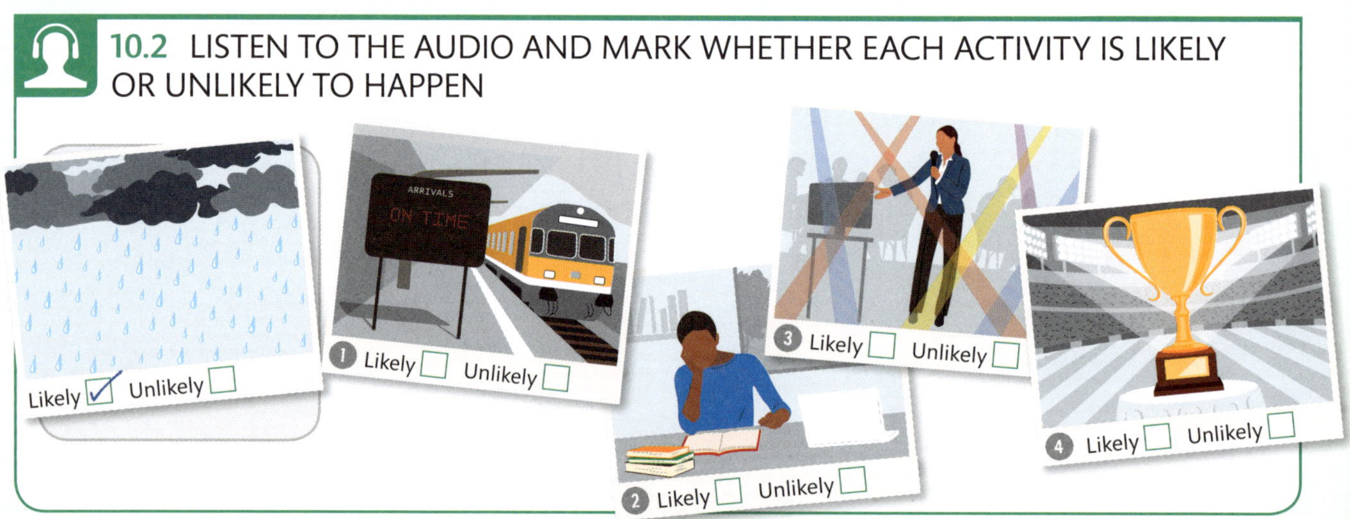

10.3 CROSS OUT THE INCORRECT WORD IN EACH SENTENCE

He looked **surprisingly** / ~~**fortunately**~~ good in his suit and tie at the wedding.

1. The internet has **fundamentally** / **essentially** changed how we book our vacations.
2. **Luckily** / **Fundamentally**, we had nice weather every day when we were on vacation.
3. **Unfortunately** / **Essentially**, Emma was sick when we were on vacation.
4. The trip home was **surprisingly** / **predictably** slow. There are always problems on that route.
5. They make their pancakes in **luckily** / **essentially** the same way that we do.
6. **Interestingly** / **Predictably**, Winston Churchill had stayed at our hotel when he was in the region.
7. **Unfortunately** / **Fortunately**, we were fit enough to be able to hike back down the coast.

10.4 SAY THE SENTENCES OUT LOUD, FILLING IN THE GAPS USING THE WORDS IN THE PANEL

Fundamentally, this is an absolutely awful hotel and I would advise you not to stay here.

1. ____________, we made it to the hotel before the reception closed for the night.
2. Windsurfing is ____________ sailing with a surfboard.
3. ____________, the hotel is completely booked up.
4. ____________, the café was also an art gallery.
5. ____________, Richard actually went in the pool. You know how he normally hates water.
6. ____________, Donald got sunburned again. He never puts any sun tan lotion on.

~~Fundamentally~~ essentially Surprisingly Predictably Unfortunately Luckily Interestingly

10.5 READ THE ARTICLE AND ANSWER THE QUESTIONS

36 CITY PULSE

CITY TO GET MEGA-MALL

Authorities announce plans to build new mega-mall in Graysonville

The local authorities have announced plans to build a new mega-mall in Graysonville. Spokesman William Peters said mega-malls are the shape of things to come and it was only a matter of time before Graysonville built one. Interestingly, the mayor of Graysonville rejected plans to build a mega-mall 10 years ago, but now he's saying that it's essentially a very positive step forward for the town. In the short-term, there's probably going to be construction work going on for the next two years. Luckily, the construction company can use the plans that were drawn up 10 years ago.

The mayor will probably make a statement to explain why the mall will be built, when this had seemed so unlikely. In the long-term, the new development means that Graysonville residents won't have to go out of town to shop because they'll have everything they need right here.

Statement	True	False	Not given
A large new mall is going to be built in Graysonville.	☑	☐	☐
1 The mall will contain over 200 shops.	☐	☐	☐
2 The spokesman thinks malls are the future of shopping.	☐	☐	☐
3 He also said it was inevitable one would be built in Graysonville.	☐	☐	☐
4 The mayor agreed to plans to build a mall 10 years ago.	☐	☐	☐
5 It's unlikely that construction work will go on for two years.	☐	☐	☐
6 It's a good thing that the old plans can be used.	☐	☐	☐
7 There's a good chance the mayor will make a statement.	☐	☐	☐
8 Graysonville residents will no longer shop in Buntstown.	☐	☐	☐
9 Residents will have all the shops they need in their city.	☐	☐	☐

11 Vocabulary

Aa 11.1 **FAMILY AND RELATIONSHIPS** WRITE THE PHRASES FROM THE PANEL UNDER THE CORRECT DEFINITIONS

Share an interest or opinion

have something in common

1. Develop from a child to an adult

2. Be a common feature of a family

3. Speak out in support of somebody

4. Agree with or have similar opinions to somebody

5. Become friendly with a person

6. Like somebody quickly and easily

7. Have a child

8. Slowly become less friendly or close to somebody

9. Meet someone unexpectedly

10. Be strict about something

11. Have respect and admiration for someone

12. A friend who you know very well

13. End a romantic relationship

put your foot down	make friends with somebody	give birth	close friend	run in the family
break up with somebody	grow up	drift apart	bump into somebody	~~have something in common~~
look up to somebody	stick up for somebody	click with somebody	see eye to eye with somebody	

12 Using discourse markers

Discourse markers can be used to show a relationship between two sentences, or parts of a sentence. This can be cause, effect, emphasis, contrast, or comparison.

New language Linking information
Aa Vocabulary Family history
New skill Talking about relationships

12.1 MATCH THE BEGINNINGS OF THE SENTENCES TO THE CORRECT ENDINGS

	I call my mother when I arrive at work, → so she knows I got there safely.	particularly chess.
1	I have bright blue eyes	especially my brother, who's a scientist.
2	We live in different countries,	as a result, he always gets socks!
3	My siblings are all very intelligent,	so she knows I got there safely.
4	My dad loves to play board games,	because we're all so busy now.
5	They like different TV channels	so he always makes dinner for us.
6	We can video chat with each other	like my mother.
7	She is interested in my life at college	especially when they all get together.
8	I enjoy going fishing	just as we used to do when we were kids.
9	My father is a great cook,	but we all get together at Christmas.
10	We only see each other once a month	because she wasn't able to go.
11	It's hard to buy a present for dad and,	since we all have smartphones or laptops.
12	We cook something different for her	so they watch them in different rooms.
13	My relatives all talk a lot,	though my family doesn't eat it often.
14	Ann and I still stay up late chatting	just as my father does. He's great at it.
15	I love cooking Chinese food,	as she's a vegetarian.

12.2 CROSS OUT THE INCORRECT WORDS IN EACH SENTENCE

I always call my mother when I have a problem **because** / ~~**though**~~ she gives me good advice. 

1 My brother loves sports, **especially** / **but** ice hockey. 

2 Our family usually goes to Greece on vacation, **since** / **though** last year we went to Turkey. 

3 My brother got great grades at school, **so** / **particularly** he studied at a good university. 

4 My dad works in the garden every day **though** / **as** he has a lot of free time after retiring. 

5 My mother loves cats **just as** / **but** my grandmother did. 

6 My sister loves music, **since** / **particularly** rock and pop bands. 

7 My mother's always wanted to go to Paris, **like** / **so** we organized a trip for her 50th birthday. 

8 We do sometimes argue with each other, **since** / **but** we never stay angry at each other for long. 

9 My two younger brothers are very close **but** / **as** they shared a room when they were growing up. 

10 My family isn't very big **like** / **since** my husband's.  

11 We will have a big family gathering this year **as** / **especially** all my cousins will be here. 

12 Sonya is a talented painter **just as** / **as a result** her grandmother was. 

13 All my relatives are good singers, **though** / **particularly** my aunt. 

12.3 MATCH THE BEGINNINGS OF THE SENTENCES TO THE CORRECT ENDINGS

	Alice was equally interested in	she decided to look at family records online.
1	She searched for her mother's last name	notably one who was an army general.
2	As a result of a friend's recommendation,	finding out more about her mother's side.
3	Her mother had many fascinating ancestors,	the history of her parents' families.
4	Whereas her mother's side was interesting,	other ancestors of hers were very interesting.
5	Therefore, she decided to concentrate on	she felt more connected to her family.
6	As well as the army general,	online, yet she didn't find anything helpful.
7	As a result of her research,	her father's ancestors were all dull.

12.4 CHOOSE THE MOST APPROPRIATE DISCOURSE MARKERS, THEN SAY THE SENTENCES OUT LOUD

I love visiting the United States, ~~notably~~ / **especially** Florida.

1 **Due to** / **Whereas** the delay to our flight from Atlanta, we missed our connecting flight.

2 It was raining heavily, **therefore** / **so** we decided to cancel the barbecue.

3 My mother is always late, **so** / **but** my father is always on time.

4 Ronald Tuft received a number of awards, **notably** / **especially** the Victoria Cross.

5 Her early work is very radical and her later work is **equally** / **whereas** innovative.

6 Hotels have to be careful **owing to** / **since** it's easy for guests to write bad reviews nowadays.

12.5 READ THE ARTICLE AND ANSWER THE QUESTIONS

GENEALOGY

Top tips for researching your family

Start by talking to your family about their memories, particularly your grandparents or older family members. Remember that they won't be around forever, so it's a good idea to record anything they tell you.

Look at any documents your family has kept. These can give important information about births, marriages, and deaths.

Censuses primarily contain information about people's ages and addresses, but they can also tell you the occupations of your ancestors.

Write down any information you find out. Make copies of family documents and keep them together with this information.

You might think family history research is something you do alone, but this doesn't have to be the case. Why not join a local family history society where you can share tips with others?

The article gives advice on how to research your family history.
True ☑ **False** ☐ **Not given** ☐

1. Don't talk to your grandparents because they can't remember anything.
True ☐ **False** ☐ **Not given** ☐

2. It's a good idea to record what your family tells you.
True ☐ **False** ☐ **Not given** ☐

3. Some types of family documents are more helpful than others.
True ☐ **False** ☐ **Not given** ☐

4. Family documents can tell you when your ancestors married and died.
True ☐ **False** ☐ **Not given** ☐

5. Censuses can tell you what jobs your ancestors did.
True ☐ **False** ☐ **Not given** ☐

6. Don't make copies of old documents because that can damage them.
True ☐ **False** ☐ **Not given** ☐

7. You have to do family history research alone.
True ☐ **False** ☐ **Not given** ☐

8. Social media can help you find out where your nearest family history society is.
True ☐ **False** ☐ **Not given** ☐

13 Past habits and states

When you talk about habits or states in the past, you can use "used to" or "would." English often uses these forms to contrast the past with the present.

New language "Used to" and "would"
Aa Vocabulary Family values
New skill Contrasting the past with the present

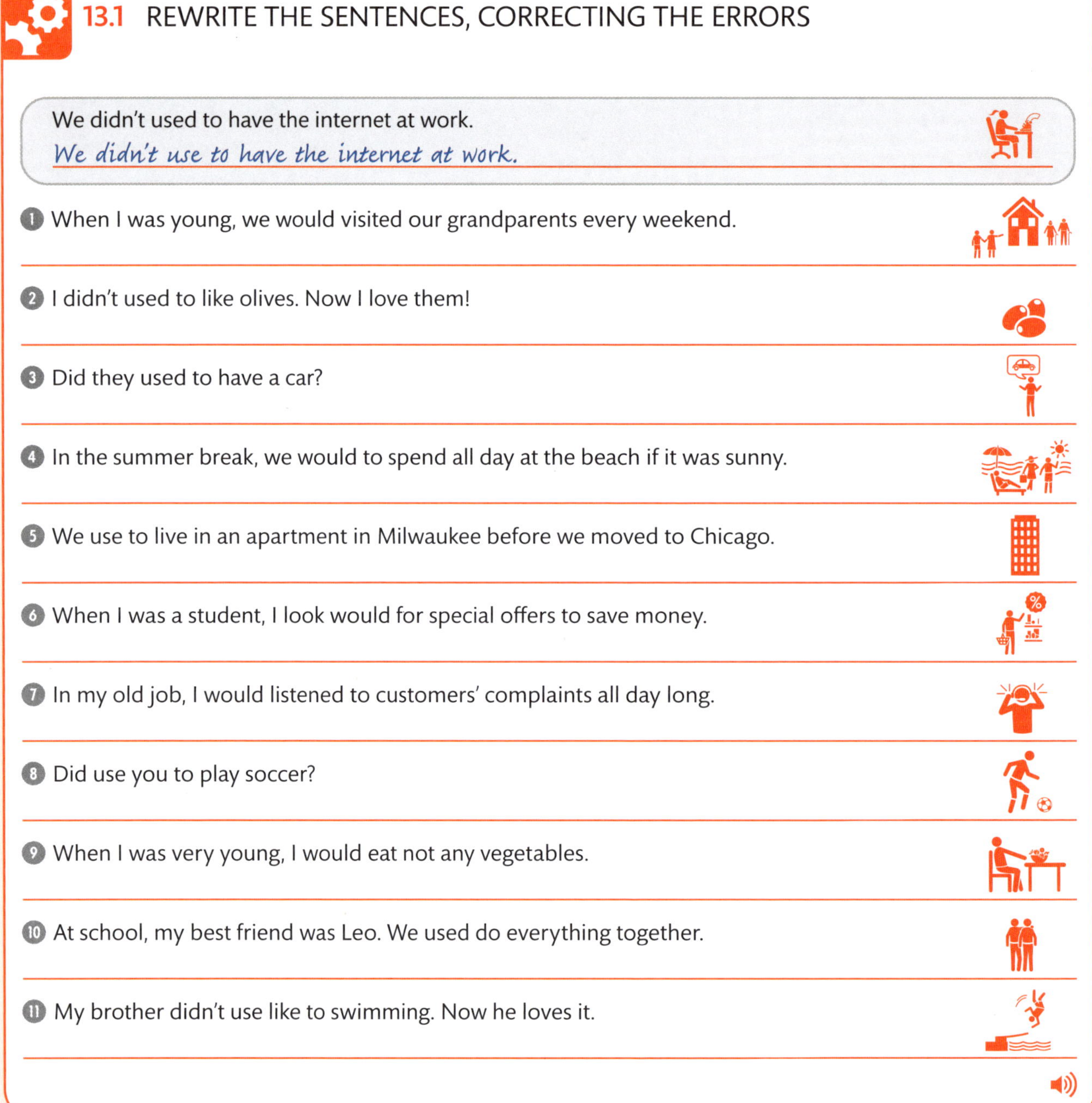

13.1 REWRITE THE SENTENCES, CORRECTING THE ERRORS

We didn't used to have the internet at work.
We didn't use to have the internet at work.

1. When I was young, we would visited our grandparents every weekend.
2. I didn't used to like olives. Now I love them!
3. Did they used to have a car?
4. In the summer break, we would to spend all day at the beach if it was sunny.
5. We use to live in an apartment in Milwaukee before we moved to Chicago.
6. When I was a student, I look would for special offers to save money.
7. In my old job, I would listened to customers' complaints all day long.
8. Did use you to play soccer?
9. When I was very young, I would eat not any vegetables.
10. At school, my best friend was Leo. We used do everything together.
11. My brother didn't use like to swimming. Now he loves it.

13.2 MARK THE SENTENCES THAT ARE CORRECT

When I was a kid, I used to hate doing homework. I would always hand it in late. ☑
When I was a kid, I use to hate doing homework. I would always hand it in late. ☐

1. Did you use to have a computer at home when you were a child? ☐
   Did you used to have a computer at home when you were a child? ☐

2. I worked in Paris from 2005 to 2009. ☐
   I used to work in Paris from 2005 to 2009. ☐

3. Liam would go to Los Angeles twice. ☐
   Liam has been to Los Angeles twice. ☐

4. We didn't used to have to wear a school uniform at my school. ☐
   We didn't use to have to wear a school uniform at my school. ☐

5. I used to ride a bicycle to school every day, even in the rain. ☐
   I use to ride a bicycle to school every day, even in the rain. ☐

13.3 REWRITE THE HIGHLIGHTED PHRASES, CORRECTING THE ERRORS

used to live

1. ______
2. ______
3. ______
4. ______
5. ______
6. ______
7. ______

BEACH LIFE

When I was 17, I got my first summer job. I worked at the beach near where I **use to live**. I **would got up** at 6am and I **would cycling** to the beach. Then I **used spend** an hour putting out sunbeds and umbrellas. For 12 hours a day, I **would got** money off the people who used them. I **use to moan** about my job endlessly. I **used complain** that I was tired, I was bored, it was hot...

Then one day, I had a revelation. I realized how lucky I really was working outdoors in the sunshine on the beach. I **never use to** complain after that!

13.4 LISTEN TO THE AUDIO AND ANSWER THE QUESTIONS

Jack and his mother are discussing the benefits of the internet.

The woman has been doing online shopping.
True ☑ **False** ☐ **Not given** ☐

1. She has bought her husband a new phone.
True ☐ **False** ☐ **Not given** ☐

2. She thinks things were better before the internet.
True ☐ **False** ☐ **Not given** ☐

3. Shopping took longer before the internet.
True ☐ **False** ☐ **Not given** ☐

4. Products on the internet are cheaper.
True ☐ **False** ☐ **Not given** ☐

5. She never had contact with her relatives before.
True ☐ **False** ☐ **Not given** ☐

13.5 LISTEN AGAIN AND MARK THE MOST ACCURATE SUMMARY

1. The son thinks the internet is a positive development, but his mom disagrees. ☐
2. The mother does not agree with most of her relatives about the internet. ☐
3. The mother has a positive attitude toward the benefits of the internet. ☐
4. The mother and son both prefer shopping online to shopping at the mall. ☐

13.6 FILL IN THE GAPS USING THE WORDS IN THE PANEL

Please don't *interrupt* me. I'm trying to make an important point.

1. Janine has similar ______________ to us. She loves animals and she's a vegetarian.
2. Your dog is so ______________ ! He's eaten a bowl of food and still wants more.
3. I take ______________ very seriously. I can't employ people who lie to me.
4. These days there is greater ______________ of people with differing points of view.
5. The best thing about Philip's ______________ is that he is so kind.

acceptance | character | greedy | honesty | ~~interrupt~~ | values

13.7 CORRECT THE ERRORS IN THE SENTENCES, THEN SAY THEM OUT LOUD

We used go the movie theater every weekend when I was a kid.

We used to go to the movie theater every weekend when I was a kid.

1. Did you used to go to dance classes when you were young?

2. I would do a lot of housework yesterday afternoon.

3. I didn't used to enjoy jogging, but now I do.

4. When I was young, my parents would taking us to the beach every summer.

13.8 REWRITE EACH SENTENCE USING "WOULD" OR "USED TO"

I would often have lunch at Rico's Café when I was working in Monterrey.

I often used to have lunch at Rico's Café when I was working in Monterrey.

1. When I was young, I didn't use to clean up my bedroom. It made my mom really angry!

2. My brother and I used to play video games for hours when we were young.

3. I wouldn't drink tea when I was little. Now I drink it all day long!

4. In college, I often used to meet my friends for coffee after classes had finished for the day.

14 Comparing and contrasting

Using "as... as" is a very flexible way to make comparisons. You can use it to compare and contrast quantities and qualities of people, objects, situations, and ideas.

New language "As... as" comparisons
Aa Vocabulary Adjective–noun collocations
New skill Comparing and contrasting

14.1 FILL IN THE GAPS USING THE EXPRESSIONS IN THE PANEL

TIP
You will need to use some of the phrases more than once.

Our chances of winning are even. We're *just as* good a team as they are.

1. This train ticket is ______________ expensive as that one because of the 50 percent discount.
2. He is ______________ intelligent as his brother. They both got high grades.
3. Peter is ______________ good at soccer as the others. He'll catch up quickly.
4. My new place is ______________ big as my old one. It only has one bedroom instead of four.
5. The new album is ______________ catchy as their old stuff. I liked their first album a little more.
6. My new computer is ______________ fast as my old one. It's actually a little slower.
7. This new soft drink tastes ______________ good as SodaUp, but it's not quite the same.
8. The car was ______________ expensive as we'd thought. It was a real bargain.
9. They both worked hard. She deserved to win ______________ much as he did.

just as | nearly as | not quite as | half as | nowhere near as

14.2 LISTEN TO THE AUDIO AND ANSWER THE QUESTIONS

Two coffee shops, Frank's and Morello's, are being compared.

Which coffee shop has better coffee?
Morello's ☑ **Frank's** ☐ **Neither** ☐

1. Which coffee shop is older?
Morello's ☐ **Frank's** ☐ **Neither** ☐

2. Which coffee shop is bigger?
Morello's ☐ **Frank's** ☐ **Neither** ☐

3. Which coffee shop has more staff?
Morello's ☐ **Frank's** ☐ **Neither** ☐

4. Which coffee shop has more customers?
Morello's ☐ **Frank's** ☐ **Neither** ☐

5. Which coffee shop provides a faster service?
Morello's ☐ **Frank's** ☐ **Neither** ☐

6. Which shop sells a wider range of pastries?
Morello's ☐ **Frank's** ☐ **Neither** ☐

7. Which coffee shop is closer to downtown?
Morello's ☐ **Frank's** ☐ **Neither** ☐

14.3 MARK THE SENTENCES THAT ARE CORRECT

She walks as silently as a mouse. ☑
She walks silently as a mouse. ☐

1. This train isn't quite as fast as we'd thought. ☐
This train isn't not as fast as we'd thought. ☐

2. He can't type quickly as she can. ☐
He can't type as quickly as she can. ☐

3. It was nowhere near as good as I'd hoped. ☐
It wasn't as half good as I'd hoped. ☐

4. It tasted just as good as it did last time. ☐
It tasted just as good it did last time. ☐

5. She doesn't shop as much as she used to. ☐
She doesn't shop she used to. ☐

6. They ran as quickly as they could. ☐
They ran quickly as they could. ☐

7. The car was as nearly as fast as we thought. ☐
The car wasn't nearly as fast as we thought. ☐

8. He told us to do it efficiently as possible. ☐
He told us to do it as efficiently as possible. ☐

9. Cooking took half as long as usual today. ☐
Cooking took as half as long as usual today. ☐

10. I wasn't as confident as I was before. ☐
I wasn't as confident I was before. ☐

11. These pastries are just good as Ann's. ☐
These pastries are just as good as Ann's. ☐

Aa 14.4 FILL IN THE GAPS USING THE COLLOCATIONS FROM THE PANEL

Louise always wears ear plugs in bed because she's such a light sleeper .

1. Most people think that if a product has a ______, it must be good quality.
2. My friend Robbie is a very ______. Nothing wakes him up!
3. I was very pleased to hear that my teacher has a ______ of me.
4. After traveling for thirty hours with very little sleep, I needed some ______.
5. Discount retailers like this one sell everything at a ______.
6. Everyone leaves work at about 5pm, so there's always ______ at that time.
7. I like ______ with lots of milk in it.

high price | low price | heavy sleeper | ~~light sleeper~~
strong coffee | weak coffee | high opinion | heavy traffic

Aa 14.5 MATCH THE BEGINNINGS OF THE SENTENCES TO THE CORRECT ENDINGS

We should grab a bite to eat → before the movie starts.

1. I love cakes and candy. You could say
2. Sometimes it's fun to spend money
3. My brother is a businessman
4. The dinner party was amazing. My friends
5. He cooked an interesting

- so he has to wine-and-dine clients.
- on a three-course meal.
- went out of their way to cook for us.
- before the movie starts.
- savory dish using tofu and fish.
- that I have a sweet tooth.

14.6 READ THE BLOG AND WRITE ANSWERS TO THE QUESTIONS AS FULL SENTENCES

CATHERINE'S BLOG

HOME | ENTRIES | ABOUT | CONTACT

POSTED FRIDAY, 6:20PM

Going back to school...

I did just as well in college as my sister did. She had become a banker and was already earning nearly as much as my dad, who's a manager in a factory. I was not quite as enthusiastic about banking as my sister was, but I thought I'd give it a try. The work was nowhere near as interesting as I'd hoped and I was working about 80 hours a week. When I talked to friends about their jobs, I found out they were working about half as many hours as me. My mom told me she was really worried about me. My dad was just as worried.

In the end, I decided I was enjoying my job nowhere near as much as I should have been and I was really depressed. I quit my job and decided to go back to college to study photography. Studying was not quite as scary the second time around because I knew how everything worked and I loved every minute. I also met other older students who were just as happy to be there as I was. I didn't miss class nearly as often as I'd done before. I was always there. The major was just as interesting as I'd thought and it helped me to develop into a photographer and a much happier woman!

How did Catherine do in college?

Catherine did just as well as her sister in college.

1. Who was more enthusiastic about a career in banking, Catherine or her sister?

   ____

2. How did Catherine's working hours compare to her friends' when she was a banker?

   ____

3. How did Catherine's parents feel about how much she was working?

   ____

4. How did Catherine's second experience of college life compare with her first?

   ____

5. How did the photography major compare with what Catherine had thought it would be like?

   ____

15 Two comparatives together

You can use two comparatives in a sentence to show the effect of an action. You can also use them to show that something is changing.

New language Two comparatives together
Aa Vocabulary Age and population
New skill Expressing cause, effect, and change

15.1 MATCH THE BEGINNINGS OF THE SENTENCES TO THE CORRECT ENDINGS

The harder I study, → the more I learn.

1. The more I think about the exam,
2. The older you are,
3. The more the boat shook,
4. The more advanced the course becomes,
5. The higher up the mountain you go,

- the wiser you become.
- the colder it gets.
- the more frightened we felt.
- the more I learn.
- the more nervous I feel.
- the more difficult it gets.

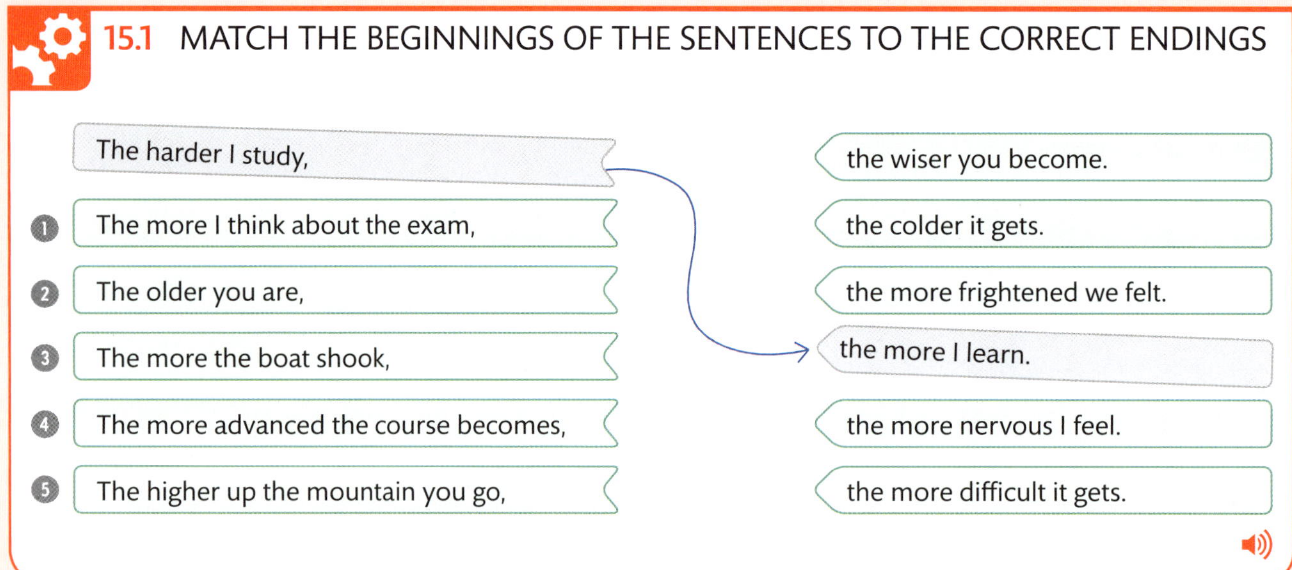

15.2 REWRITE THE SENTENCES, PUTTING THE WORDS IN THE CORRECT ORDER

The | terrified | he | more | drives, | become. | faster | the | I

The faster he drives, the more terrified I become.

1. The | I | earn, | more | I | more | the | save.

2. The | time | happier | we | more | we | spend | outdoors, | the | feel.

3. The | becomes. | the | Joel | works, | harder | he | unhappier

15.3 REWRITE THE SENTENCES, CORRECTING THE ERRORS

Later I watch TV, more bad the shows become.

The later I watch TV, the worse the shows become.

1. The most difficult a challenge is, the most I enjoy it.

2. The early you start working on the project, sooner you'll finish.

3. Long an action film is, less I want to watch it.

4. The hottest it is, thirstiest I become in the summer months.

5. The more angry Peter gets, the lesser sure I become of how to react.

6. More successful my sister becomes, more stressed she gets.

7. The friendly a person is, the more popular they are at work.

8. The more I study, the less certainer I become of what I know.

9. The dangerous an adventure sport is, the more I like it.

10. Further you swim in the mornings and evenings, fitter you'll become.

11. The least junk food you eat in the day, the slimmest you'll get.

12. More interviews with successful people I read, more I realize success is down to hard work.

15.4 LISTEN TO THE AUDIO AND ANSWER THE QUESTIONS

Linda bumps into her old friend Chloe. They talk about their busy lives.

Linda thinks that as you get older, time goes...
quicker and quicker ☑
quicker and longer ☐
quicker and slower ☐

1. Chloe says her life is...
   busier and busier ☐
   easier and easier ☐
   more and more interesting ☐

2. Chloe is feeling more...
   and more depressed about life ☐
   and more lonely ☐
   and more tired ☐

3. Chloe's attitude toward going to bed is...
   the later the better ☐
   the earlier the better ☐
   the quieter the better ☐

4. Dan's job is becoming more...
   and more exciting ☐
   and more stressful ☐
   and more rewarding ☐

5. Chloe's attitude towards her vacation is...
   the more relaxing the better ☐
   the hotter the better ☐
   the sooner the better ☐

15.5 FILL IN THE GAPS USING THE PHRASES IN THE PANEL

The days in November and December become *shorter and shorter*.

1. Because of climate change, temperatures on Earth are getting ________________.
2. In developed countries, people are getting ________________. Is this fair?
3. Ben practices the piano every day so he's getting ________________.
4. Every time I look at my baby daughter she seems ________________ to me.
5. I waved as the boat got ________________ away, and a tear slid down my cheek.

better and better | farther and farther | hotter and hotter | more and more beautiful | richer and richer | ~~shorter and shorter~~

16 Vocabulary

Aa 16.1 STUDYING WRITE THE PHRASES FROM THE PANEL UNDER THE CORRECT DEFINITIONS

Consider and describe how things are alike

compare similarities

7. Finish something within a given time

1. Register to start something

8. A significant level of difference

2. Go to lessons or lectures

9. Fail to finish something within a given time

3. Surprisingly not alike

10. Grading based on work done over a long period

4. Answer questions or perform actions to show how much you know about something

11. Study carried out following graduation from a first degree

5. Consider and describe how things are different

12. Provide comments and advice on how somebody is doing something

6. Someone studying for a first degree at college or university

13. An obvious difference

clear distinction | give someone feedback on something | meet a deadline | ~~compare similarities~~
undergraduate | attend classes | postgraduate | contrast differences | continuous assessment
take a test / take an exam | a world of difference | miss a deadline | strikingly different | enrol in

17 Taking notes

Discourse markers can help you to organize language to make it easier for the listener or reader to follow. Listening for them is very useful when taking notes.

New language Organizing information
Aa Vocabulary Academic life
New skill Taking notes

17.1 MATCH THE DISCOURSE MARKERS TO THEIR SYNONYMS

second → next	for example
1 such as	in addition
2 additionally	in conclusion
3 furthermore	next
4 therefore	moreover
5 to conclude	as a result

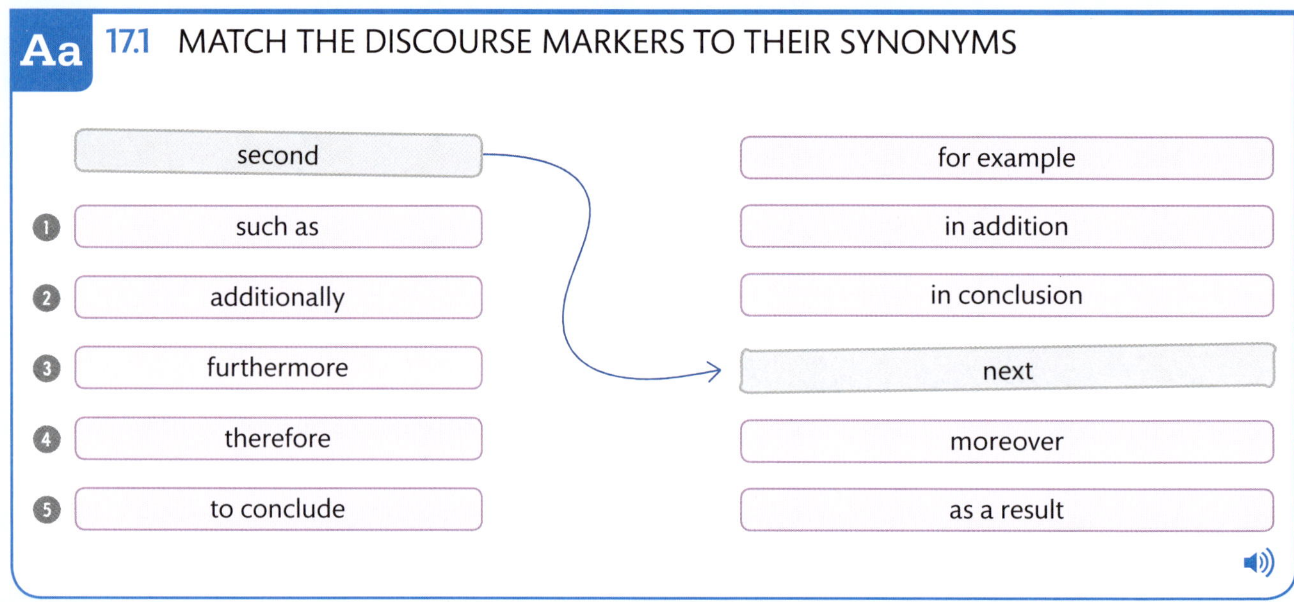

17.2 MATCH THE BEGINNINGS OF THE SENTENCES TO THE CORRECT ENDINGS

To sum up, studying abroad → has both advantages and disadvantages.	what the benefits would be.
1 It is, therefore, easier to study	example, studying at a university.
2 There are a lot of possibilities. For	in a place where you know the language.
3 First, you have to think about	has both advantages and disadvantages.
4 In conclusion, I think studying	go to a Spanish-speaking country.
5 Moreover, you also have the chance	abroad is something everyone should try.
6 If you know Spanish, for instance,	to meet people from other countries.

17.3 LISTEN TO THE AUDIO AND ANSWER THE QUESTIONS

A university professor is addressing a group of first-year students who have just enrolled at the university.

The speaker is talking to people who are studying English. True ☑ False ☐

1. Students can attend classes as and when they choose to do so. True ☐ False ☐
2. The first point she makes is the importance of speaking English in class. True ☐ False ☐
3. The last of her three points is the importance of studying outside of class. True ☐ False ☐
4. The teacher will never assign extra reading. True ☐ False ☐
5. Students have access to an online platform during their course. True ☐ False ☐
6. There is only one way that students can study outside of class. True ☐ False ☐

17.4 READ THE EMAIL AND PUT THE DISCOURSE MARKERS INTO THE CORRECT CATEGORIES

SEQUENCING

first

____

____

ADDING

____

____

EXAMPLES

____

____

____

CONCLUDING

____

____

To: Sam Jones

Subject: Re: Studying overseas

Hi Sam,

You're right. I noticed some differences between being a student in the UK and in France when I studied abroad. First, the days on campus were long. We had to be in class for six or eight hours every day, for example. Second, the classes were more like lessons than lectures. The teacher would give us homework, for instance, and this would be things such as exercises from a book. Third, the atmosphere at the university was much more relaxed. Additionally, there were a lot of clubs to get involved in. Overall it was a fantastic experience. Moreover, it helped me to improve my French a lot. In conclusion, I would recommend studying abroad to anyone.

Best wishes,

John

17.5 REWRITE THE FIRST CONDITIONAL SENTENCES, CORRECTING THE ERRORS

Unless you write the essay by Friday, you have to leave the class.
Unless you write the essay by Friday, you will have to leave the class.

1. If they will want to go on the trip, they'll need to sign up today.

2. Unless we will get three more registrations, we won't be able to run the class.

3. If he wants to join the Spanish class, he is needing to email me this evening.

4. If you will join the committee, you will have to give up a lot of your free time.

5. If you want to meet up for coffee later, I will be being in the library.

6. I will having to cancel Tuesday's class unless we can find another room.

7. If they will want to find out more about our club, we are at the fair tomorrow.

8. Unless we will hear from them in the next five minutes, we will start without them.

9. If you will be biology student, you will need to buy a lab coat by Friday.

10. If you are needing a study partner next semester, I might be available.

11. If they will be able to come to the film night, it will be a great evening.

17.6 MATCH THE BEGINNINGS OF THE SENTENCES TO THE CORRECT ENDINGS

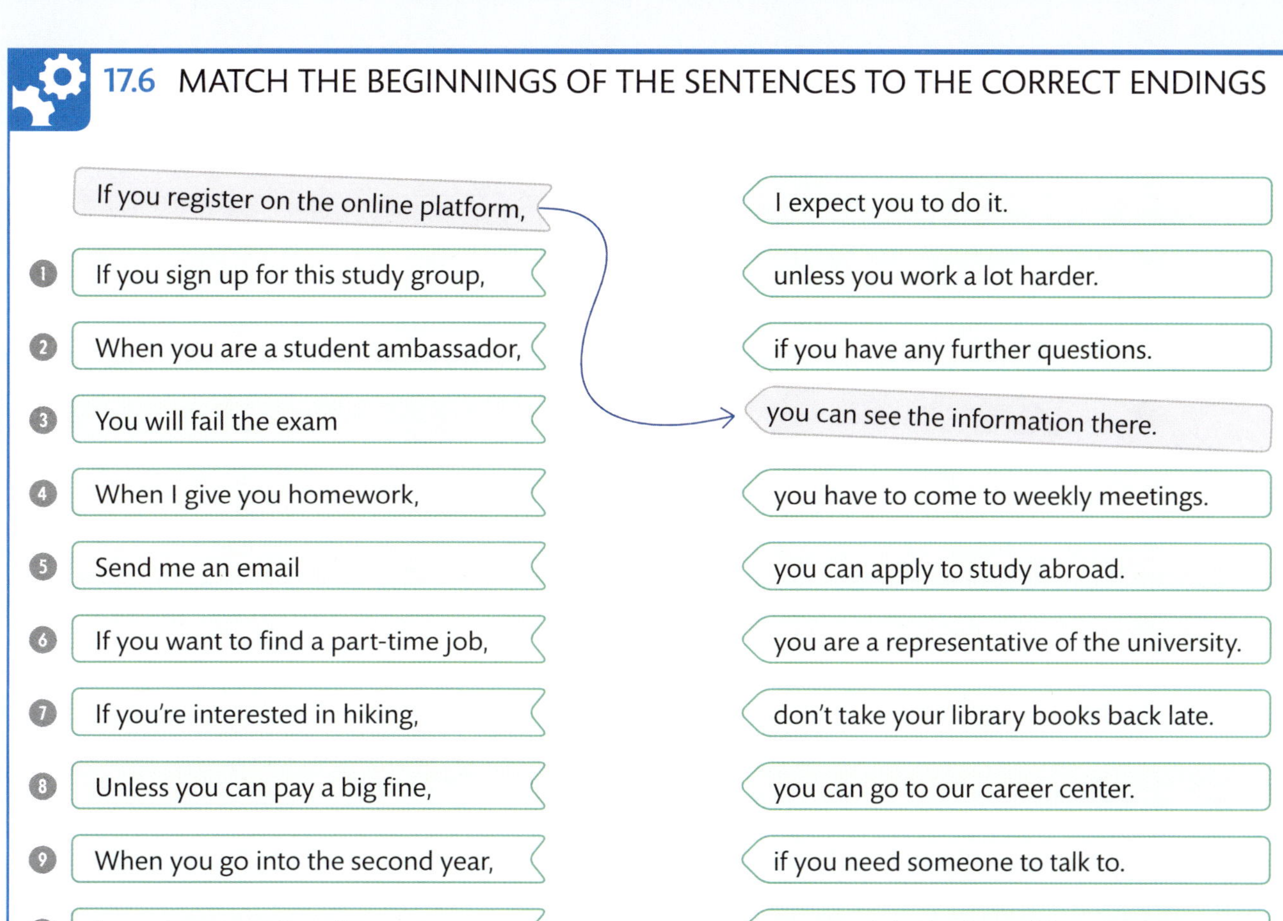

If you register on the online platform, → you can see the information there.

1. If you sign up for this study group,
2. When you are a student ambassador,
3. You will fail the exam
4. When I give you homework,
5. Send me an email
6. If you want to find a part-time job,
7. If you're interested in hiking,
8. Unless you can pay a big fine,
9. When you go into the second year,
10. I am always ready to listen
11. If you want to study French,
12. Unless you attend classes regularly,

- I expect you to do it.
- unless you work a lot harder.
- if you have any further questions.
- you can see the information there.
- you have to come to weekly meetings.
- you can apply to study abroad.
- you are a representative of the university.
- don't take your library books back late.
- you can go to our career center.
- if you need someone to talk to.
- you can join the Expeditions Society.
- you will not understand this subject.
- you should visit the language center.

17.7 LISTEN TO THE AUDIO AND MARK THE CORRECT SUMMARY

A counselor at a university is informing students about the options available to them for their year abroad.

1. Only rich students can study during their year abroad. Everyone else will need to work. ☐
2. The best option is to combine work experience and studying while you're abroad. ☐
3. Students can choose whichever of the three options for their year abroad they prefer. ☐

18 Speaking approximately

English has a number of useful phrases to describe approximate quantities and amounts. You can use them when a number is unknown or roughly accurate.

New language Generalization
Aa Vocabulary Approximate quantity phrases
New skill Talking about numbers

Aa 18.1 MATCH THE PICTURES TO THE CORRECT DESCRIPTIONS

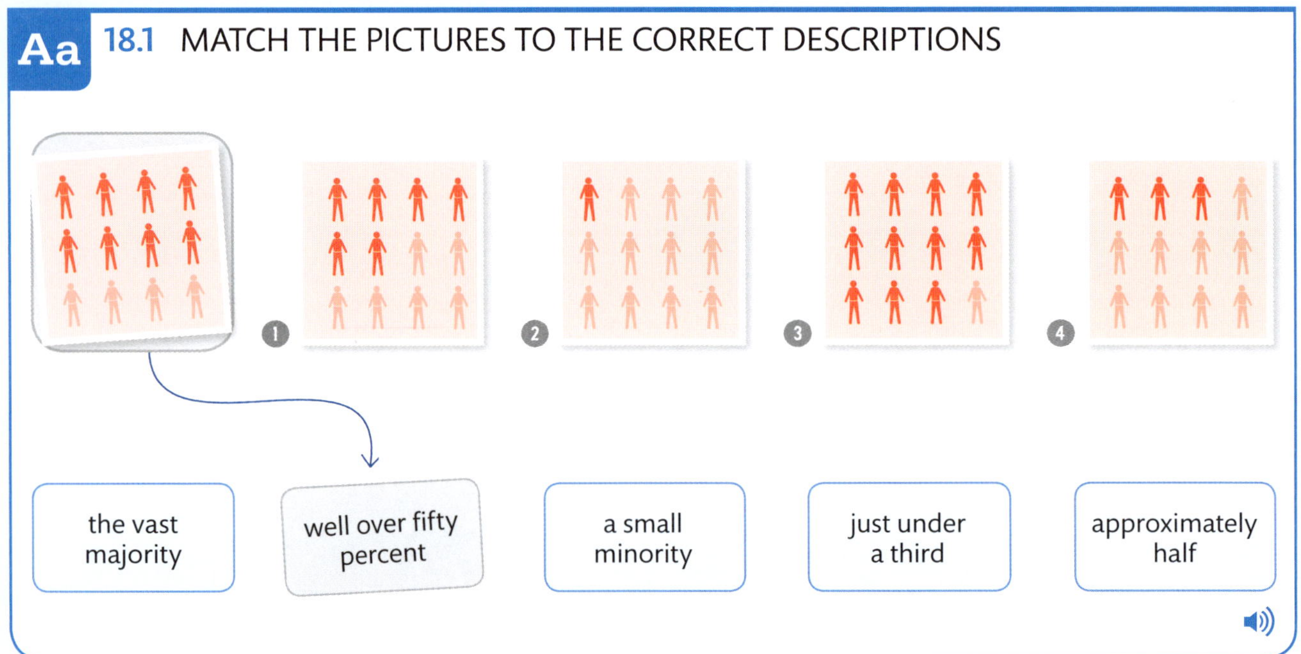

18.2 CROSS OUT THE INCORRECT WORDS IN EACH SENTENCE

52% Approximately / ~~Well over~~ half of the students in the college in the current year are male.

1. 8% In a few / the majority of cases students are asked to retake the year.
2. 9% In a number / approximately half of cases students drop out and leave college.
3. 7% In some / most cases students can ask to defer and start college a year later.
4. 91% In a majority / third of cases students make friends for life while in college.
5. 95% In a minority of / most cases students live on campus in their first year.
6. 23% Just under / Well over a quarter of students have part-time jobs.

18.3 READ THE EMAIL AND ANSWER THE QUESTIONS

To: College Governors

Subject: Student numbers report

Dear Governors,

Please find below the latest figures on our student body this year.

Students: 1,672 undergraduates, 329 graduates. 54 percent female, 46 percent male. 89 international students (60 from Asia, three from South America, 26 from North America).

Campus: 320 acres, 15 minutes from Riverside city center. 98 percent of students live on campus.

Subjects: 32 different degree subjects in Arts (35 percent), Sciences (41 percent), Humanities (11 percent) and Engineering (13 percent).

Clubs: 47 different clubs ranging from skiing to chess to hot-air ballooning. Most students can find a club for something they are interested in.

Meet and Greet: Last year, 1,480 students attended the Meet and Greet. This year's Meet and Greet takes place at the Union Hall, 7pm on October 3.

The majority of students at the college are undergraduates. **True** ☑ **False** ☐ **Not given** ☐

1. Just under half of students are female. **True** ☐ **False** ☐ **Not given** ☐
2. There are some students from South America. **True** ☐ **False** ☐ **Not given** ☐
3. In most cases, international students are Asian. **True** ☐ **False** ☐ **Not given** ☐
4. The college campus is much bigger than at most colleges. **True** ☐ **False** ☐ **Not given** ☐
5. A vast majority of students live on campus. **True** ☐ **False** ☐ **Not given** ☐
6. Just under a third of students study an arts subject. **True** ☐ **False** ☐ **Not given** ☐
7. Biology is the most popular subject. **True** ☐ **False** ☐ **Not given** ☐
8. There are just under 50 different clubs. **True** ☐ **False** ☐ **Not given** ☐
9. In a few cases, students can't find a club that interests them. **True** ☐ **False** ☐ **Not given** ☐
10. You need lots of other students in order to start a club. **True** ☐ **False** ☐ **Not given** ☐
11. Well over 2,000 students went to last year's Meet and Greet. **True** ☐ **False** ☐ **Not given** ☐

18.4 FILL IN THE GAPS USING THE WORDS AND PHRASES IN THE PANEL

92% In *the majority of* cases, foreign language students study abroad for one year.

1. 15% In a ______ cases, the company will hire candidates who do not have a degree.
2. 67% Approximately ______ of students regularly buy fast food.
3. $180 I'm not prepared to pay as ______ as $180 to go to a music festival.
4. 20% In ______ cases, patients are asked to stay at home so they don't infect others.
5. $30 The plane tickets are really cheap. They cost as ______ as $30.
6. 90/120 Can you believe it? Out of 120 professors, as ______ as 90 can speak three languages.
7. 96% ______ 90 percent of students complete their studies.
8. 30% In a ______ of cases, students will have to find their own accommodation.
9. 84% In ______ cases, you'll feel much better within a week.
10. 3 The yoga class isn't very popular. There are as ______ as three people at most classes.
11. 23% ______ a quarter of students take more than a year to find a job.
12. 53% ______ half of students meet their future partner in college.

few ~~the majority of~~ Just over Just under little Well over many
minority most much some few two-thirds

18.5 LISTEN TO THE AUDIO AND ANSWER THE QUESTIONS

The majority of students at Jeremy's college join a sports club. True ☑ False ☐ Not given ☐

1. Most students who join a club have never tried the sport. True ☐ False ☐ Not given ☐
2. There are lots of female students in the soccer club. True ☐ False ☐ Not given ☐
3. In most cases, it costs no more than $5 per semester to join a club. True ☐ False ☐ Not given ☐
4. Students can choose from over 70 clubs. True ☐ False ☐ Not given ☐
5. In your first year, you can only join six clubs. True ☐ False ☐ Not given ☐
6. You have to apply for membership two weeks before you join. True ☐ False ☐ Not given ☐

18.6 RESPOND TO THE AUDIO, FILLING IN THE GAPS IN THE SENTENCES

Most of the people who go to this college end up in really low-paid jobs.

Is that right? I heard completely *the opposite.*

1. Unfortunately, the class sizes are really big.

   Really? I heard that the class sizes are ______

2. The professors are really uninspiring and have nothing new to say.

   Is that so? My experience is very ______ from that.

3. I've been told that the student accommodation is dirty and dark.

   Is that right? I heard that it is ______

really small. | clean and comfortable. | ~~the opposite.~~ | different

19 Changing emphasis

There are a number of ways that you can change emphasis in English. One way is to use a less common grammatical structure, such as the passive voice.

New language The passive voice
Aa Vocabulary Online learning
New skill Changing sentence emphasis

19.1 READ THE BLOG POST AND CHOOSE THE BEST SUMMARY

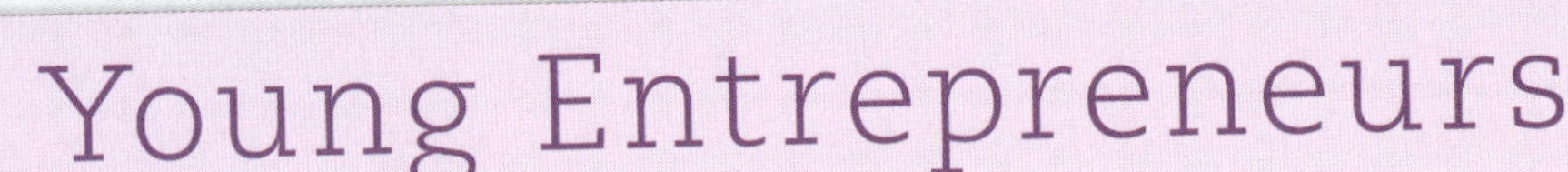

HOME | ENTRIES | ABOUT | CONTACT

POSTED THURSDAY, 8.20AM

A piece of cake

More and more people are now using crowdfunding websites to set up their own businesses. Just post some information about your business idea online and people will transfer money to your account. We talked to Rachel from London, who started using a crowdfunding website a few years ago.

"I started my business, Tea and Cakes, after I graduated from college. I used my savings to buy some basic equipment and started off at small local events. It went well, so I decided to make the business into my full-time job."

That was when Rachel started using the internet where she read about a crowdfunding website she could use. Within about an hour of joining, eight people had offered to fund Rachel's business and within a week it was 200!

Rachel started to expand the business, but after a while she realized that she would need to find a funding model that is appropriate for a larger company. "That was when I found another site where you can get investment in return for shares in your business and some of the investors on there were interested in me! It was a bit scary because I had to write a proper business plan and send it to them."

Rachel is now going to open a tea shop of her own in London. Her advice to other entrepreneurs? "Don't be afraid to try crowdfunding," she says. "It worked for me."

1. Entrepreneurs are being given training in how to set up their own businesses by crowdfunding websites. ☐
2. Crowdfunding websites are being used by entrepreneurs like Rachel to raise funds for their business. ☐
3. Crowdfunding is being used to raise large amounts of money for companies that are active on social media. ☐
4. A business advisor helped Rachel to put together a business plan and find funding for her business online. ☐

19.2 CROSS OUT THE INCORRECT WORDS IN EACH SENTENCE

Crowdfunding websites ~~are using~~ / are being used by more and more people today.

1. Money for setting up a new business can raise / can be raised through these websites.
2. Rachel had been selling / had been sold at local events before she decided to get serious.
3. Rachel found out that social media was using / was being used by other entrepreneurs.
4. Rachel set up / was set up her own website by using a simple web platform.
5. Within a week, Rachel had offered / had been offered funding by eight investors online.
6. Rachel took on / was taken on someone to work for her as her business grew.
7. Later Rachel found / was found another crowdfunding website.
8. Rachel's new tea shop will locate / will be located in London.

19.3 REWRITE THE SENTENCES USING THE PASSIVE VOICE

Entrepreneurs set up new businesses.
New businesses *are set up by entrepreneurs.*

1. They were selling their products at the baseball club last weekend.
   Their products ______________________________
2. Entrepreneurs can easily use social media to promote their businesses.
   Social media ______________________________
3. We will write our detailed business plan for the next 12 months this weekend.
   Our detailed business plan ______________________________
4. He had already sold his old catering business when he bought the hairdressing business.
   His old catering business ______________________________
5. Someone delivered all of the cooking equipment to our new shop yesterday.
   All of the cooking equipment ______________________________

19.4 SAY THE SENTENCES OUT LOUD USING THE WORDS FROM THE PANEL

TIP
Nouns formed from phrasal verbs are spoken with the stress on the first syllable.

Here are the login details you need to use this website.

1. __________ time at this hotel is 2pm. Your room won't be free until then.
2. Just put the __________ in the fridge. We'll have them for lunch tomorrow.
3. Don't forget to make a __________ of your files.
4. The police are looking for an __________ who may have seen the bank robbers.
5. Let me make it clear from the __________ what I expect from you.
6. In the first part of the lesson I'll give you a lot of __________ and then you'll be able to use it.
7. Getting angry with the boss in the boardroom was his __________. He'll never work here again.
8. The police have announced a __________ on bicycle thieves.

downfall · onlooker · crackdown · backup · outset · input · leftovers · ~~login~~ · Check-in

19.5 READ THE ARTICLE AND ANSWER THE QUESTIONS

All hotel guests are able to sleep in until noon before checking out.
True ☐ False ☑

1. There are more budget hotels today than there were in the past.
True ☐ False ☐

2. Guests at budget hotels have early check-in times.
True ☐ False ☐

3. Budget hotels have had a negative effect on other hotels.
True ☐ False ☐

4. A receptionist will always be there when you check into a budget hotel.
True ☐ False ☐

TRAVEL TIPS

The rise and rise of the budget hotel

The days when hotel guests could enjoy sleeping in until noon before checking out are gone. As the number of budget hotels rises, they are making stricter rules for their guests and one of them is earlier check-out times and later check-in times. Such hotels have been the downfall of some of the more expensive hotel chains, which are no longer attracting as many guests as they used to.

Budget hotels will provide you with the services you expect, but from the outset you will notice that they also do everything they can to ensure savings. If you arrive in the evening, for example, you might have to go to a computer terminal to check in. There usually won't be a receptionist there to do it for you. You may also find that your room isn't as clean as you would like it to be.

19.6 MATCH THE BEGINNINGS OF THE SENTENCES TO THE CORRECT ENDINGS

From the outset, → we were told about the challenges.

1. When my dad cooks,
2. After losing my data, I know
3. Never share your login
4. There has been a crackdown
5. I always prefer an early check-in
6. The police put up a line

- it's essential to have a backup.
- on social media use during class.
- to hold back onlookers.
- we were told about the challenges.
- to make the journey easier.
- with anyone for security reasons.
- there are never any leftovers.

20 Things that might happen

There are many ways to talk about hypothetical future situations. You can use different structures to indicate whether you think a hypothesis is likely or unlikely.

New language "What if," "suppose," "in case"
Aa Vocabulary Exams and assessment
New skill Talking about hypothetical situations

20.1 MATCH THE SITUATIONS TO THE LIKELY CONSEQUENCES

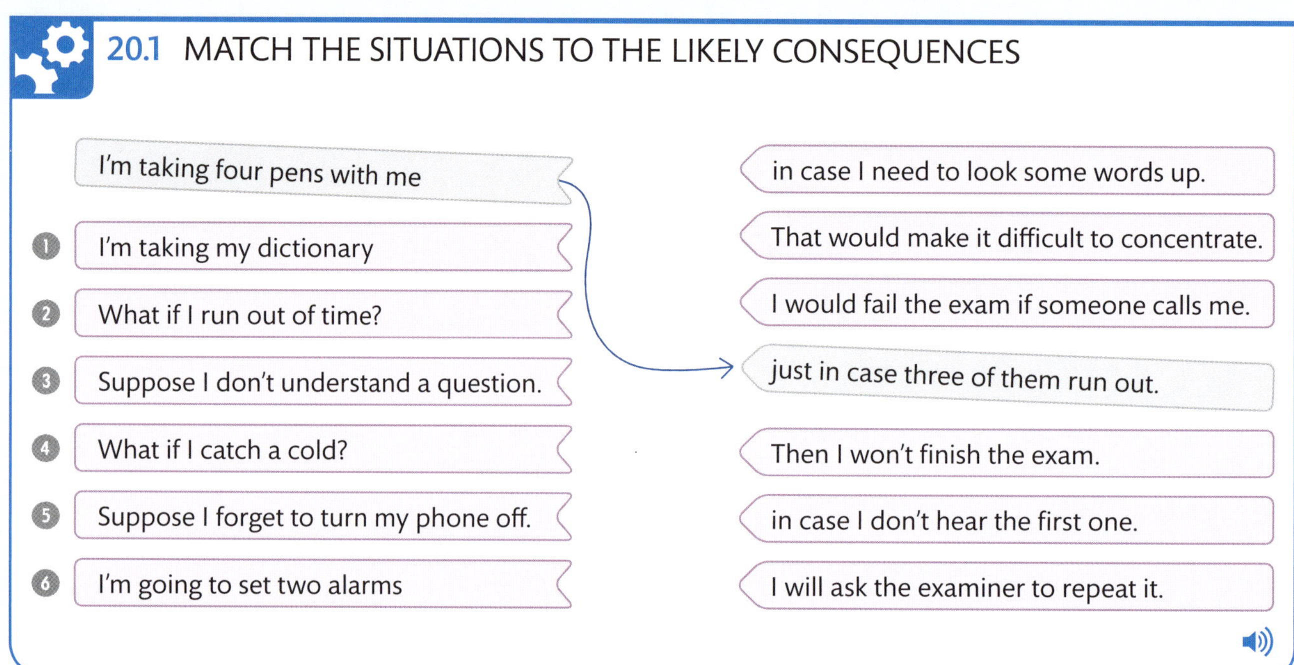

20.2 MARK WHETHER THE OUTCOMES ARE LIKELY OR UNLIKELY

Suppose I won the lottery? I could buy my own car. **Likely** ☐ **Unlikely** ☑

1. What if we all fail the test? We'll have to take it again. **Likely** ☐ **Unlikely** ☐
2. Suppose I wrote a book. I could become famous. **Likely** ☐ **Unlikely** ☐
3. I'm taking two pens in case my old one stops working. **Likely** ☐ **Unlikely** ☐
4. What if I misunderstood the road signs? I could get lost. **Likely** ☐ **Unlikely** ☐
5. Suppose I got a job. I could move to a new house. **Likely** ☐ **Unlikely** ☐
6. It's supposed to be rainy, so I'll get my raincoat. **Likely** ☐ **Unlikely** ☐

20.3 CROSS OUT THE INCORRECT VERB FORM IN EACH SENTENCE

What if you ask / ~~asked~~ the teacher for some help? He won't mind.

1  I know it's not likely, but suppose I have / had an accident on the way to school.

2  What if I help / helped you review and you help me with my essay?

3  Suppose we find / found a rat in our classroom and the test was delayed.

4  You should ask if you can have more time just in case they say / said yes.

5  Suppose another fire alarm goes / went off during the exam. Will they give us more time?

6  What if we don't / didn't know the answers to any of the questions? What would we do?

20.4 FILL IN THE GAPS BY PUTTING THE VERBS IN THE CORRECT TENSES

I would be surprised if that topic ___was___ (be) in the exam. It seems unlikely.

1 If you ____________ (get) 100 percent in the biology exam on Monday, I would be amazed.

2 We ____________ (learn) much more quickly if we use an app to help us learn the words.

3 What if it ____________ (snow) and we couldn't get to school on the day of the exam?

4 If my brother ____________ (win) the prize for the best student, I would be shocked.

5 My parents will be happy if I ____________ (pass) the chemistry exam.

6 If we bought a new car, we ____________ (not be) late so often!

7 She ____________ (not finish) in time if she doesn't start her project soon.

8 It would be so much less stressful if the teachers ____________ (give) us some help.

20.5 RESPOND TO THE AUDIO OUT LOUD, SAYING WHAT MIGHT HAPPEN

Suppose you were a teacher. What subject would you teach?

I'd teach biology because that's my favorite subject.

1. Suppose you could decide how long the weekend was. How many days would it have?

2. Suppose you have some time to watch TV this evening. What will you watch?

3. If you could spend six months anywhere in the world, where would you go?

4. If you could have dinner with anyone, who would you choose?

5. Suppose you had the chance to study abroad. Where would you go?

6. If you won the lottery, what would be the first thing you'd buy?

7. Suppose you got two free tickets to a concert. Who would you go with?

21 Vocabulary

Aa 21.1 **WORKING** WRITE THE PHRASES FROM THE PANEL UNDER THE CORRECT DEFINITIONS

Do more than you are required to do

go the extra mile

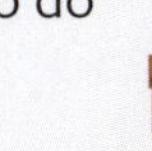

1. A position without many prospects

2. Aim to achieve a particular goal

3. The knowledge and skill gained through doing something yourself

4. Make more progress than others

5. Be forced to leave your job for doing something wrong

6. Have too much work to do

7. Deal with something directly

8. Suddenly begin to have more success

9. A position with the lowest level of responsibility or compensation

10. A job with regular hours

11. Made to leave a job because there is not enough work available

12. Compromise

13. The conditions in which you work

hands-on experience | bottom of the career ladder | be snowed under | nine-to-five | give and take | ~~go the extra mile~~ | set your sights on something | get ahead | dead-end job | take off | tackle something head-on | be fired | working environment | laid off

22 Job applications

In English, prepositions can only be followed by a noun phrase or a gerund. This is particularly important when talking about the order of events.

New language Prepositions and gerunds
Aa Vocabulary Job applications
New skill Writing a résumé and cover letter

22.1 FILL IN THE GAPS USING THE WORDS IN THE PANEL

Since ___*leaving*___ my old job and going back to college, I've started a better-paid job.

1. After ______________ my studies I decided to take a year off and go traveling.
2. ______________ original and innovative products is something I'm particularly interested in.
3. ______________ spending the summer having fun, I want to get a job and earn some money.
4. ______________ attending a workshop on project management, I have a deeper understanding of this area.
5. I've applied ______________ so many jobs, but I haven't had a single interview.
6. ______________ starting my studies, I had earned very high grades at school.
7. While ______________ at a school in Peru, I realized how much I enjoy helping other people.
8. ______________ giving me a strong theoretical grounding, my degree also gave me practical skills.
9. ______________ work at your company immediately would be perfect for me.
10. They're ______________ doing interviews for the job, they're also asking people to take a test.
11. ______________ completing my studies, I have gained some work experience in marketing.
12. After ______________ the job ad, I knew this job was the one for me and I applied for it.
13. ______________ working in human resources for 10 years, I wouldn't be able to take on this role.
14. Since ______________ as a doctor, I've started working at a local hospital.
15. ______________ out into the community to work with people has been very valuable.

Going | As well as | Before | Without | Since | seeing | After | completing
for | Instead of | not only | volunteering | Starting | Developing | qualifying | ~~leaving~~

22.2 READ THE JOB ADVERTISEMENT AND WRITE ANSWERS TO THE QUESTIONS AS FULL SENTENCES

VACANCIES

Job opening

Digital Marketing Manager: Transvan logistics

We are looking for an experienced and enthusiastic individual to coordinate marketing activities across desktop and mobile digital platforms. With at least five years' experience in a similar position, you will be responsible for growing the number of visitors to our website. We are a logistics company, so any experience in the logistics industry would be particularly relevant and desirable.

About you: You will be happy to get involved with all aspects of our marketing activities. Ideally, we want someone who will stay with us for a long time and who will be an active part of the young, fun team we've built up.

Must haves:

- Five or more years' experience in digital marketing
- A Bachelor's degree or higher
- Perfect spoken and written English skills
- Excellent communication skills
- Previous experience working for a logistics company (desirable, not essential)
- A great eye for detail

How to apply: Please send a résumé and cover letter by March 26.

How much experience in digital marketing would the ideal candidate for this job have?

The ideal candidate would have at least 5 years' experience in digital marketing.

1. Experience of which industry would be particularly desirable?

2. What will the candidate be responsible for?

3. How long would the ideal candidate stay with the company for?

4. What academic qualifications do you need to have to apply for this job?

5. Which language do you need to be able to speak and write perfectly?

6. What do you have to send to the company if you want to apply for this job?

22.3 REWRITE THE SENTENCES, CORRECTING THE ERRORS

I write to apply for the position of sales representative advertised on your website.
I'm writing to apply for the position of sales representative advertised on your website.

1. I have recently completing a degree in mechanical engineering.

___

2. This has prepared me very good for working in the area of product management.

___

3. One course I made on brand design is particularly relevant to this position.

___

4. I have a keen interest in follow developments in the food industry.

___

5. Thank you for taking the time to consider my application and I look forward to hear from you.

___

22.4 FILL IN THE GAPS USING THE PHRASES IN THE PANEL

I have been *responsible for* teams of up to 10 people in my previous positions.

1. The contents of my degree course have prepared me very well for ________.
2. I have a ________ in the energy sector and have work experience in this area.
3. You will find that I'm a fast and accurate writer with a keen ________.
4. I would be able to ________ the responsibility that this position involves.
5. The experience I have gained in my previous jobs is ________ to this position.

eye for detail	particularly relevant	take on
strong interest	~~responsible for~~	this position

22.5 MARK THE MORE FORMAL SENTENCE IN EACH PAIR

A lot of the stuff I studied during my degree would be relevant to this job. ☐
A lot of the courses I did during my degree would be relevant to this job. ☑

1. I can see myself being an awesome boss one day. ☐
   I think I would make an excellent office supervisor at some point in the future. ☐

2. My first job was a complete nightmare because my colleagues weren't very nice to me. ☐
   In my old job I experienced some conflict with colleagues. ☐

3. I've organized lots of events like trade fairs and product launches. ☐
   I've organized a lot of events such as trade fairs and product launches. ☐

4. Since graduating from college, I've gained a lot of experience in public relations. ☐
   Since graduating from college, I've got loads of experience in PR. ☐

5. I may look to move into a managerial job in a few years' time. ☐
   Maybe I'll move into a managerial job in a few years' time. ☐

6. I want to do stuff like organize marketing campaigns. ☐
   I would like to be involved with the organization of marketing campaigns. ☐

7. As you can see, I have extensive work experience in the area of retail. ☐
   As you can see, I have lots of work experience in retail. ☐

8. My skills are significantly superior to those of the average candidate. ☐
   My skills are way better than the skills most people have. ☐

9. It would be great if you could look at my application. ☐
   Thank you for taking the time to consider my application. ☐

10. My work experience is particularly relevant to this position. ☐
    My work experience is really great for this position. ☐

11. I have an in-depth knowledge of product development processes. ☐
    I know lots about product development processes. ☐

12. I've wanted to be an electrician for ages. ☐
    I've wanted to be an electrician for a very long time. ☐

13. I very much look forward to hearing from you. ☐
    I hope you'll write back to me soon. ☐

23 Asking polite questions

In English, asking questions directly can sometimes be seen as impolite. It is very common for English speakers to make their questions more indirect.

New language Direct and indirect questions
Vocabulary Job interviews
New skill Asking questions politely

23.1 REWRITE THE DIRECT QUESTIONS AS INDIRECT QUESTIONS

Do you have any weaknesses?
Could you tell me if *you have any weaknesses?*

1. Do you have any relevant experience in this area?
   Could you tell me if ______
2. Are your studies relevant to this area?
   I was wondering whether ______
3. Have you applied for any other jobs?
   We'd like to know whether ______
4. Do you like working on a team?
   I was wondering if ______
5. Are you a good team player?
   We'd like to know if ______
6. What would you like to be doing in 10 years' time?
   Do you have any idea what ______
7. What are your weaknesses?
   Could you tell me what ______
8. Where did you work after completing your studies?
   I was wondering where ______
9. Where in China did you study?
   I'm curious to know where ______
10. Which area of our activities are you particularly interested in?
    Could you tell us which ______
11. Have you ever worked abroad?
    I'd like to know if ______

23.2 REWRITE THE INDIRECT QUESTIONS, PUTTING THE WORDS IN THE CORRECT ORDER

last | wondering | you | left | job. | why | I | was | your

I was wondering why you left your last job.

1. on? | tell | which | us | Could | you've | projects | you | worked

2. know | how | plan | you | to | work | for | I'd | us. | like | long | to

3. abroad. | was | where | I | wondering | studied | you

4. further | to | if | you'd | to | training. | do | know | like | We'd | like

23.3 SAY THE DIRECT QUESTIONS OUT LOUD AS INDIRECT QUESTIONS

What are your goals?

I was wondering *what your goals are.*

1. How did you get along with your last boss?

   Could you tell us ________

2. Where do you want to be in five years' time?

   Do you have any idea ________

3. Have you ever worked with children before?

   I'm curious to know if ________

4. Have you ever managed a website before?

   I was wondering whether ________

5. Why should we employ you?

   Could you tell us ________

23.4 MATCH THE QUESTIONS TO THEIR ANSWERS WITH STALLING TECHNIQUES

Would you be able to work weekends? → Good question. I'm not sure. Let me check with my family.

1. Would you be prepared to travel a lot?
2. Would you like to lead a team one day?
3. Could you come in for an interview?
4. Could you send us references from your previous employers?
5. Can we count on you to stay with us long-term?

- Well, I don't know. Managing a team is something I might be interested in.
- Good question. I'm not sure. Let me check with my family.
- Let me see. I'll check my schedule and let you know.
- Well, yes, that should be possible. I'll check with them.
- Maybe we should wait and see how I settle in here first.
- Let's see. It would depend where you wanted me to go.

23.5 LISTEN TO THE AUDIO AND ANSWER THE QUESTIONS

Mr. James is interviewing Rose for the position of Head of Communications.

How many other offers has Rose gotten so far?

None ☐
One ☑
A lot of companies ☐

1. Which of the following is not important to Rose?
   - **How close the company is to her home** ☐
   - **How many people are on her team** ☐
   - **How challenging the job is** ☐

2. What is Rose's greatest weakness?
   - **She wants to push herself all the time** ☐
   - **She likes to control everything** ☐
   - **She doesn't cope well in a crisis** ☐

3. What is one of Rose's strengths as a manager?
   - **Her energy inspires the people on her team** ☐
   - **She communicates well with her team** ☐
   - **She wants to give her team new challenges** ☐

4. What does Rose say about her salary?
   - **She would be willing to earn less than before** ☐
   - **She wouldn't want to earn less than before** ☐
   - **She wants to earn more than before** ☐

5. What is Rose going to do about her salary?
   - **Rose wants Mr. James to decide her salary** ☐
   - **Rose will call Mr. James and let him know** ☐
   - **Rose will think about what she would expect** ☐

23.6 RESPOND TO THE AUDIO, SPEAKING OUT LOUD AND ADDING APPROPRIATE STALLING PHRASES FROM THE PANEL

Is this the only job you've applied for?

Well, to be honest with you, I have applied for a few other jobs, too.

1 Could you tell us something about yourself?

__________ I'm a dedicated worker and a great communicator.

2 Where do you want to be in 10 years' time?

__________ I'd like to have a position in management.

3 How do you feel about working as part of a team?

__________ it's something that I enjoy and would like to continue doing.

4 Could you tell me what your strengths are?

__________ I have a keen eye for detail and I always give 100 percent.

5 Do you have any experience of holding a leadership role?

__________ I did once take over from my boss while he was on vacation.

6 Would you be able to do overtime if we needed you to?

__________ It would depend how much you needed me to do.

7 How soon would you be able to start if we offer you the job?

__________ I could start next month.

Yes, where to start? ~~Well, to be honest~~ Let's see. I suppose Let me see.

I'm not sure. Oh, let me see. Well, Good question, let me see.

24 Complex verb patterns

There are several different patterns that verbs can follow, including whether they can be followed by an infinitive or a gerund.

New language Verb + infinitive / gerund
Aa Vocabulary World of work
New skill Using complex verb patterns

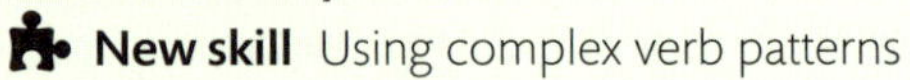

24.1 REWRITE THE SENTENCES, CORRECTING THE ERRORS

She hates people to make decisions without consulting her.
She hates people making decisions without consulting her.

1. She finally managed cutting down the number of hours she works from 40 to 35.

2. I think our manager should allow us leaving work a bit earlier on Friday afternoon.

3. This new piece of software enables me to making updates very quickly.

4. Sam threatened leaving if the boss doesn't find a new employee to help him.

5. I'm the person in my office who always volunteering to stay late.

6. This is the first time that a colleague has invited me having dinner at their home.

7. The merger deal we completed last month has caused our profits increase.

8. He doesn't like people to tell him what to do while he's at work.

9. The boss has offered sending me on a training course to improve my computer skills.

10. He enjoys to play the role of the hot-shot manager when visitors come.

24.2 CROSS OUT THE INCORRECT WORDS IN EACH SENTENCE

I was glad that I managed ~~finishing~~ / to finish all my work on Friday afternoon. Now I can relax.

1. My colleague enjoys hearing / to hear from satisfied customers.
2. My new smartphone enabling / enables me to stay connected with my office wherever I am.
3. She hates her colleagues telling / to tell her what she should do in her department.
4. We like our customers giving / to give us feedback on the services we provide them.
5. My boss offered / offered to give me an office of my own next year.

24.3 READ THE ARTICLE AND ANSWER THE QUESTIONS

EMPLOYEES AND EMPLOYERS

Why people quit jobs

Rudeness and work/life balance are the top factors

Companies are advised to hold on to their employees for as long as possible. Losing employees is expensive and threatens to lower the morale on the teams that the employees leave behind. According to a recent survey, the thing that causes the largest number of employees to resign is rudeness. People just don't like their colleagues being rude to them. Another reason given by a lot of people is having a job that doesn't enable them to have a good work/life balance. Some people are being forced to do two people's jobs and, as a result, they have to work long hours and weekends.

	True	False	Not given
Companies should try to keep employees as long as they can.	☑	☐	☐
1. It doesn't cost companies much money when employees leave.	☐	☐	☐
2. Other employees' morale might be lower when a colleague leaves.	☐	☐	☐
3. More than 80 percent of people resign because of rudeness.	☐	☐	☐
4. Having a good work/life balance is important to a lot of people.	☐	☐	☐
5. Some people volunteer to do two people's jobs.	☐	☐	☐

24.4 FILL IN THE GAPS USING THE WORDS IN THE PANEL

I was surprised when my daughter told me she would like *to study* in Canada next year.

1. She always stops ______ at what's on at the movie theater when we walk past it.
2. I remember ______ that movie with Brian Owen, but it was a very long time ago.
3. She reminded him ______ to the supermarket after work, but he still forgot!
4. I wish they would stop ______ at us like that. They're making me nervous.
5. He finally remembered ______ me some flowers for my birthday. He usually forgets.
6. When I was a child, my mother always encouraged me ______ fruit and vegetables.
7. The turbulence caused the airplane ______ from side to side for about 10 minutes.
8. He knew that we weren't interested in what he had to say, but he still went on ______ .
9. I would advise you ______ an aspirin for your headache.
10. Did you see Donald volunteering ______ the office party this year?
11. He tried ______ the table through the door of our new living room, but it was too big.
12. The boss threatened ______ us work all weekend if we didn't finish the project by Friday.

to move	to take	watching	to eat	looking	to buy	
to organize	to look	to go	to push	talking	~~to study~~	to make

24.5 MARK THE SENTENCES THAT ARE CORRECT

I forgot to tell something important to my boss at the meeting. ☐
I forgot to tell my boss something important at the meeting. ☑

1. Jade remembered giving that doll me as a birthday present when I was a child. ☐
   Jade remembered giving me that doll as a birthday present when I was a child. ☐

2. The inspector advised us to change our safety procedures in the factory. ☐
   The inspector advised us changing our safety procedures in the factory. ☐

3. She likes people talking about how great she is. She has a very big ego! ☐
   She likes people talk about how great she is. She has a very big ego! ☐

4. The loan we got from the bank enabled us to build an extension on our house. ☐
   The loan we got from the bank enabled us building an extension on our house. ☐

5. I'll write a note to remind myself to bring that book with me next week. ☐
   I'll write a note to remind myself bringing that book with me next week. ☐

24.6 READ THE EMAIL AND ANSWER THE QUESTIONS

How does Lynn feel about her job at the moment?
Lynn isn't enjoying her job.

1. What does Jackie advise Lynn to do with her boss?

2. What does Jackie suggest that Lynn's boss could do?

3. What should Lynn do if she can't fulfill her potential?

4. What positive quality does Jackie believe Lynn has?

5. What does Jackie think that Lynn shouldn't accept?

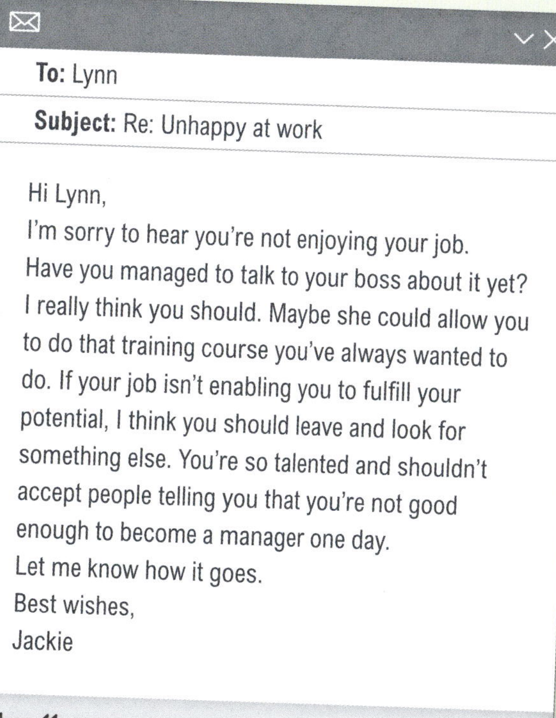

To: Lynn

Subject: Re: Unhappy at work

Hi Lynn,
I'm sorry to hear you're not enjoying your job. Have you managed to talk to your boss about it yet? I really think you should. Maybe she could allow you to do that training course you've always wanted to do. If your job isn't enabling you to fulfill your potential, I think you should leave and look for something else. You're so talented and shouldn't accept people telling you that you're not good enough to become a manager one day.
Let me know how it goes.
Best wishes,
Jackie

25 Double object verbs

Some verbs can be followed by both a direct object and an indirect object. Sentences using these verbs can be ordered in a number of different ways.

New language Double object verbs
Vocabulary New businesses
New skill Talking about starting a business

25.1 REWRITE THE SENTENCES, CORRECTING THE ERRORS IN THE ORDER OF THE WORDS

He bought a new book his daughter.
He bought his daughter a new book.

1. Jake lent a pencil me.
2. The teacher offered some help me.
3. She borrowed from Liz a book.
4. Susanne sent a postcard from her vacation me.
5. We donated to the families some old clothes.
6. They paid for the book 20 dollars.
7. John sent an email me yesterday.
8. I'm sure she told the truth you.
9. We gave some biscuits the dog.
10. He brought to her house his computer.
11. Joanne gave her notes him.
12. She lent to her son her car.
13. They bought some chocolates the teacher.
14. Brian the message passed on to Fiona for me.
15. Richard lent his pen me.
16. She always gives a ride to work me.
17. The teacher gave to those students bad grades.
18. Jason passed to me a note in class.
19. Kathryn lent some money her son.
20. They brought to the discussion a lot of energy.
21. He sold to the neighbor his old car.
22. They gave some candy her.
23. She gave to them some books she didn't need.

25.2 REWRITE THE SENTENCES, PUTTING THE WORDS IN THE CORRECT ORDER

daughter | She | 50 | lent | her | dollars.

She lent her daughter 50 dollars.

1. Robert | a | me | of | help. | lot | gave

2. gave | to | Emma | that | me. | book

3. lent | bike | a | He | his | friend. | to

4. message | me. | the | They | on | to | passed

5. present. | He | wife | a | great | gave | his | birthday

25.3 MATCH THE SENTENCES THAT DESCRIBE THE SAME EVENT

The students received a lot of homework. → The teacher gave them a lot of homework.

1. Another student bought his books.
2. The daughter received a car.
3. She received a message from him.
4. The charity received money from them.
5. He borrowed some money from his dad.
6. He received an email from me.

They donated money to the charity.

I sent him an email.

He lent some money to his son.

The teacher gave them a lot of homework.

He sold his books to another student.

He passed the message on to her.

She bought a car for her daughter.

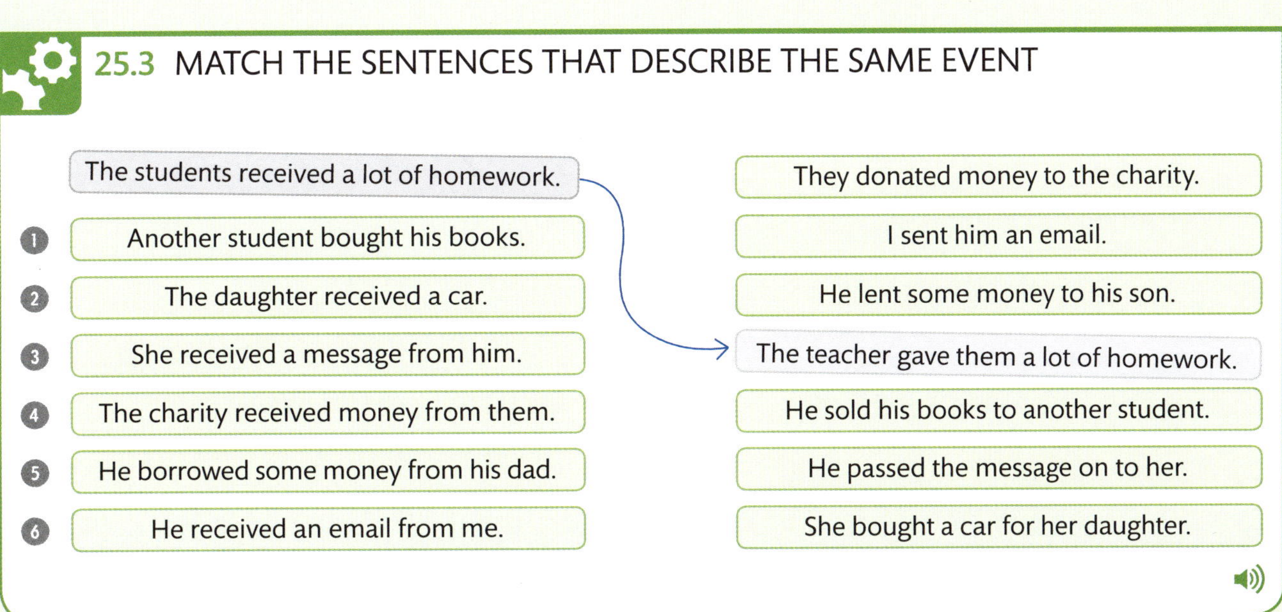

25.4 READ THE BLOG AND ANSWER THE QUESTIONS

The Neighbor Network is a supermarket chain.
True ☐ False ☑ Not given ☐

1. *The Neighbor Network* is a new company.
True ☐ False ☐ Not given ☐

2. *The Neighbor Network* was set up by two entrepreneurs.
True ☐ False ☐ Not given ☐

3. You access *The Neighbor Network* through the internet.
True ☐ False ☐ Not given ☐

4. You use *The Neighbor Network* to contact neighbors.
True ☐ False ☐ Not given ☐

5. You can borrow things through *The Neighbor Network*.
True ☐ False ☐ Not given ☐

6. There is a monthly charge for using the site.
True ☐ False ☐ Not given ☐

25.5 FILL IN THE GAPS USING THE IDIOMS IN THE PANEL

At first I was worried about all of the *red tape* I would have to deal with.

1. However, I thought ______________________ and I decided to just go for it anyway.
2. Things really took off when I met an angel investor who basically wrote me a ______________.
3. Her faith in my abilities was the ______________ that gave me an edge over the competition.
4. As a result, I was able to ______________ and everyone was coming to me.
5. I had really ______________ there.

cornered the market | ~~red tape~~ | ace up my sleeve | blank check
nothing ventured, nothing gained | hit the ground running

26 Vocabulary

Aa 26.1 **MEETING AND PRESENTING** WRITE THE PHRASES FROM THE PANEL UNDER THE CORRECT DEFINITIONS

Arrive at a point of agreement

reach a consensus

1. Write a record of what was said during a meeting

2. Present a formal talk for a group of people

3. Listen to and answer questions

4. Start working or doing something that you have to do

5. Conclude

6. A vote performed by raising hands to show agreement to a proposal

7. Arrange a date in the future

8. Have no time left for something

9. Included on the list of things to discuss

10. A group of people who manage a business or organization

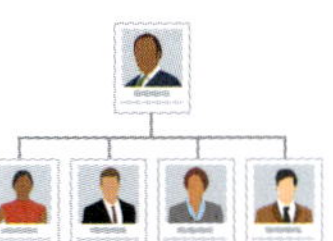

11. Go to a meeting

12. A telephone call with a number of people at the same time

13. Not present

get down to business · show of hands · take minutes · absent · ~~reach a consensus~~ · attend a meeting · take questions · on the agenda · conference call · give a presentation · board of directors · run out of time · sum up · set a date

27 Reflexive pronouns

Reflexive pronouns show that the subject of a verb is the same as its object. They can also be used in other situations to add emphasis.

New language Reflexive pronouns
Aa Vocabulary Workplace language
New skill Talking about work issues

27.1 FILL IN THE GAPS USING REFLEXIVE PRONOUNS

The company director *himself* came to our team meeting.

1. Anna, you're welcome to help ______ to tea or coffee and cookies.
2. I taught ______ to use this computer program.
3. He is very proud of ______ for getting the highest grade in his class.
4. You can all sit ______ down anywhere you like.
5. We helped ______ to the free food at the staff party.
6. I'm annoyed with ______ for not thinking about that.
7. She accidentally cut ______ while she was cooking.
8. The members of the team argued among ______ for about half an hour.
9. They're very pleased with ______ because their boss praised their work.
10. I often ask ______ why I decided to leave the country and move to the city.
11. He felt that he had let ______ down.

27.2 CROSS OUT THE INCORRECT WORD IN EACH SENTENCE

I've emailed the presentation to ~~me~~ / myself so I don't forget to look at it.

1. My grandparents are 90 years old, but they can still do everything for them / themselves.
2. He prides him / himself on his honesty and integrity.
3. Ramona is really busy today. Could you take this package to the post office for her / herself?
4. You don't need to translate that for me. I can do it for me / myself.
5. They got the contract because they worked much harder than us / ourselves.
6. You are all very welcome. Please make yourself / yourselves at home here.
7. Our neighbors were shouting at each other / themselves until 10 o'clock last night.

27.3 SAY THE SENTENCES OUT LOUD, FILLING IN THE GAPS WITH THE CORRECT REFLEXIVE PRONOUNS

I bought a book and the author *herself* signed it! She was really sweet.

1. We want you to prepare the presentations __________ .
2. The CEO __________ mentioned me during his annual speech.
3. I am very proud! I repaired the bike __________ .
4. We should be proud that we've achieved all of this by __________ .
5. Food __________ is changing and so are our eating habits.
6. They congratulated __________ on a job well done.
7. The shop manager __________ came down to apologize to me for her mistake.

27.4 FILL IN THE GAPS USING THE REFLEXIVE PRONOUNS IN THE PANEL

The winners of the competition will be able to enjoy *themselves* at this luxury hotel in the Caribbean.

1. I'm glad that we were able to do it ______________ without asking the boss for help.
2. The presentation ______________ went well, but the meeting afterwards went badly.
3. All of the children behaved ______________ really well during the flight.
4. The president's wife ______________ came to shake my hand and give me the award.
5. I felt very pleased with ______________ when I found out that my painting had won the prize.
6. This is the first time that he's been able to walk by ______________ since the accident.
7. I'm looking forward to having the house to ______________ while my parents are away.
8. You should all help ______________ to any books on my bookcase that you're interested in.
9. Your mother isn't going to wash your clothes anymore. You'll have to do it ______________ .

himself | ourselves | ~~themselves~~ | yourselves | herself
myself | yourself | myself | itself | themselves

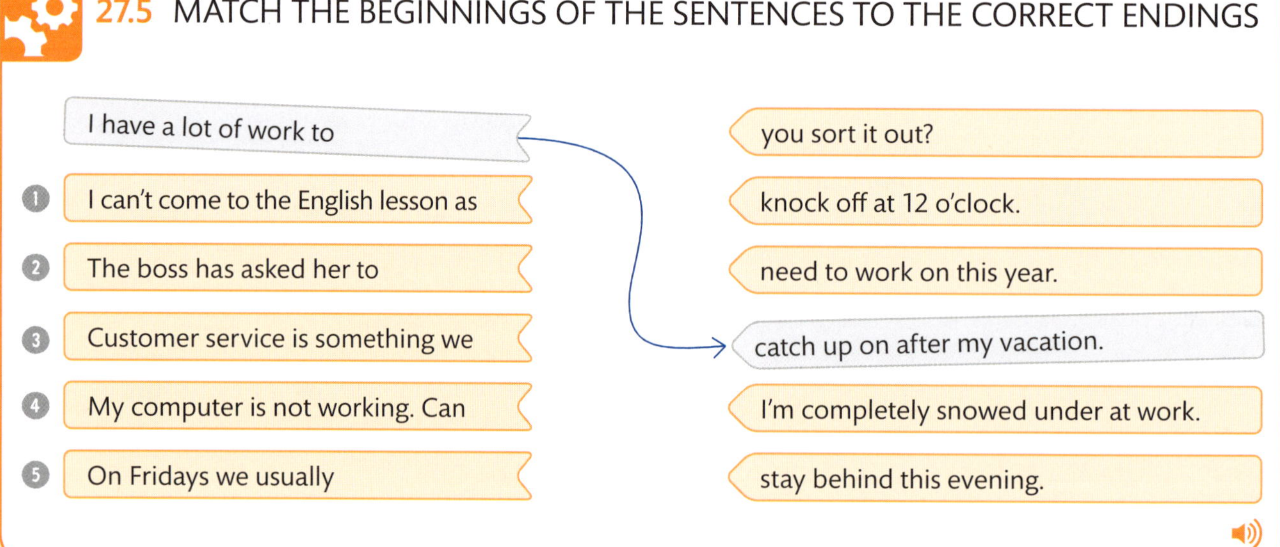

27.5 MATCH THE BEGINNINGS OF THE SENTENCES TO THE CORRECT ENDINGS

I have a lot of work to → catch up on after my vacation.

1. I can't come to the English lesson as
2. The boss has asked her to
3. Customer service is something we
4. My computer is not working. Can
5. On Fridays we usually

- you sort it out?
- knock off at 12 o'clock.
- need to work on this year.
- catch up on after my vacation.
- I'm completely snowed under at work.
- stay behind this evening.

27.6 REWRITE THE SENTENCES, CORRECTING THE ERRORS

It's so busy that I think I'll have to stay after at work this evening.
It's so busy that I think I'll have to stay behind at work this evening.

1. Sometimes, I'm so snowed over at work that I don't have time to eat my lunch.

2. I need to sort up these customer queries.

3. She allowed her enough time to drive to the bank and park her car before the meeting.

4. Our project manager has given ourselves more responsibility.

5. I'm still trying to catch off with the work I should have done last week.

6. We can't tear him up from the video game he's playing for more than 10 minutes.

7. I think I have taken under too much work. I'm absolutely exhausted!

8. I always ask for challenging projects, but my boss never lets myself do them.

9. Here's the safety information for working in this building. Could you all familiarize itself with it?

10. I'm sorry, but I'll have to ask Jason to deal with this. I'm completely snowed on at the moment.

11. When students fail their exams, they usually don't blame themself.

12. When I take my children on the train, I bring some toys that they can occupy them with.

28 Meeting and planning

Many verbs can be followed by another verb. This can be a "to" infinitive ("want to eat") or a gerund ("enjoy cooking").

New language Combining verbs
Vocabulary Office tasks
New skill Taking part in meetings

28.1 FILL IN THE GAPS USING THE VERBS IN THE PANEL

I hate _traveling_ by train. There are always delays and the seats usually aren't very clean.

1. He can't stand ______ for people. He doesn't understand why people can't be on time.
2. I have to say that I prefer ______ for myself to eating out. I can eat whatever I want then.
3. I hate ______ , but fresh flowers make a new house feel more like home.
4. How would you propose ______ the big problems that we have?
5. Your flight had such a long delay that I began ______ if you would ever make it back home.
6. He likes ______ to a concert or the opera once a month or even more frequently if he can.
7. You continued ______ my concerns even after you had seen the negative effects yourself.
8. I love ______ outdoors in a lake or in the ocean, even if the water's quite cold.
9. We started ______ our wedding last year as we knew it would take a long time.

to wonder / waiting / to plan / solving / to ignore / cooking / to go / moving / ~~traveling~~ / swimming

28.2 MATCH THE BEGINNINGS OF THE SENTENCES TO THE CORRECT ENDINGS

When we were young we **started** → collecting stamps and now we have 5,000!

1. In our family we usually **prefer**
2. The design department **proposed**
3. Despite being tired, he **continued**
4. We've always really **loved**
5. When I was younger I **hated**
6. I have to say I **can't stand**
7. The music was so good that I **started**
8. Ten years ago he **began**
9. Marjorie **proposed**

- to run for the last six miles.
- getting up early, but now I like it.
- walking in the countryside.
- collecting stamps and now we have 5,000!
- saving money so he could buy a house.
- beach vacations to city breaks.
- putting more time between our meetings.
- making some changes to the sizes.
- dancing along to it.
- hearing music from people's phones.

28.3 CROSS OUT THE INCORRECT WORD IN EACH SENTENCE

I'll never forget ~~to see~~ / **seeing** my daughter receive her degree certificate. I felt so proud of her.

1. Now I regret **to ask** / **asking** him about his family. I had no idea what had happened to them.
2. He graduated at the top of his class and we think that he will go on **to be** / **being** a successful lawyer.
3. We regret **to inform** / **informing** you that on this occasion your application was not successful.
4. I remember **to put** / **putting** my car keys on the table, but then someone must have moved them.
5. Don't worry, he won't forget **to call** / **calling** you when he arrives in Australia.
6. After our success this season, we're sure the hotel will go on **to be** / **being** popular next season.
7. Please remember **to write** / **writing** to catering and ask if they can cater for 80 instead of 60.
8. Can we stop **to buy** / **buying** some snacks and get coffee at the next service station we get to?

28.4 MATCH THE DEFINITIONS TO THE HIGHLIGHTED VERBS

proceed to do something in the future	They **went on** celebrating until 2am.
1 stop doing something to do something else	I **remembered** to buy her a present.
2 not forget to do something	Did you **forget** going to Paris with me?
3 wish you hadn't done something	She'll **go on** to be a great teacher.
4 have no memory of having done something	I **regret** to inform you about the changes.
5 continue doing something	We **stopped** to get coffee.
6 no longer do something	I **remember** visiting you when I was a child.
7 not remember to do something	I **regret** telling him that.
8 feel bad about having to do something	I **stopped** going to the gym in February.
9 have a memory of having done something	Sometimes I **forget** to charge my phone.

28.5 MARK THE SENTENCES THAT ARE CORRECT

I stopped to smoke cigarettes last year. I live much more healthily nowadays. ☐
I stopped smoking cigarettes last year. I live much more healthily nowadays. ☑

1 I forgot to ask Valerie if she wanted to join us for dinner this evening. ☐
I forgot asking Valerie if she wanted to join us for dinner this evening. ☐

2 I always remember to close all of the windows when I leave the house. ☐
I always remember closing all of the windows when I leave the house. ☐

3 Who would have thought he would go on to be such a successful ballet dancer in the future? ☐
Who would have thought he would go on being such a successful ballet dancer in the future? ☐

4 The views along the coast road were so beautiful we decided to stop to take photos. ☐
The views along the coast road were so beautiful we decided to stop taking photos. ☐

5 I regret to say that he doesn't work as hard as everyone else. He hasn't spoken to me since. ☐
I regret saying that he doesn't work as hard as everyone else. He hasn't spoken to me since. ☐

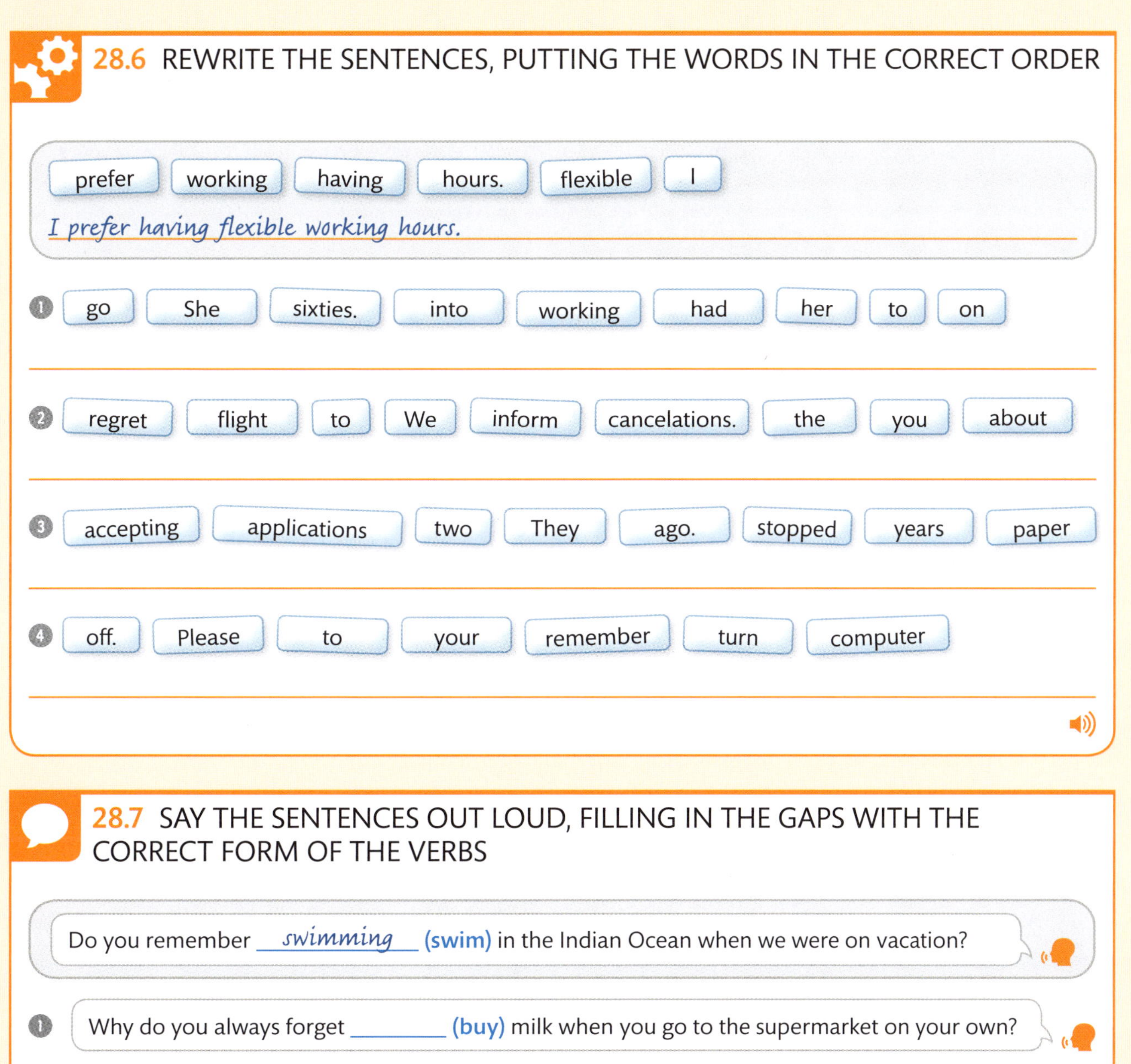

28.6 REWRITE THE SENTENCES, PUTTING THE WORDS IN THE CORRECT ORDER

prefer | working | having | hours. | flexible | I

I prefer having flexible working hours.

1. go | She | sixties. | into | working | had | her | to | on

____

2. regret | flight | to | We | inform | cancelations. | the | you | about

____

3. accepting | applications | two | They | ago. | stopped | years | paper

____

4. off. | Please | to | your | remember | turn | computer

____

28.7 SAY THE SENTENCES OUT LOUD, FILLING IN THE GAPS WITH THE CORRECT FORM OF THE VERBS

Do you remember *swimming* (swim) in the Indian Ocean when we were on vacation?

1. Why do you always forget ________ (buy) milk when you go to the supermarket on your own?
2. When are you going to stop ________ (work) there and do something you really want to do?
3. Do you regret ________________ (get) that tattoo of a dolphin on your neck now?
4. Do you think you would like ________________ (run) the whole company one day?
5. Can we stop ____________ (have) dinner at that nice restaurant in town on our way home?

29 Qualifying descriptions

There are many ways to qualify or add further detail to adjectives. Some types of adjectives can only be modified in certain ways.

New language Non-gradable adjectives
Aa Vocabulary Qualifying words
New skill Adding detail to descriptions

29.1 FILL IN THE GAPS USING THE WORDS IN THE PANEL

The concert venue was ___*enormous*___. Seventy thousand people could fit in there.

1. She's a ______ scientist. I'm sure she'll win the Nobel Prize for physics one day.
2. The fact that smoking can damage your health was ______ to most people until the 1970s.
3. It's amazing that such a ______ chip can contain so much data.
4. This scarf was handmade in Malaysia and the design is completely ______.
5. Could you please send me this document in a ______ format? I can then upload it to our site.
6. The weather was ______ last weekend. It wouldn't stop raining and it was really cold, too.
7. I think it's ______ that there's so much bacteria on our phones.
8. She tries to avoid using cosmetic products that have too many ______ ingredients in them.
9. We're very proud of our ______ heritage, such as these 19th-century factory buildings.

brilliant awful disgusting unique ~~enormous~~
chemical industrial unknown tiny digital

29.2 MARK THE SENTENCES THAT ARE CORRECT

It's not very economical to leave the lights on all night. Your electricity bill will be high! ☑
It's not completely economical to leave the lights on all night. Your electricity bill will be high! ☐

1. They had a very fantastic trip to South Africa. They're already planning their next trip. ☐
   They had an absolutely fantastic trip to South Africa. They're already planning their next trip. ☐

2. He's absolutely fascinated by trains so we decided to buy him a train set for his birthday. ☐
   He's very fascinated by trains so we decided to buy him a train set for his birthday. ☐

3. The delegates at the conference were very European with a few North Americans. ☐
   The delegates at the conference were largely European with a few North Americans. ☐

4. We wanted to create a very digital product for today's young people. ☐
   We wanted to create a completely digital product for today's young people. ☐

5. It's very impossible to put this table together. I'll never be able to do it. ☐
   It's completely impossible to put this table together. I'll never be able to do it. ☐

29.3 CROSS OUT THE INCORRECT WORD IN EACH SENTENCE

If you use our new heating system, you'll be **very** / ~~completely~~ hot even on cold winter nights.

1. It's **hugely** / **absolutely** important that as many people as possible see these billboards.
2. This product is **totally** / **extremely** useful if you don't have very much time to spend on housework.
3. We think that our customer base will be **rather** / **perfectly** interested in this new feature.
4. Our competitors' products are **extremely** / **wholly** inadequate to deal with these challenges.
5. The first design was **absolutely** / **slightly** awful, so we had to get rid of it and create a new one.
6. The coffee machine has a **totally** / **very** unique feature that enables you to make hot or cold milk.
7. I'm **utterly** / **rather** exhausted after putting so much effort into the product launch last week.
8. The CEO can speak **slightly** / **quite** good English, but he's much better at Spanish or Portuguese.
9. Have you noticed that our new packaging designer is **completely** / **really** talented?

29.4 RESPOND TO THE AUDIO, SPEAKING OUT LOUD AND FILL IN THE GAPS USING THE WORDS IN THE PANEL

How would you feel if you got a hundred percent on an English test?

I'd feel *extremely happy* if I got a hundred percent on an English test.

1. What did you think of the film?

   I loved it! I thought it was ______________________ and very funny.

2. How would you feel about giving a presentation in front of a thousand people?

   I'm shy, so I'd feel ______________________ if I had to do that.

3. How would you feel if you lost your cell phone?

   It would be so inconvenient! I'd be ______________________ .

absolutely terrified | thoroughly enjoyable | utterly miserable | ~~extremely happy~~

29.5 MATCH THE BEGINNINGS OF THE SENTENCES TO THE CORRECT ENDINGS

The last product was really → successful and this one will be, too.

1. I thought the test was fairly
2. Our product will be really
3. The presentation was pretty
4. My boss sometimes gets quite

- interesting and I learned a lot from it.
- annoyed if we fall behind schedule.
- difficult, but my friend found it easy.
- successful and this one will be, too.
- popular with consumers everywhere.

29.6 READ THE PRODUCT DESCRIPTION AND ANSWER THE QUESTIONS

HOME SHOPPING TODAY

TurboTravel XS

The travel accessory that will change your flying experience

The TurboTravel XS is a brand new product for business travelers that packs several essential travel accessories inside a comfortable cushion. We're fairly sure that you've never seen a product quite like this before.

What makes the TurboTravel XS completely unique is its extra features, such as a phone charger, light, and pen. The technology it uses is relatively low-tech, but it gives business travelers exactly what they need.

A cable enables you to connect the cushion to your phone and charge it up using an electrical power pack inside the cushion. The light and pen enable you to fill in customs forms really easily.

When it comes to price, the TurboTravel retails at $69.99 so it's quite an expensive, high-end product. However, tests with consumer groups have shown that it's also an extremely reliable travel accessory. To sum up, the TurboTravel XS is a product worth investing in for any business traveler looking for a wholly innovative new combination of comfort and convenience.

Statement	True	False	Not given
The TurboTravel XS is a completely new product.	✓		
1 Its makers are absolutely sure you've never seen a product like it.			
2 It has features that no other product of its type has.			
3 One of its extra features is an eye mask.			
4 The technology it uses it fairly low-tech.			
5 The light and pen make it easy to fill in forms.			
6 It's quite an expensive, high-end product.			
7 It's available for business travelers to buy online.			
8 It's already been on sale for a long time.			
9 Consumers think the product is not reliable.			
10 It's perfectly acceptable to use it at work.			

30 Expressing purpose

There are a number of ways to express the purpose of, or reason for, an action. You use different expressions to describe the purpose of an object.

New language "In order to," "so that"
Vocabulary Language of apology
New skill Expressing purpose

30.1 MATCH THE BEGINNINGS OF THE SENTENCES TO THE CORRECT ENDINGS

	We organized a training course	in order to find the items I needed.
1	He wrote a bad review of the movie	to complain about a rude waiter.
2	She took the toaster back	to find out when they will connect us.
3	I looked everywhere in the store	to let everyone know about safety.
4	The store gave them a voucher	in order to get your money back.
5	He called the restaurant manager	to let everyone know it's terrible.
6	She raised her voice	so as to keep their business.
7	We called the airline	not to get a new one, but to get a refund.
8	You need to fill in this form	to let them know they're being too noisy.
9	I called our internet provider	so that everyone would hear her.
10	I talked to our neighbors	to find out about vacancies.
11	Now we check all of the pallets	to ask them to cancel our flights.
12	He looked for the company online	in order to complain about her haircut.
13	I called the HR department	to find out what others think about it.
14	He asked to speak to the chef	to ensure the goods in them aren't broken.
15	She talked to the salon manager	in order to protect them.
16	I covered the goods in shrink wrap	to compliment his cooking.

30.2 REWRITE THE SENTENCES USING "SO THAT" TO JOIN THEM TOGETHER

He decided to advertise his business online. He wanted more people to know what he does.
He decided to advertise his business online so that more people would know what he does.

1. She took her car to the garage. She needed the mechanics to fix it.

____

2. We use RFID technology. This enables us to track the goods.

____

3. He wrote a positive review of the hotel. He wanted other people to know how good it is.

____

4. I usually get up at 5am. I like to go running before I go to work.

____

5. She spent a lot of time planning her presentation. She wanted to be well-prepared.

____

30.3 FILL IN THE GAPS USING "FOR" OR "TO"

This device is *for* monitoring your heartbeat.

1. Our products are made _______________ withstand all temperatures.
2. Our career website is _______________ busy professional people.
3. You can use this little USB stick _______________ connect to the internet in any location.
4. This headset is _______________ video-chatting and web-conferencing.
5.  This hi-fi system is only _______________ serious music fans, as it's very expensive.

30.4 SAY THE SENTENCES OUT LOUD, CHOOSING THE CORRECT WORDS

I'm calling **to complain** / ~~complaining~~ about the service I received at this store yesterday.

1. Can we offer you a voucher **to show** / **showing** we are sorry for the inconvenience caused.
2. I will be making a **complain** / **complaint** about your airline as soon as I get home.
3. I'm not very satisfied **for** / **with** the product I received from the company two days ago.
4. Could you **let** / **tell** me know when the basket of fruit that I ordered last week will arrive?
5. These workers are employed **to** / **for** pick and pack the goods in the factory outside the city.
6. Thank you for your prompt **assist** / **assistance** with the ongoing matter of delayed product delivery.
7. You can use this device **to** / **for** cleaning the windows in your house quickly and effectively.
8. I recently **delivered** / **ordered** a pair of running shoes from you as a gift for my sister.
9. I need a **replace** / **replacement** for this kettle as soon as possible, or else I will require a refund.
10. I look forward **to hear** / **to hearing** from you about the meeting next week.

31 Vocabulary

Aa 31.1 **ENVIRONMENTAL CONCERNS** WRITE THE PHRASES FROM THE PANEL UNDER THE CORRECT DEFINITIONS

Gases that cause the greenhouse effect, heating up the Earth

greenhouse gases

1 No longer existing

2 Causing damage to the environment

3 A place with many turbines for generating wind power

4 Use a supply of something, such as fuel or energy

5 Fuels based on oil, coal, and gas

6 Energy from sources that do not run out

7 At risk of extinction

8 Equipment needed to turn sunlight into electricity

9 The act of damaging something so badly that it cannot survive or be repaired

10 Changes in the Earth's weather patterns

11 Lower the level of carbon dioxide produced by your actions

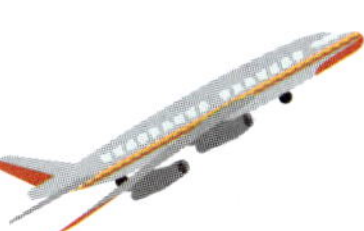

12 The increase in the Earth's temperature

13 Energy that does not use fossil fuels

harmful to the environment · renewable energy · climate change · endangered · ~~greenhouse gases~~ · extinct · global warming · reduce your carbon footprint · consume · solar panel · alternative energy · destruction · fossil fuels · wind farm

32 Conditional tenses

You can use the third conditional to describe an unreal past, or events that did not happen. This is useful for talking about regrets you have about the past.

New language The third conditional
Vocabulary Environmental threats
New skill Talking about an unreal past

32.1 FILL IN THE GAPS BY PUTTING THE VERBS IN THE CORRECT TENSES TO MAKE SENTENCES IN THE THIRD CONDITIONAL

If I *had been* (be) in London yesterday, I *would have seen* (would / see) the parade.

1. If I ______ (know) it was raining, I ______ (would / bring) my umbrella.
2. I ______ (would / not know) the party was canceled if he ______ (not tell) me.
3. If I ______ (arrive) at the station earlier, I ______ (would not / miss) the train.
4. If they ______ (study) more, they ______ (might / pass) the exam.
5. If I ______ (know) you didn't like onions, I ______ (would / not use) them.
6. If I ______ (not go) to college, I ______ (might / take) a gap year.
7. We ______ (would / not put) the box there if we ______ (know) that it would fall.
8. If I ______ (realize) he was unhappy, I ______ (could / talk) to him about it.
9. I ______ (would / wear) a suit if I ______ (know) the CEO was coming to visit us.
10. If we ______ (give) out more samples, we ______ (would / sell) more products.
11. If she ______ (know) there was a test, she ______ (would / prepare) .

32.2 SAY THE SENTENCES OUT LOUD USING THE CONTRACTED FORMS

If we had known the play was that bad, we would not have gone to see it.

If we'd known the play was that bad, we wouldn't have gone to see it.

1. If we had known there was a train strike on, we would have driven there.

2. If I had not gone to that party, I would not have met my husband.

3. If I had worked harder, I might have been promoted last year.

32.3 REWRITE THE SENTENCES, CORRECTING THE ERRORS

If you hadn't come to this school, where would you study?
If you hadn't come to this school, where would you have studied?

1. I would have called you if I had knew you were in town.

2. If we had taken a taxi, we won't have missed our flight.

3. If I would have left the house at nine, I would not have been late for the interview.

4. I would made it home by 7 o'clock if my train had left on time.

5. If we had known the movie was that good, we should have gone to see it.

32.4 READ THE NEWS STORY AND ANSWER THE QUESTIONS

96 MOUNTAINEERING WEEKLY

TIMELY RESCUE

Pete Falconer recounts his harrowing experience in California

Pete Falconer has been mountain climbing since he was seven years old. The 32 year old thought that he had seen everything and was prepared for any situation, but one day that all changed. It was a hot August day in California and Pete was out climbing with a group of friends. "That day started just like any other. If you'd have told me what was going to happen later on, I would never have believed you," Pete told us. He decided to move ahead of the rest of the group and started climbing up the face of a mountain known as The Antelope. If he'd stayed with the others, they would have been able to reach him faster or even catch hold of him to stop him falling, but Pete was out there all alone when he lost his footing and fell down into a canyon. "I knew right away that my leg was broken," Pete continued. "And even if I hadn't been injured, I don't think I would have been able to climb out of that narrow canyon." Pete called out to his friends for help, but they were still a hundred meters away. "After what felt like an hour, but was probably only about 15 minutes, I heard footsteps overhead and called out for help again. My friends quickly realized what had happened and called the emergency services. If I'd been out there on my own, with

no reception on my cell phone, I doubt I would have made it out of there alive, but the emergency services came in a helicopter and used specialist equipment to get me out of there. I was so grateful to be alive and I decided that from now on, I'll always stay close to the group when I go out climbing."

Pete is an experienced climber.	True ☑	False ☐	Not given ☐
1 Pete knew that day was going to be different right from the start.	True ☐	False ☐	Not given ☐
2 Pete was using the latest climbing equipment.	True ☐	False ☐	Not given ☐
3 Pete was climbing a mountain called The Deer.	True ☐	False ☐	Not given ☐
4 Pete could have called the emergency services himself.	True ☐	False ☐	Not given ☐
5 Pete realized his leg was broken as soon as he fell.	True ☐	False ☐	Not given ☐
6 Pete's friends found him after four hours.	True ☐	False ☐	Not given ☐
7 Pete has decided to stay with other climbers in future.	True ☐	False ☐	Not given ☐

32.5 CROSS OUT THE INCORRECT WORDS IN EACH SENTENCE

I wish we **had stayed** / ~~**stayed**~~ somewhere closer to downtown. It would've been easier to get around.

1. If only we **had asked** / **asked** for a room on the second or third floor. It wouldn't have been so noisy.
2. I wish we had been able to spend more time at that museum. It **would be** / **was** really interesting.
3. If only we had been there in summer. We **could have taken** / **could take** a boat trip on the river.
4. I wish we **had gone** / **went** to the Eiffel Tower earlier. We might not have had to wait so long.
5. I wish we **had read** / **read** the reviews of that restaurant before we decided to eat there.
6. I love that band. If only we **had known** / **knew** they were doing a concert down the road from the hotel.
7. If only we had taken the train to the airport. We **would have arrived** / **had arrived** there faster.

32.6 FILL IN THE GAPS USING AN "I WISH" OR AN "IF ONLY" SENTENCE

I find this subject so difficult! I wish *I'd studied more* **(study / more)**.

1. My brother always makes fun of me. If only ______________ **(have / a sister instead)**!
2. Why didn't I take your advice? I wish ______________ **(listen / to you)**.
3. I left my wallet on the train. I wish ______________ **(not forget /it)**.
4. My presentation was awful. If only ______________ **(practice / more)**.
5. I got soaked outside. If only ______________ **(bring /my umbrella)**.
6. I'm so bored at work. I wish ______________ **(take / time off)**.
7. I hate walking. If only ______________ **(not crash / my car)**.

33 Past regrets

You can use "should have" or "ought to have" to talk about past mistakes. They both signal that you wish you had done something differently in the past.

New language "Should have" and "ought to have"
Aa Vocabulary Time markers
New skill Expressing regret about the past

33.1 FILL IN THE GAPS USING "SHOULD," "SHOULD NOT," OR "OUGHT"

Your company ___should___ have reduced its pollution levels.

1. You ______________ have separated your waste for recycling.
2. We ______________ to have bought fair trade chocolate.
3. She ______________ have wasted so much paper.
4. The company ______________ have dumped their waste in the river.
5. They ______________ have used wood from sustainable forests.
6. We ______________ have found out about the risks beforehand.
7. You ______________ have changed to energy-saving light bulbs.
8. He ______________ have turned the lights off when he left.
9. They ______________ to have reduced the amount of traveling their employees do.
10. We ______________ have cut down so much of the rainforest.
11. You ______________ to have drunk tap water instead of bottled water.
12. She ______________ have showered for so long. She's wasting water!
13. They ______________ have flown the goods halfway across the world.
14. We ______________ to have talked to the local community about this.
15. Governments ______________ have made a law to stop this happening.
16. We ______________ have buried the waste in that landfill.
17. He ______________ to have turned his computer off at night.
18. You ______________ have stopped using new plastic bags every time you go shopping.

TIP
"Ought not to..." is not incorrect, but is not commonly used.

33.2 MATCH THE PICTURES TO THE SENTENCES

We should not have dumped the waste in the river.

We ought to have dealt with the causes of climate change earlier.

1 

We ought to have switched to greener cars sooner.

2 

We should have protected the wildlife from the oil spill.

3 

We should not have overfished the oceans.

4 

We should not have used so many pesticides in these fields.

5 

We should have thought about the effects of the mine on the river.

6 

33.3 REWRITE THE SENTENCES, PUTTING THE WORDS IN THE CORRECT ORDER

stopped | oil | the | that | into | should | We | have | sea. | all | leaking

We should have stopped all that oil leaking into the sea.

1 built | there. | dam | should | We | the | not | have

____

2 ought | started | renewable | earlier. | using | We | to | energy | have

____

3 recycled | They | have | waste | all | materials. | should | their

____

4 it | We | left | the | as | island | to | was. | ought | have

____

5 orangutans' | not | destroyed | the | habitat. | We | should | have

____

6 impact | have | They | thought | should | the | fish | on | supplies. | about

____

7 said. | ignored | should | We | not | what | the | have | protesters

____

8 stored | more | those | chemicals | We | to | carefully. | ought | have

____

9 the | controls | have | more | had | We | at | power | should | plant.

____

33.4 READ THE CLUES AND WRITE THE ANSWERS IN THE CORRECT PLACES ON THE GRID

1 o v e r c o n f i d e n t

1. Too sure of yourself
2. Too much weight or pressure
3. People packed in close to each other
4. Too much to do
5. Never takes a risk

overworked | overcautious | ~~overconfident~~ | overloaded | overcrowded

33.5 LISTEN TO THE AUDIO AND FILL IN THE GAPS USING THE WORDS IN THE PANEL

Initially, it was just the one rig in the Gulf of Mexico that was contaminated.

1. However, ______ the original explosion, a large oil leak was discovered.
2. It is estimated that oil was flowing into the sea at a rate of 62,000 gallons a day ______.
3. Oil continued to flow into the ocean at this rate ______ the next six weeks.
4. Efforts were made to stop the flow of oil ______ that time, but none of them proved successful.
5. ______, the oil spill has become known as one of the worst manmade disasters in recent history.

Since then | by that time | throughout | ~~Initially~~ | following | during

34 Actions and consequences

Unlike many parts of speech, prepositions often have little meaning in themselves, but work to change the meaning of the words around them.

New language Dependent prepositions
Aa Vocabulary Actions and consequences
New skill Changing sentence stress

Aa 34.1 FILL IN THE GAPS USING THE DEPENDENT PREPOSITION PHRASES IN THE PANEL

Is he a famous scientist? I've never ___*heard of*___ him before.

1. I'm ______ getting trapped in an elevator, so I always take the stairs.
2. In recent years, there's been a huge ______ smartphone ownership.
3. My children sometimes ______ who gets to watch TV.
4. I always ______ a window seat when I fly so I can look out the window.
5. We'll never ______ how to raise children.
6. I think he'll win. All of the signs ______ his direction.
7. There's been a ______ the number of letters people have written in the last decade.
8. The economic situation had the ______ pushing house prices down.
9. There's a ______ interest in the project among the people in my team.
10. I'm afraid I'm going to be ______ our appointment this morning.
11. They're really ______ all of the opportunities they've been given.
12. We ______ my previous work experience and career goals.
13. There's been a ______ the number of people watching live television in recent years.
14. When I call my sister, we ______ absolutely everything that's been going on in my life.

talked about · ~~heard of~~ · increase in · talk about · effect of
afraid of · late for · decline in · argue about · decline in
lack of · point in · agree about · grateful for · ask for

34.2 FILL IN THE GAPS USING THE CORRECT PREPOSITIONS

There's been a massive **increase** ___*in*___ the number of people using social media.

1. My husband and I sometimes **argue** __________ whose turn it is to do the dishes.
2. Frank is never **late** __________ any meetings in the office.
3. The course was canceled due to a **lack** __________ interest by students.
4. I know a lot of people who are **afraid** __________ spiders and snakes.
5. She's very **grateful** __________ the chance to study medicine in the US.
6. Marlon will **talk** __________ his travels in the Amazon rainforest this evening.
7. I'm so **grateful** __________ the opportunity you have given me.

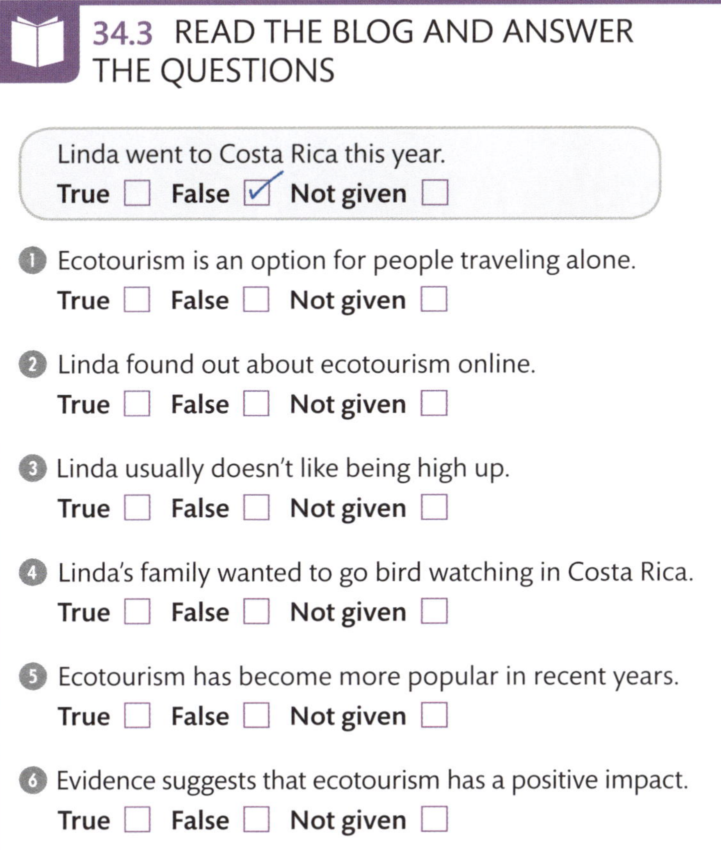

34.3 READ THE BLOG AND ANSWER THE QUESTIONS

Linda went to Costa Rica this year.
True ☐ **False** ☑ **Not given** ☐

1. Ecotourism is an option for people traveling alone.
   True ☐ **False** ☐ **Not given** ☐
2. Linda found out about ecotourism online.
   True ☐ **False** ☐ **Not given** ☐
3. Linda usually doesn't like being high up.
   True ☐ **False** ☐ **Not given** ☐
4. Linda's family wanted to go bird watching in Costa Rica.
   True ☐ **False** ☐ **Not given** ☐
5. Ecotourism has become more popular in recent years.
   True ☐ **False** ☐ **Not given** ☐
6. Evidence suggests that ecotourism has a positive impact.
   True ☐ **False** ☐ **Not given** ☐

Travel Blog

HOME | ENTRIES | ABOUT | CONTACT

POSTED MONDAY, 12:25AM

ECOTOURISM

My name's Linda and last year my family and I went to Costa Rica, where we discovered ecotourism. It's suitable for solo travelers, couples, and families.

When deciding on our vacation last year, we all agreed that we wanted to trek through rainforests and see animals living in the wild. Our travel agent then suggested ecotourism in Costa Rica, which is about visiting parts of the world where you can experience interesting or unique wildlife and cultural heritage while having a minimal impact on the natural environment and the local culture. It's popularity has increased in recent years, as more people are realizing the importance of responsible travel.

34.4 CROSS OUT THE INCORRECT PREPOSITIONS

There's no doubt that an increase in fuel consumption leads **to** / ~~**in**~~ higher pollution levels.

1. We are currently searching **for** / **about** a suitable location for a new offshore wind farm.

2. The Prime Minister apologized **to** / **for** the public for not giving them all of the facts.

3. I'm so bored **about** / **with** news stories about how the Earth is getting hotter. It's freezing today!

4. If we reduce the amount of packaging we use, that will result **to** / **in** us having less waste.

34.5 UNDERLINE THE WORDS YOU NEED TO STRESS AND SAY EACH SENTENCE OUT LOUD

We can't undo what humans have already done to the environment.

[It's not possible to change this.]

1. Environmentally-friendly farming practices help farmers grow more food.

[Other farming practices don't.]

2. This government isn't going to stand by and do nothing about climate change.

[Other governments have.]

3. What changes can you make in your everyday life to make it a healthier one?

[I'm just interested in what you can do and your life.]

4. There isn't a future for the nuclear power industry in this country.

[I know you think there is.]

34.6 REWRITE THE HIGHLIGHTED PHRASES, CORRECTING THE ERRORS

YOUR FOOD

Food security

Explaining food security and related concepts

One of the big issues facing governments around the world this century is food security. Just in case you've never heard for it before, when we talk over food security, we mean a state where everyone has access to an amount of food that is suitable of their needs. Those of us lucky enough to be food secure should be grateful over it because a lot of people live in a state of food insecurity and this number is set to grow. Long-term food insecurity leads in hunger and large-scale food-insecurity becomes famine when it has the effect at forcing more than 20 percent of a country's population to live without the food they need.

Experts can't agree for exactly how many people worldwide are food insecure, but the evidence points at the direction of it being over 1.2 billion and we're likely to see an increase of that number in the years to come.

The expression "food desert" refers to places with limited access to healthy, nutritious food. "Food deserts" tend to be low-income areas and are found in developed as well as developing countries. People living in "food deserts" become used to this lack in choice and, even when there is an option, they're more likely to ask of a burger and chips than a fresh salad at a restaurant. It's almost as if

they're afraid over healthy eating. The results are high obesity levels as people eat large amount of high-fat and high-sugar foods with little nutritional value. Social factors may be to blame in developed countries and especially the decline of the number of families who sit down together to eat a home-cooked meal.

Politicians have argued on what the best way to deal with food security is, but they haven't reached a consensus on what action to take yet.

heard of

1 ______

2 ______

3 ______

4 ______

5 ______

6 ______

7 ______

8 ______

9 ______

10 ______

11 ______

12 ______

13 ______

35 Few or little?

The words used to describe quantities vary according to a number of factors, including whether you are talking about something countable or uncountable.

New language "Few," "little," "fewer," "less"
Aa Vocabulary Nature and environment
New skill Describing quantities

35.1 CROSS OUT THE INCORRECT WORDS IN EACH SENTENCE

I'm so excited. I've got ~~few~~ / a few hours to explore the city tonight.

1  I'm not rich, but I try to donate little / a little money to charity every month.

2  Sadly, there are few / a few Sumatran tigers left in the world today.

3  I have little / a little patience for people who are always late. I'm always on time!

4  There are very few / a few people I would lend money to. But my brother is one of them.

5  Little / A little can be done to completely stop climate change in our time.

6  Do you need some help to finish that report? I have little / a little time I can spare.

7  There are few / a few paintings in the museum I haven't seen. Can we stay a bit longer?

8  There's little / a little point in explaining it to Jen. She never listens to what I say.

9  I know you're on a diet, but would you like little / a little bit of chocolate?

10  There are very few / a few old buildings left in this city. It's sad that we've lost so much history.

11  I don't have lots of friends, but I've got few / a few that I'm really close to.

35.2 MATCH THE BEGINNINGS OF THE SENTENCES TO THE CORRECT ENDINGS

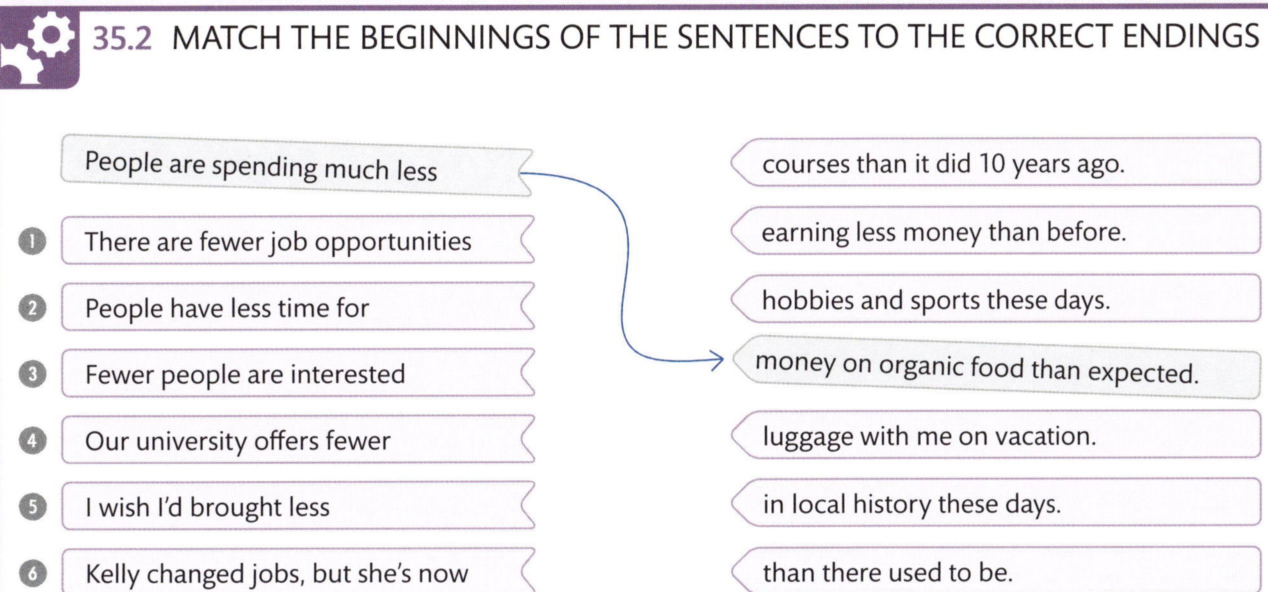

35.3 MARK THE SENTENCES THAT ARE CORRECT

There are fewer whales in the ocean. ☑
There are less whales in the ocean. ☐

1. Fewer money is spent on care for the elderly. ☐
   Less money is spent on care for the elderly. ☐
2. We all need to use fewer electricity. ☐
   We all need to use less electricity. ☐
3. Fewer people are worried about pollution. ☐
   Less people are worried about pollution. ☐
4. I wish I had fewer work to do. ☐
   I wish I had less work to do. ☐
5. People are having fewer children. ☐
   People are having less children. ☐
6. Fewer people enjoy gardening nowadays. ☐
   Less people enjoy gardening nowadays. ☐

35.4 LISTEN TO THE AUDIO AND ANSWER THE QUESTIONS

Stuart Brookes is fighting to save the endangered red squirrel.

Stuart Brookes began his fight 15 years ago.
True ☑ **False** ☐

1. The planned road was not close to his home.
   True ☐ **False** ☐
2. The road would have helped protect the squirrel.
   True ☐ **False** ☐
3. There are 2.5 million gray squirrels in the UK.
   True ☐ **False** ☐
4. There are just 140,000 red squirrels in the UK.
   True ☐ **False** ☐
5. The initial group had fewer than five members.
   True ☐ **False** ☐

35.5 FILL IN THE GAPS USING "FEW" OR "BIT"

I have quite a *few* questions.

1. She has been working for quite a ________ years.
2. I've earned quite a ____________ of money.
3. Amal has quite a ________ of work experience.
4. There are quite a ________ students in this class.
5. I've spent quite a ________ of time on this report.
6. Jo has made quite a _______ friends at university.
7. There's quite a ________ of rice left over.
8. There are quite a ________ things I have to do.
9. It took quite a ________ of effort to finish the race.
10. I've got quite a ________ pairs of sneakers.
11. We've got quite a ________ vacations planned.
12. She gave me quite a ________ of useful advice.
13. There's quite a ________ of garbage on the floor.

35.6 CROSS OUT THE INCORRECT WORDS IN EACH SENTENCE

We go on holiday to France in ~~fewer than~~ / less than four weeks.

1. The park is empty. There must be fewer than / less than 10 people here.
2. My daughter's school is tiny. It has fewer than / less than five teachers.
3. Seattle is fewer than / less than 20 miles from here. It won't take long to drive there.
4. Applicants should supply no fewer than / less than two references.
5. The plane leaves in fewer than / less than half an hour. We'd better hurry!
6. I've got fewer than / less than $2 in cash. Could you lend me some money, please?
7. The company had to cut some jobs, so we now have fewer than / less than 15 employees.
8. It's fewer than / less than 10 minutes until the game starts. I'm so excited!
9. I'm afraid the course is canceled because fewer than / less than 10 people signed up.
10. Jeremy is being paid fewer than / less than all his friends. He wants a new job.
11. I always pack light. My suitcase weighs fewer than / less than 12 pounds.
12. It's very disappointing that fewer than / less than eight countries signed the agreement.

36 Vocabulary

Aa 36.1 TRADITION, LUCK, AND SUPERSTITION WRITE THE PHRASES FROM THE PANEL UNDER THE CORRECT DEFINITIONS

A single piece of good fortune

a stroke of luck

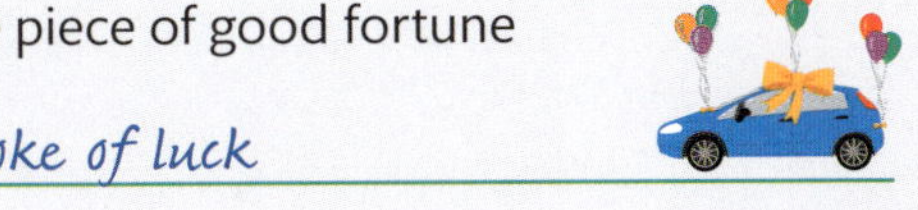

1 Hope for something to happen

2 A group of values

3 Have strong feelings that something is not right

4 A positive / negative sign about something that will happen

5 Talk about other people, often in a negative way

6 Information or news transmitted by people telling other people

7 Say something indirectly

8 Good fortune with no skill involved

9 Stories, sayings, and traditions from a certain area or culture

10 A modern story which is untrue but believed by many

11 Have good fortune the first time you do something

12 To start / continue saying things that may or may not be true

13 Think that something exists or is true

gossip | make a wish | beginner's luck | have serious misgivings / doubts | pure luck | ~~a stroke of luck~~ | start / spread a rumor | word of mouth | drop a hint | folklore | set of beliefs | urban myth | good / bad omen | believe in something

37 Past possibility

You can use a variety of language to talk about possible events in the past, and to indicate whether you agree or disagree with speculation.

New language "Might / may / could" in the past
Aa Vocabulary Urban myths
New skill Talking about past possibility

37.1 CROSS OUT THE INCORRECT WORDS IN EACH SENTENCE

I feel a bit sick. I **might** / ~~may not~~ / ~~could not~~ have eaten something bad earlier.

1. Chris hasn't turned up for training. He **might** / **might not** / **could not** have realized it was today.
2. Your phone **may** / **might not** / **could not** have been stolen. Have you checked in your desk?
3. I found a wallet. It **might** / **might not** / **could not** have been dropped by someone walking to the station.
4. Liz isn't answering her emails. She **may** / **may not** / **could not** have gone away.
5. I **may** / **might not** / **could not** have forgotten to send Lola a birthday card. I'm not sure.
6. That strange noise **could** / **may not** / **could not** have been a fox outside. There are a lot of them in this area.
7. I'm sure Les **may** / **might not** / **could not** have sent such a rude message. He's usually such a gentleman.
8. Jen and Will are late. They **might** / **might not** / **could not** have missed the train.
9. Helena **may** / **might not** / **could not** have grown 20 inches last year. That's too much in 12 months!
10. That bag is a fake. You **might** / **might not** / **could not** have bought a real one. It was far too cheap.
11. You **may** / **might not** / **could not** have caught the flu. It might just be a bad cold.
12. I **may** / **may not** / **could not** have left my glasses at work. I can't find them.
13. You **might** / **might not** / **could not** need an operation. You might just need to take some medicine.
14. You **could** / **might not** / **could not** have seen Sally in town yesterday. She's in China.
15. It **might** / **might not** / **could not** have been Sally I saw in town. But it was someone who looks like her.
16. Your purse **could** / **may not** / **could not** have been stolen when you were waiting in line at the market.
17. We **may** / **may not** / **could not** have bought the right ingredients for the cake. I'm not sure. Let's check.

37.2 MATCH THE PICTURES TO THE CORRECT SENTENCES

1 

2 

3 

4 

5 

6 

They may have forgotten to turn down the hob.

They might have forgotten to turn the iron off.

They may not have remembered to close the window.

She couldn't have gone out. All her clothes are dirty!

Anyone could have left the freezer door open.

They might have made a big dinner for lots of people.

They may have had a party.

37.3 MARK THE SENTENCES THAT ARE CORRECT

My arm is red and itchy. I might have been bitten by a mosquito. ☑
My arm is red and itchy. I could not have been bitten by a mosquito. ☐

1. My car has a scratch on it. Someone could reverse into it in the parking lot. ☐
   My car has a scratch on it. Someone could have reversed into it in the parking lot. ☐

2. Your email could have gone into my junk folder. I'll check again. ☐
   Your email could gone into my junk folder. I'll check again. ☐

3. You may have visited my old school. It was turned into an office in 2012. ☐
   You could not have visited my old school. It was turned into an office in 2012. ☐

4. You might have spoken to Jill on the phone. She's flying to Brazil right now. ☐
   You could not have spoken to Jill on the phone. She's flying to Brazil right now. ☐

5. I might have said the right thing to Annabel. She looked a bit upset. ☐
   I might not have said the right thing to Annabel. She looked a bit upset. ☐

37.4 REWRITE THESE STATEMENTS USING REPORTED SPEECH

I saw it with my own eyes! **(tell)** = He *told me that he had seen it with his own eyes.*

1. We couldn't believe what we were seeing. **(say)** = They ________
2. I'm not lying. **(say)** = She ________
3. I don't believe in things like ghosts. **(tell)** = She ________
4. I heard a terrible scream last night. **(say)** = He ________
5. I'll never stay in a castle ever again. **(say)** = She ________
6. I took a photo and there is a ghost in it. **(say)** = She ________
7. We had a lot of fun on Halloween. **(tell)** = He ________
8. We were so scared that we couldn't move. **(tell)** = They ________

37.5 REWRITE THE QUESTIONS AS REPORTED QUESTIONS USING "I ASKED"

What are you doing tonight? **(she)**
I asked her what she was doing tonight.

1. How much was your new jacket? **(he)**
2. Do you feel tired? **(he)**
3. Are they going to get married? **(she)**
4. What did you do last weekend? **(he)**
5. Is Carina good enough to play for the team? **(she)**
6. Are you busy right now? **(he)**
7. Where did you go on vacation? **(he)**
8. Will you call me back when you're free? **(she)**
9. Is Robert the new office manager? **(she)**

37.6 WRITE REPORTED QUESTIONS TO MATCH THE ANSWERS

She said she was looking for her husband.
I asked her what she was doing.

1. She said her favorite food was pasta.
2. He told me he was nervous about the exam.
3. He said he played tennis at the sports center.
4. He told me she wasn't easy to talk to.
5. She said they weren't a difficult team to play.
6. They told me they were away next week.
7. He said he was sad because his cat was missing.

38 Speculation and deduction

You can use modal verbs to describe past events with varying degrees of certainty. These constructions are useful for speculating about events you haven't witnessed.

New language More uses for modal verbs
Aa Vocabulary Phrasal verbs with "out"
New skill Speculating and making deductions

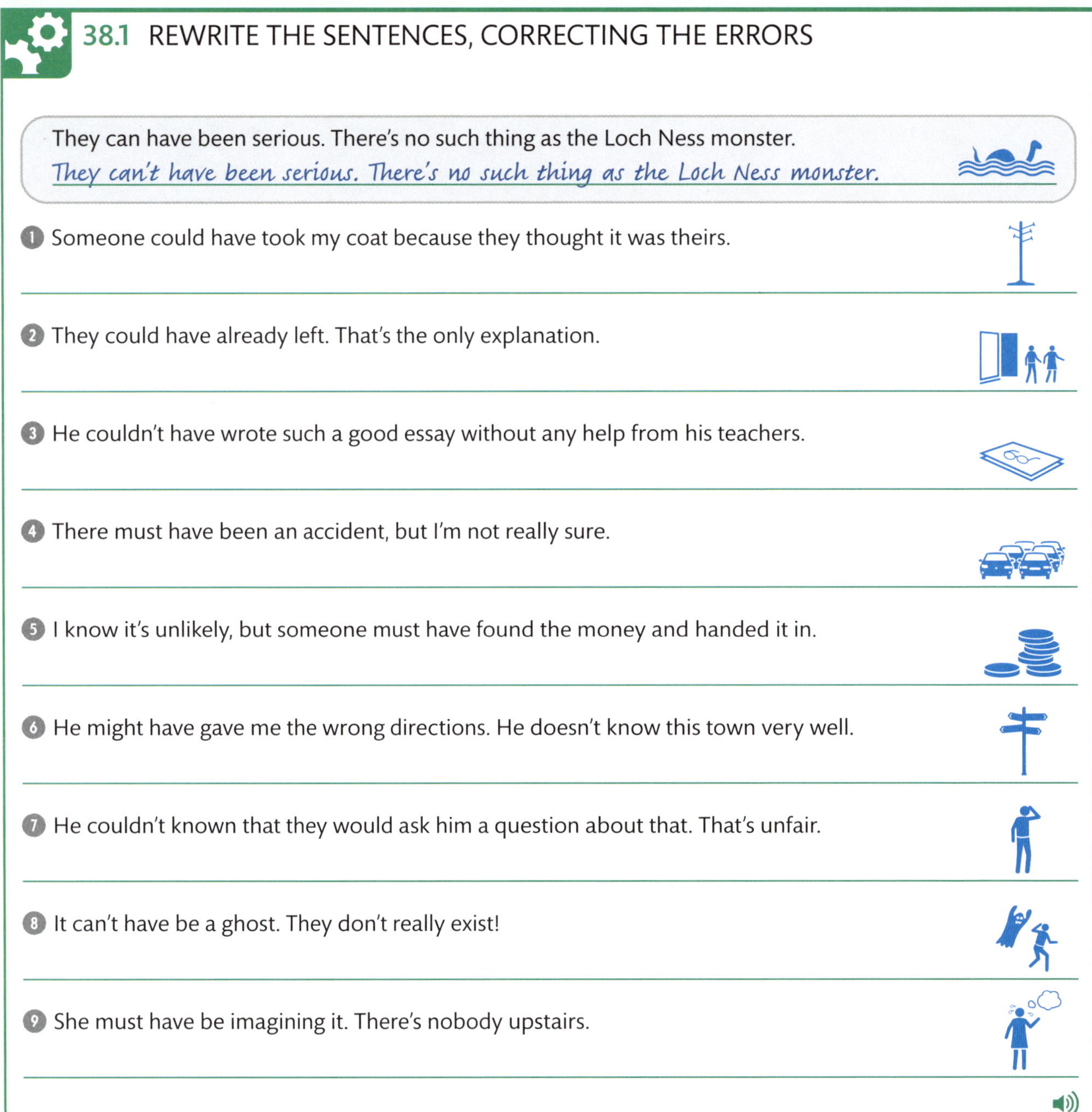

38.1 REWRITE THE SENTENCES, CORRECTING THE ERRORS

They can have been serious. There's no such thing as the Loch Ness monster.
They can't have been serious. There's no such thing as the Loch Ness monster.

1. Someone could have took my coat because they thought it was theirs.

2. They could have already left. That's the only explanation.

3. He couldn't have wrote such a good essay without any help from his teachers.

4. There must have been an accident, but I'm not really sure.

5. I know it's unlikely, but someone must have found the money and handed it in.

6. He might have gave me the wrong directions. He doesn't know this town very well.

7. He couldn't known that they would ask him a question about that. That's unfair.

8. It can't have be a ghost. They don't really exist!

9. She must have be imagining it. There's nobody upstairs.

38.2 MATCH THE PAIRS OF SENTENCES TOGETHER

It's twenty past two now. → He must have forgotten about our meeting.

1. Have you checked your phone?
2. He's not answering the door.
3. I still can't get through to her.
4. They must have changed their address.
5. Have you looked in the top drawer?
6. Their plane might have been delayed.
7. You must have dialled the wrong number.
8. We may have lost James and Katie.
9. He can't have thrown the tickets away!

- That's why our letters keep being returned.
- Nobody called Sheila lives here.
- Is there anything on the arrivals board?
- He must have forgotten about our meeting.
- She could have tried to call you.
- They must be here somewhere.
- She might have left her phone at home.
- He might have left already.
- He might have left the keys there.
- They're no longer following behind us.

38.3 CROSS OUT THE INCORRECT WORDS IN EACH SENTENCE

We ~~can't~~ / ~~couldn't~~ / may have stayed too long. I think they were glad when we left.

1. I can't / couldn't / might have won the competition if my entry had arrived in time.
2. They can't / may / might have lost their way. They know this area very well.
3. I can't / couldn't / must have done something to upset her. She's not speaking to me.
4. She couldn't / may / must have opened that door. She doesn't have a key for it.
5. They can't / couldn't / may have destroyed those documents. We haven't found them.

38.4 FILL IN THE GAPS BY PUTTING THE VERBS IN THE CORRECT FORM

He couldn't *have been* (be) at that meeting because he was in France at the time.

1. You must ______________ (deal with) a lot of customers over the last 20 years.
2. Mom and Dad might ______________ (hide) our presents in this cupboard.
3. He can't ______________ (leave) without saying goodbye. He must still be here.
4. The children might ______________ (outgrow) these toys. They prefer video games now.
5. They must ______________ (run) very fast to finish the race in such good time.
6. They can't ______________ (tell) you everything. There's a lot more that you need to know.
7. The students might ______________ (go) to the classroom we were in last semester instead.

38.5 LISTEN TO THE AUDIO AND ANSWER THE QUESTIONS

Jason and Valerie are talking about their colleague Richard, who they cannot find in the office.

Valerie thinks Richard couldn't have gone to the cafeteria.
True ☐ **False** ☑

1. Jason says Richard may have gone to see a client.
   True ☐ **False** ☐
2. Valerie thinks Richard may have gone home early.
   True ☐ **False** ☐
3. Valerie says Richard must have gone to buy a present for his wife.
   True ☐ **False** ☐
4. Valerie says Richard couldn't have left a note for Jason on his desk.
   True ☐ **False** ☐
5. Jason thinks Richard might have forgotten their meeting.
   True ☐ **False** ☐

39 Mixed conditionals

You can use different types of conditional statements to talk about hypothetical situations. Mixed conditionals use more than one of these types in the same statement.

New language Mixed conditionals
Aa Vocabulary Personality traits
New skill Talking about hypothetical situations

39.1 FILL IN THE GAPS USING THE PHRASES IN THE PANEL

If you ___were___ fitter, you would have been able to keep running.

1. If he ________ more organized, he wouldn't have been late for work again today.
2. If I had lost my job, ________ living with my parents again now.
3. If he had kept on learning English, he ________ fluent by now.
4. If they ________ how stormy it would be, they wouldn't be outside today.
5. If your aunt hadn't lent you money, you ________ buy a house now.
6. If he ________ more confident, he wouldn't have failed his driving test.
7. If you had gone to college, you might ________ a good job by now.
8. If they had finished painting the bedroom, we ________ sleep in the loft tonight.

I would be | were | wouldn't have to | were | wouldn't be able to | ~~were~~ | have | would be | had known

39.2 MATCH THE BEGINNINGS OF THE SENTENCES TO THE CORRECT ENDINGS

	He wouldn't be so good at swimming	if his Dad had shown him how to do it.
1	I would wear my coat	you would not be where you are today.
2	If we had saved more money,	you wouldn't think that the test was easy.
3	If you had believed what they said,	if he hadn't trained so hard over the years.
4	He wouldn't be so bad at cooking	if she had bought herself a new watch.
5	He might be more patient	we wouldn't have to be so thrifty now.
6	If he had reserved a seat on the train,	if I hadn't forgotten it.
7	She wouldn't always be late	he wouldn't have to stand for two hours.
8	If you had read all of the questions,	if he hadn't already been waiting so long.

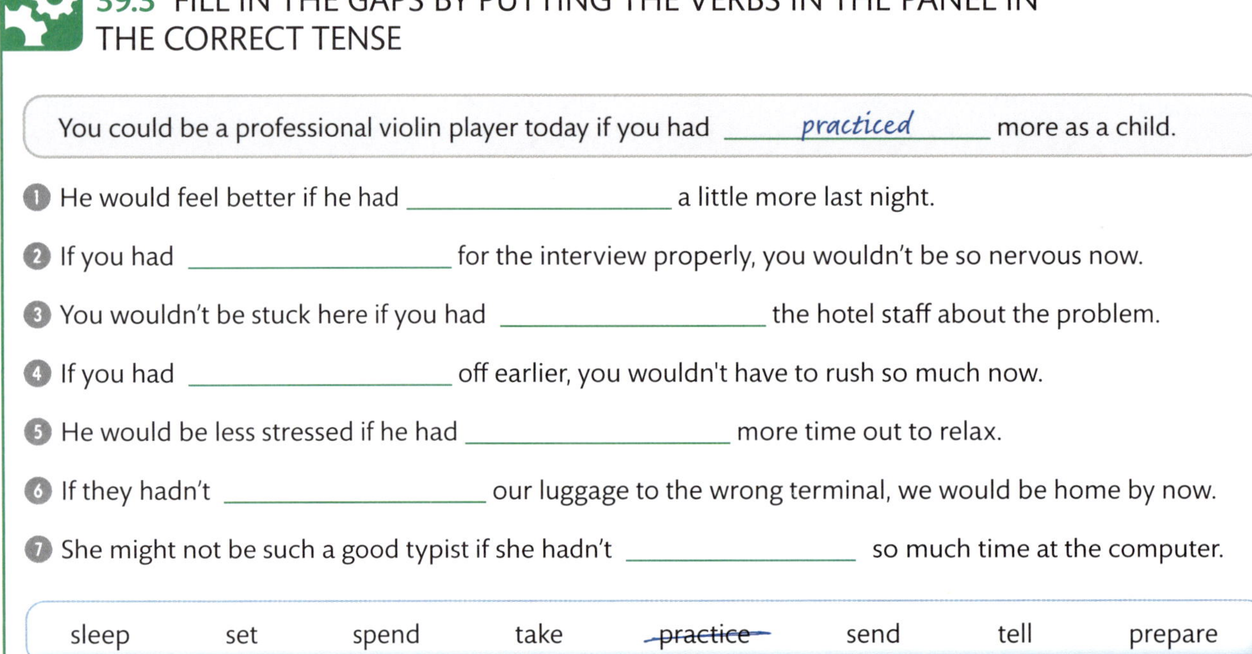

39.3 FILL IN THE GAPS BY PUTTING THE VERBS IN THE PANEL IN THE CORRECT TENSE

You could be a professional violin player today if you had *practiced* more as a child.

1. He would feel better if he had ____________ a little more last night.
2. If you had ____________ for the interview properly, you wouldn't be so nervous now.
3. You wouldn't be stuck here if you had ____________ the hotel staff about the problem.
4. If you had ____________ off earlier, you wouldn't have to rush so much now.
5. He would be less stressed if he had ____________ more time out to relax.
6. If they hadn't ____________ our luggage to the wrong terminal, we would be home by now.
7. She might not be such a good typist if she hadn't ____________ so much time at the computer.

sleep | set | spend | take | ~~practice~~ | send | tell | prepare

39.4 REWRITE THE MIXED CONDITIONAL SENTENCES, CORRECTING THE HIGHLIGHTED ERRORS

If you **had be** there, you would have a Christmas present, too.

If you had been there, you would have a Christmas present, too.

1. If he **have told** me how upset he was, I would still be there comforting him.

2. If I were a good cook, I **would invited** you to lunch at our place by now.

3. He **would have stroke** Fido if he wasn't so scared of dogs.

4. If they weren't going to France tomorrow, they **would have went** to your party.

5. We **could have go** to the theater if we weren't busy tonight.

6. I would be surprised if Katherine **had want** me to go to the ball with her.

7. If the teacher were here, she **would have tell** you all to be quiet.

8. If I **had move** to America, I might be rich and happy now.

9. I would be happy to help you if I **haven't already agreed** to help Jack.

10. If they **had learn** to ski, they could go on a skiing vacation next year.

11. If we **had look** at the map earlier, we wouldn't be so lost!

12. If I had taken that job, I **would been** earning a lot more money now.

40 Adding "-ever" to question words

Adding "-ever" to question words changes their meaning. These new words modify the question words to mean "no matter" or it "doesn't matter."

New language Words with "-ever"
Aa Vocabulary Chance and weather phrases
New skill Joining a clause to a sentence

40.1 FILL IN THE GAPS USING THE WORDS IN THE PANEL

Whoever James marries will be a very lucky lady. He's handsome, intelligent, and charming.

1. I can't remember what we decided about the color, but I'm sure it'll be bright, ______ it is.
2. ______ I go on vacation abroad, I always try the dishes that are typical for that country.
3. I'm sure the new boss will do a good job and treat everyone fairly, ______ he or she is.
4. They always believe that they will win the lottery one day, ______ small the chances are.
5. She always ignores any criticism she gets, ______ anyone says about her.
6. ______ I fly, I always make sure that I get to the airport two hours before my flight time.
7. I don't think I'll be able to find the answer to this math problem, ______ hard I try.
8. We could talk about this on the phone or I could arrange a meeting, ______ you prefer.
9. He always finds the time to call and say goodnight to me ______ he is in the world.

whoever	Whenever	whichever	however	wherever
whatever	however	Whenever	whatever	~~Whoever~~

40.2 CROSS OUT THE INCORRECT WORD IN EACH SENTENCE

Whatever / ~~Whichever~~ you decide, you can be sure that we'll support you.

1. Whoever / However completes the questionnaire first will win an exciting prize.
2. We always stay in touch by text message or email whenever / wherever we're apart.
3. I won't give up until I reach the top of the mountain, whichever / however hard it gets.
4. I can pick you up at the airport or you can take the train, whichever / whoever you prefer.
5. I'm not going to put up with this kind of behavior from him, whatever / whoever he is.
6. We can have Chinese or Italian food or something else, whatever / wherever you want to do.
7. I always take a little first aid kit with me whenever / whatever I go on vacation.
8. I'm sure she'll look beautiful in her dress, whichever / whatever one she chooses.
9. She's determined to change his mind about the Nigeria project, however / whatever long it takes.

40.3 MATCH THE BEGINNINGS OF THE SENTENCES TO THE CORRECT ENDINGS

Let's meet on Friday the 13th or the next day, → whichever you prefer.

1. I always fear I'm going to have a bad day
2. Whatever happens in my life,
3. Whoever told you that
4. My mother believes in superstitions,
5. Whenever a family member gets married,
6. This horse shoe will bring me luck,
7. She always wears that ring,
8. Whenever she sees a black cat,

- however often they prove to be false.
- I give them something blue for luck.
- however strange it looks.
- whichever you prefer.
- she thinks that it'll bring her bad luck.
- whenever I walk under a ladder.
- my superstitions bring me comfort.
- must be very superstitious.
- however difficult life gets.

40.4 MATCH THE DEFINITIONS TO THE PHRASES

decline an invitation until a later date → take a rain check

1. no matter what happens
2. behave recklessly
3. extremely happy
4. something sudden and unexpected
5. do something before someone else does it
6. healthy or well

- right as rain
- throw caution to the wind
- take a rain check
- a bolt from the blue
- come rain or shine
- on cloud nine
- steal someone's thunder

40.5 REWRITE THE SENTENCES, CORRECTING THE ERRORS

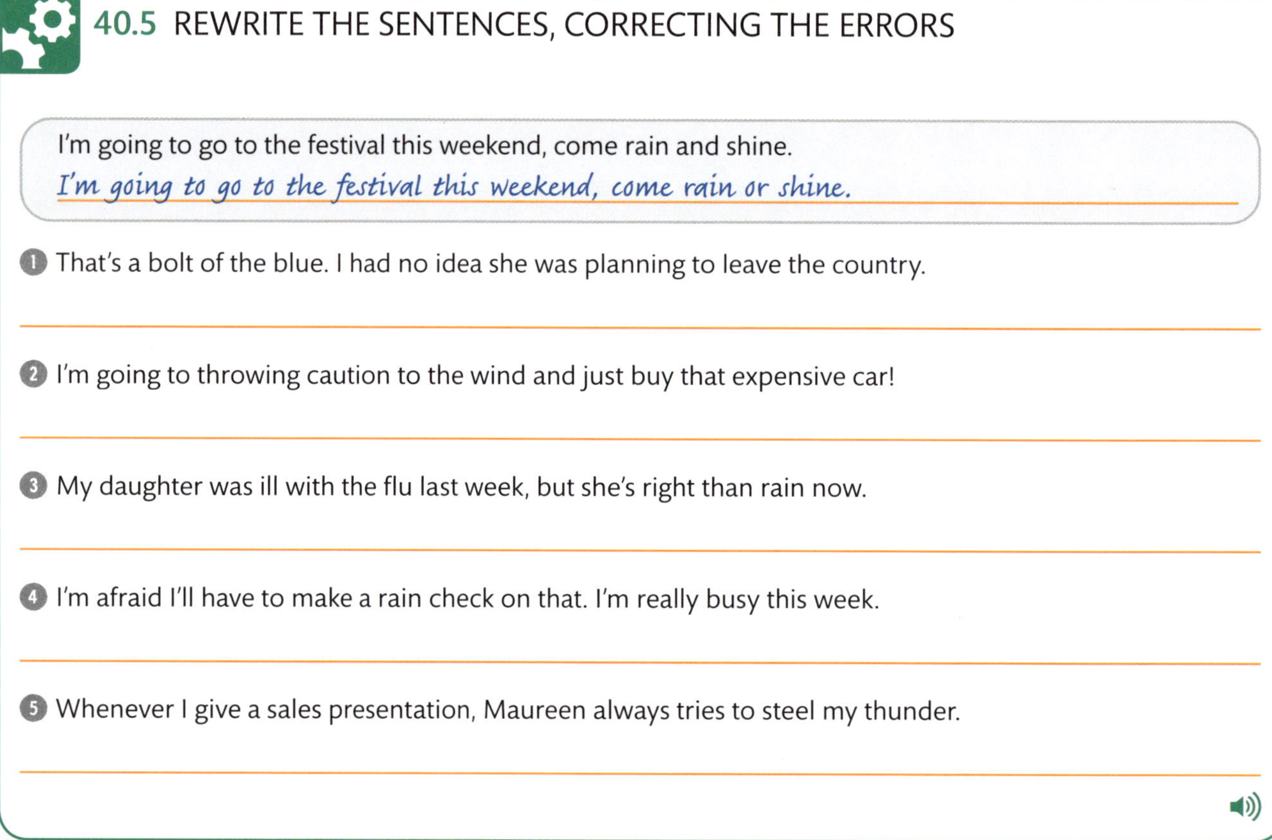

I'm going to go to the festival this weekend, come rain and shine.
I'm going to go to the festival this weekend, come rain or shine.

1. That's a bolt of the blue. I had no idea she was planning to leave the country.

2. I'm going to throwing caution to the wind and just buy that expensive car!

3. My daughter was ill with the flu last week, but she's right than rain now.

4. I'm afraid I'll have to make a rain check on that. I'm really busy this week.

5. Whenever I give a sales presentation, Maureen always tries to steel my thunder.

41 Vocabulary

Aa 41.1 **MEDIA AND CELEBRITY** WRITE THE PHRASES FROM THE PANEL UNDER THE CORRECT DEFINITIONS

An interview that no other source has obtained
exclusive interview

7 Become a famous person

1 Be known by most people

8 A show based on or around real-life events

2 Something designed to get your attention quickly

9 A very rapid rise, often in a career

3 The first night of a show or film

10 Make something more dramatic or exciting than it is

4 A carpet for important guests to walk or stand on at an event

11 The popular culture which surrounds famous people

5 Photographers who take pictures of famous people without their consent

12 News that is widely reported

6 A competition with performances by entertainers showcasing their skills

13 The large text at the top of a a newspaper page

celebrity culture | become a celebrity | paparazzi | newspaper headline | red carpet | talent show | ~~exclusive interview~~ | opening night | sensationalize | attention-grabbing | headline news | be a household name | reality show | meteoric rise

42 Reporting with passives

One way to distance yourself from facts is to use the passive voice and reporting verbs. This device is commonly used in newspaper and television journalism.

New language Passive voice for reporting
Aa Vocabulary Reporting language
New skill Distancing yourself from facts

42.1 FILL IN THE GAPS USING THE WORDS IN THE PANEL

It has been ___claimed___ that eating processed meat is as dangerous as smoking.

1. These items have been ______________ in our new factory.
2. It has been ______________ that a hurricane will hit the coast this evening.
3. Those tests have been ______________ out in our new laboratory next door.
4. Following the meeting, it has been ______________ that we will increase our prices.
5. He has been ______________ by the pharmaceutical company as their new CEO.
6. Our products have been ______________ all over the world since 1995.
7. The proposal has been ______________ by all the members of the board.
8. There are ______________ to have been a series of crimes committed by this gang.
9. It has long been ______________ that money isn't his main motivation.

reported	produced	exported	carried	rejected
believed	~~claimed~~	alleged	named	decided

42.2 MATCH THE BEGINNINGS OF THE SENTENCES TO THE CORRECT ENDINGS

She is understood to have been → working in Ethiopia for the last six months.

1. It is understood that there
2. Our organization is thought to
3. It has been reported that
4. It was announced that the company
5. He is thought to have been
6. There are said to be
7. It is hoped that the next generation
8. Norway is believed to be

- there will be massive job cuts.
- would recall its latest products.
- some nice walking trails around here.
- working in Ethiopia for the last six months.
- be a trailblazer in the area we work in.
- have been many flight cancelations.
- among the most beautiful countries.
- the most successful CEO we ever had.
- will continue the work we've been doing.

42.3 CROSS OUT THE INCORRECT WORDS IN EACH SENTENCE

Safety glasses must ~~worn~~ / **be worn** at all times in the laboratory.

1. This essay **should have been** / **should be** handed in two weeks ago!
2. Unfortunately, the project couldn't **completed** / **be completed** on time.
3. It must **have taken** / **be taken** us four hours to get here because of all the traffic jams.
4. She must **have thought** / **be thought** that the meeting started at 11am instead of 10am.
5. Any feedback you may have should **sent** / **be sent** to our administrator.
6. The machine may **have broken down** / **have broke down** because there was some dust in it.
7. Traffic could **been redirected** / **be redirected** here during the festival.
8. Free samples can **obtained** / **be obtained** from our store on the first floor.
9. The booking should **have been made** / **be made** earlier. Then we would have better seats.

42.4 MARK THE SENTENCES THAT ARE CORRECT

It was hoped that we could resolve the differences between them without any arguments. ☑
There was hoped that we could resolve the differences between them without any arguments. ☐

1 The bell must have rang 10 times, but he still didn't come to the door. ☐
The bell must have rung 10 times, but he still didn't come to the door. ☐

2 There has been understood to be a car accident on Station Road this evening. ☐
There is understood to have been a car accident on Station Road this evening. ☐

3 All of the books we sent should have been delivered to the venue by now. ☐
All of the books we sent should be delivered to the venue by now. ☐

4 It was announced yesterday that students can now apply for scholarships for next year. ☐
It has been announced yesterday that students can now apply for scholarships for next year. ☐

5 The driver is thought to have lost his way while driving from the airport back to the city. ☐
The driver is thought to have lose his way while driving from the airport back to the city. ☐

42.5 LISTEN TO THE AUDIO AND ANSWER THE QUESTIONS

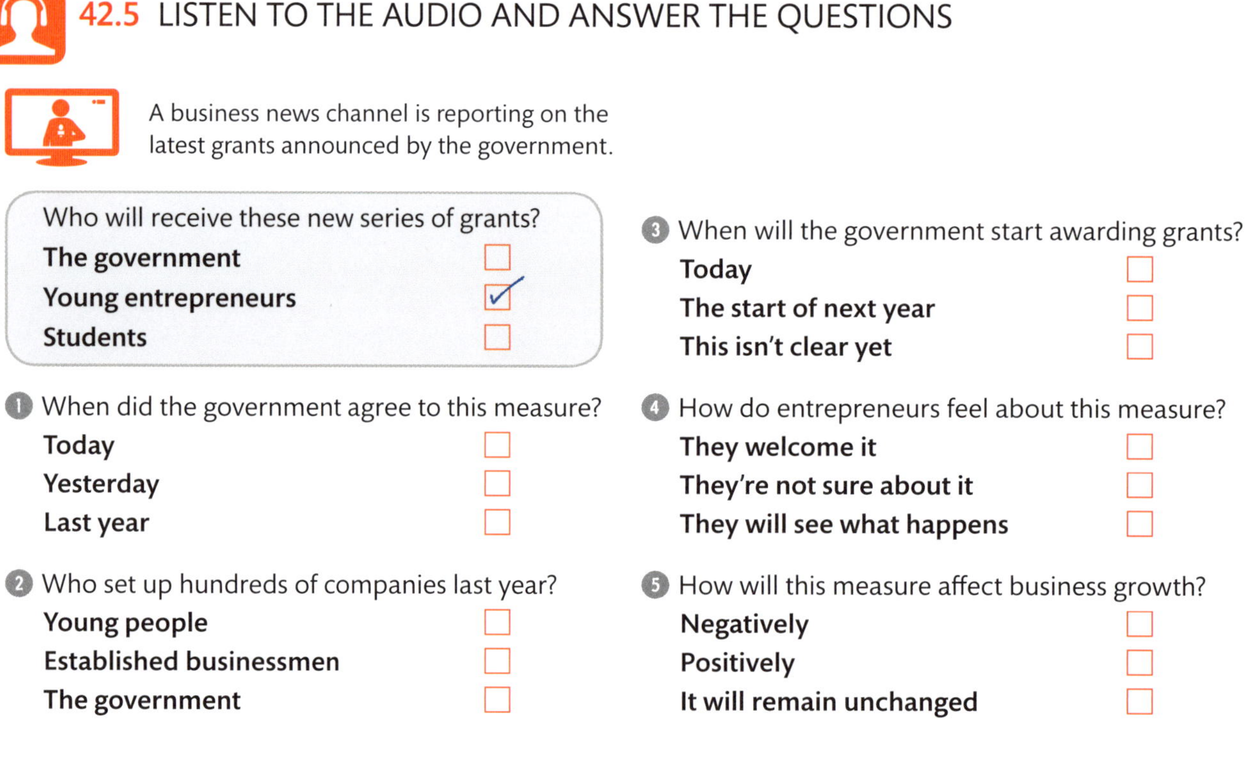

A business news channel is reporting on the latest grants announced by the government.

Who will receive these new series of grants?
The government ☐
Young entrepreneurs ☑
Students ☐

1 When did the government agree to this measure?
Today ☐
Yesterday ☐
Last year ☐

2 Who set up hundreds of companies last year?
Young people ☐
Established businessmen ☐
The government ☐

3 When will the government start awarding grants?
Today ☐
The start of next year ☐
This isn't clear yet ☐

4 How do entrepreneurs feel about this measure?
They welcome it ☐
They're not sure about it ☐
They will see what happens ☐

5 How will this measure affect business growth?
Negatively ☐
Positively ☐
It will remain unchanged ☐

42.6 REWRITE THE SENTENCES USING THE PASSIVE VOICE

He has extensively rewritten the text to make it a lot clearer.
The text *has been extensively rewritten to make it a lot clearer.*

1. We bottled a million gallons of water at this plant last year.
   A million gallons of water ______________________
2. Business travelers rent our cars at the airport.
   Our cars ______________________
3. We could organize another conference for next September.
   Another conference ______________________
4. Our chefs make all of our dishes by hand.
   All of our dishes ______________________
5. They hope that the supplier will accept the new terms and conditions.
   It is hoped ______________________
6. According to reports, the government will change traffic laws this year.
   It is reported ______________________
7. We service all of the company cars in this garage.
   All of the company cars ______________________
8. A Spanish company installed the solar panels on our roof last month.
   The solar panels on our roof ______________________
9. Everyone agrees that he would make an excellent team leader.
   It is agreed ______________________
10. They could have unloaded the trucks in half the time that they actually took.
    The trucks ______________________
11. She announced that she would be stepping down from the committee.
    It was announced ______________________
12. Some students claimed that they didn't get enough help from their teachers.
    It was claimed ______________________

43 Making indirect statements

Sometimes you may wish to avoid giving definite facts or personal opinions. This is known as "hedging." Certain words and indirect statements can help you with this.

New language Indirect statements
Vocabulary Hedging language
New skill Expressing uncertainty

43.1 FILL IN THE GAPS USING THE WORDS AND PHRASES IN THE PANEL

___Often___ people use hedging language if they do not have exact figures.

1. ________ 40,000 spectators watched the game at the national stadium.
2. The figures ________ that our population is aging rapidly.
3. Harris Mode is ________ the most handsome man alive today.
4. To ________, we can all do more to improve the state of our health.
5. ________ that unless we stop climate change, the ice caps will melt.
6. It has been ________ that the witness lied during the trial.
7. People who purchase violent video games ________ to be young men.
8. ________ like we've missed the bus. We're going to be late again.
9. It ________ that the jewelry had been stolen in the early hours of the morning.

appeared · tend · arguably · indicate · It looks
~~Often~~ · suggested · Approximately · some extent · It has been said

43.2 MATCH THE BEGINNINGS OF THE SENTENCES TO THE CORRECT ENDINGS

These new figures indicate → a downward turn in sales.

1 The teacher suggested that
2 If I don't have coffee in the morning,
3 There are approximately 15,000
4 It appears that the company
5 The soccer players allegedly
6 It has been said that
7 People often say

is going to make a loss this year.
I tend to get a headache.
they don't have the time to exercise.
a downward turn in sales.
people in the town where I live.
accepted money to lose games.
Lilian should expect good exam results.
there's no fool like an old fool.

43.3 SAY THE SENTENCES OUT LOUD, CHOOSING THE CORRECT WORDS

How disappointing! It would **appear** / ~~**tend**~~ that someone has eaten the cupcakes.

1 The test results **suggest** / **tend** that this is a new kind of bacteria.

2 **To some extent** / **Often**, I'm glad Gina canceled her party. I don't feel very well.

3 Jess **seems** / **suggests** to have gone home early.

4 Carren Lake is **arguably** / **approximately** the most successful British tennis player ever.

5 It **looks** / **appears** that we have no food left in the fridge.

6 It would **tend** / **seem** that Clarissa is not answering my text messages.

43.4 READ THE ARTICLE AND WRITE ANSWERS TO THE QUESTIONS AS FULL SENTENCES

58 **CITY TODAY**

OH, DEER!

The curious incident of a deer that walked into a hospital

News stations in Banff have been reporting the story of arguably the smartest deer in Canada. Medical staff at Banff General Hospital were surprised to see what appeared to be a deer walking into the Emergency Room yesterday. It was indeed a deer, who seemed to have been injured in an accident on the roads. The deer must have walked approximately 10 kilometers from the scene of the accident to get to the hospital. Medical staff were at hand to pick him up and take him to a nearby vet, who said it looked like the animal would make a full recovery.

What is the story that the news stations have been reporting?

The news stations have been reporting about a deer that walked into a hospital.

1. Where did the incident take place?

2. What surprised the medical staff at the hospital?

3. What seemed to be the reason for the deer's injury?

4. How many kilometers must the deer have walked to get to the hospital?

5. What did the medical staff do once the deer got to the hospital?

6. What did the vet say about the animal's condition?

43.5 LISTEN TO THE AUDIO AND ANSWER THE QUESTIONS

A news item on the radio talks about a criminal who made a foolish mistake.

Alfie Richardson was found guilty of forging paintings. True ☐ False ☑ Not given ☐

1. He committed a robbery about once every six months. True ☐ False ☐ Not given ☐
2. Richardson's mistake seems to be that he got lazy. True ☐ False ☐ Not given ☐
3. There were approximately 20 customers in the post office. True ☐ False ☐ Not given ☐
4. Richardson erased everything on the phone before he used it. True ☐ False ☐ Not given ☐
5. The selfies Richardson took were uploaded to an online account. True ☐ False ☐ Not given ☐
6. The photos led the police to Alfie Richardson. True ☐ False ☐ Not given ☐

43.6 REWRITE THE SENTENCES, CORRECTING THE ERRORS

There are approximate 25 students in my class.
There are approximately 25 students in my class.

1. To some extents, the project we worked on last month was a waste of time.

____

2. It would seem than someone has hacked into our database.

____

3. He has alleged stolen $2 million from his employer.

____

4. It has been say that absence makes the heart grow fonder.

____

5. It appear that you have forgotten to pay your bill.

____

44 Adding emphasis

You can add emphasis, or even a sense of drama, to a statement through grammar and pronunciation. Inversion is one effective way to do this.

New language Inversion after adverbials
Aa Vocabulary Media and celebrity
New skill Adding emphasis to statements

44.1 CROSS OUT THE INCORRECT WORDS IN EACH SENTENCE

Not ~~when~~ / **until** I was 18 did I start to cook for myself.

1 Only after trying to reach the summit three times **he did** / **did he** give up.

2 Little **she does** / **does she** know that we're planning a surprise party for her.

3 Only **when** / **until** it starts to snow do I stop gardening.

4 Not since the 1980s **the team has** / **has the team** won a major trophy.

44.2 MATCH THE BEGINNINGS OF THE SENTENCES TO THE CORRECT ENDINGS

Not only is the hotel luxurious, → but it's also in a great location.

1 Only after living there for five years
2 Not only is she a great mother,
3 Little did they realize
4 Only when she read their stories
5 Not since his childhood
6 Only after studying the instructions

did he understand how it worked.
that they were in for a big surprise.
did she realize how well they can write.
but it's also in a great location.
did he master the Spanish language.
but she's also a top business executive.
had he ridden a skateboard.

44.3 MARK THE SENTENCES THAT ARE CORRECT

Only when she moved away from home did she become independent. ☑
Only when she moved away from home she did become independent. ☐

1. Little I did know that I would meet my future husband that evening. ☐
   Little did I know that I would meet my future husband that evening. ☐

2. Not only is he a talented pianist, is he also a writer. ☐
   Not only is he a talented pianist, he is also a writer. ☐

3. Only until he came on stage did the fans start to scream. ☐
   Only when he came on stage did the fans start to scream. ☐

4. Only after living there for six months they did talk to the neighbors. ☐
   Only after living there for six months did they talk to the neighbors. ☐

5. The movie was also entertaining, not only informative. ☐
   Not only was the movie informative, but it was also entertaining. ☐

44.4 USING THE PROMPTS, REWRITE THE SENTENCES TO SHIFT THE EMPHASIS

I trained for nine months and then I felt ready to run the marathon. **[only after]**
Only after training for nine months did I feel ready to run the marathon.

1. My son asked me to help him with his homework the moment I arrived home. **[no sooner]**

2. She didn't know that she would stay for 40 years when she started working there. **[little]**

3. This is the first time that people from both communities have worked together. **[never before]**

4. The last time I cried this much at a film was when I went to see *Sally's Song*. **[not since]**

5. You don't often see a dog and cat that get along with each other so well. **[rarely]**

44.5 FILL IN THE GAPS USING THE PHRASES IN THE PANEL

Not only ___do we___ have a buffet, you can also order from the menu.

1. ______________ have I seen so many people running together.
2. Little ______________ know that we would end up living in Italy.
3. ______________ had I reached the station than the train arrived.
4. Not since 1988 ______________ had such a hot summer.
5. ______________ did she know that she would win an award that evening.
6. Never before ______________ a child who loves reading as much as she does.
7. Only when I'd had time to recover ______________ realize what a lucky escape I'd had.
8. Only after experiencing it ourselves ______________ understand how difficult it is.
9. ______________ preparing for six months did they feel ready to take the exam.
10. ______________ my teenage years have I been so excited about a concert.
11. ______________ had he started to speak when someone interrupted him.
12. ______________ do we produce these dolls here, but we make them all by hand.

Only after	~~do we~~	Rarely	Little	did I	could we	have I seen
did we	Hardly	No sooner		Not only	Not since	have we

44.6 LISTEN TO THE AUDIO AND ANSWER THE QUESTIONS

A news station is reporting on a fire that broke out during an awards ceremony in Los Angeles.

More people attended the ceremony this year than ever before. **True** ☑ **False** ☐ **Not given** ☐

1. The guests were able to go into the auditorium at 6pm. **True** ☐ **False** ☐ **Not given** ☐
2. The fire started in the middle of the ceremony. **True** ☐ **False** ☐ **Not given** ☐
3. About 5,000 people were evacuated from the building. **True** ☐ **False** ☐ **Not given** ☐
4. It's unusual to see so many famous people waiting around outside. **True** ☐ **False** ☐ **Not given** ☐
5. Everyone was allowed back inside once the firefighters had left. **True** ☐ **False** ☐ **Not given** ☐

44.7 REWRITE THE SENTENCES, PUTTING THE WORDS IN THE CORRECT ORDER

after | yes. | did | thought | say | it | giving | I | Only | some

Only after giving it some thought did I say yes.

1. we | pitched | Hardly | rain. | to | our | had | it | when | tent | began

2. as | I | when | feel | alone. | as | Rarely | I'm | do | happy

3. was | girl | a | I | young | Not | since | danced. | I | have

4. up. | after | times | calling | five | pick | him | he | Only | did

45 Shifting focus

You can add emphasis to part of a sentence in English by splitting it into two clauses. This allows you to focus attention on the the new or important information.

New language Focusing with clauses
Aa Vocabulary Phrases for emphasis
New skill Shifting focus

45.1 REWRITE THE SENTENCES USING "WHAT" CLAUSES TO CHANGE THE FOCUS

I dislike people who put their bags on available seats in trains.
What I dislike is people who put their bags on available seats in trains.

1. I would prefer to take the train to the international airport.

2. I really want to hike the Inca Trail in Peru with my friends this year.

3. I would really appreciate some help with using the software to sort data.

4. She was most surprised by the party they threw for her birthday yesterday.

5. We really need some more time to get the booth ready for the annual fair.

6. I hate it when people play music on their phones without using headphones.

7. I really enjoyed the day we spent at the local spa last weekend.

8. He realized that he didn't want to do that boring job for the rest of his life.

9. I understood that they aren't very happy about the sudden changes we're making.

45.2 FILL IN THE GAPS USING THE WORDS IN THE PANEL

The ___country___ I'd most like to visit is Japan because it really fascinates me.

1. The ______ I'd most like to go back to is Ancient Rome so I could visit the Colosseum.
2. The ______ that I enjoy making the most is spaghetti carbonara. It's quick and easy.
3. The ______ I liked the most at school was science, so I became a science teacher.
4. The ______ that I'll always remember is my twenty-first, when I had a huge party.
5. The ______ that I like the most is winter. I love walking in the snow.
6. The ______ I'd most like to have met is Alasdair Rove. I love his music and his style.
7. The ______ who influenced me the most is probably Mr. Lucas, my English teacher.
8. The ______ that reminds me the most of my childhood is *Little Tim*. I loved it!
9. The ______ that always gets me up and dancing at a party is *Dancing Bells* by Claude Robert.

famous person	time	~~country~~	birthday	teacher
song	subject	season	meal	movie

45.3 CROSS OUT THE INCORRECT WORDS IN EACH SENTENCE

~~Where~~ / The city I enjoyed visiting the most on the cruise was Venice.

1. Why / The reason do you always take on more than you can actually do in a day?
2. Where / The place that I would most like to be right now is a Caribbean beach.
3. Who / The person I most admire and look up to is probably Shakespeare.
4. What / The thing he absolutely hates is people who talk while they're eating.
5. Where / The school is Jonathan doing his Master's degree?
6. The time of day / When I like the most is first thing in the morning when I'm alone.

45.4 MATCH THE QUESTIONS TO THE CORRECT ANSWERS

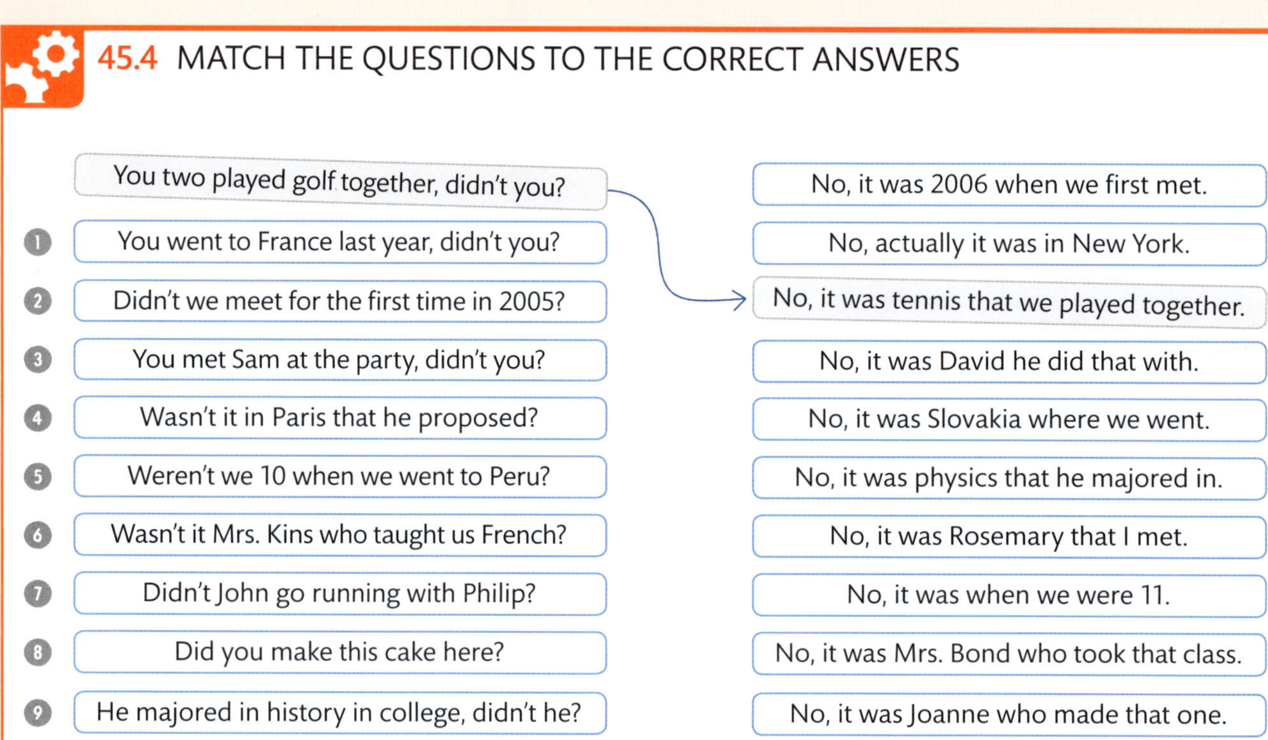

45.5 MARK THE SENTENCES THAT ARE CORRECT

That was the strawberry farmer it was that we talked to on the way home. ☐
It was the strawberry farmer that we talked to on the way home. ☑

1. It was the young man at the visitor center which helped us a lot in New York. ☐
It was the young man at the visitor center that helped us a lot in New York. ☐

2. It was an old lady helped us find the way when we were lost in that Greek village. ☐
It was an old lady that helped us find the way when we were lost in that Greek village. ☐

3. It was your colleague Charles that I met at the Christmas party last year. ☐
It was your colleague Charles where I met at the Christmas party last year. ☐

4. It was at a restaurant in Florence where we ate the delicious steak by the river. ☐
It was a restaurant in Florence where we ate the delicious steak by the river. ☐

5. I think it was our second year in college when the two of us first met. ☐
I think it was our second year in college where the two of us first met. ☐

46 Vocabulary

Aa 46.1 **CRIME AND THE LAW** WRITE THE PHRASES FROM THE PANEL UNDER THE CORRECT DEFINITIONS

Financial, nonviolent crime

white-collar crime

7 Crime committed in a public space

1 (Without) uncertainty about somebody's guilt

8 Break the law

2 Find somebody guilty of a crime

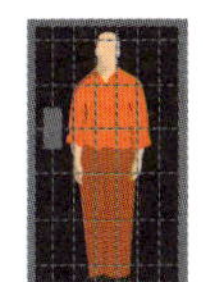

9 Say what punishment a criminal will have

3 A lot of crimes happening suddenly in the same area

10 A list of crimes a person has committed

4 Say that you know nothing about something or somebody

11 Come to a decision about somebody's guilt or innocence

5 Use the power of the law to take and question somebody

12 Request that an insurance company pays you money

6 The people who decide whether a person is guilty of a crime

13 Be covered by insurance

jury | commit a crime | criminal record | reach a verdict | arrest
~~white-collar crime~~ | convict a criminal | pass sentence | deny all knowledge
be insured | street crime | make a claim | crime wave | (beyond) reasonable doubt

47 Relative clauses

Relative clauses are sections of a sentence that provide more information about a noun in the main statement. They can be defining or non-defining.

New language Relative clauses
Aa Vocabulary Crime and criminals
New skill Specifying and elaborating

47.1 MARK WHETHER THE RELATIVE PRONOUN IS THE SUBJECT OR THE OBJECT OF THE RELATIVE CLAUSE

I'm writing about people **who** have been to prison for theft and robbery. **Subject** ☑ **Object** ☐

1. There's the woman **who** called the police. **Subject** ☐ **Object** ☐
2. The diamond necklace **which** they stole belonged to my grandmother. **Subject** ☐ **Object** ☐
3. The website **which** stole people's identities is based abroad. **Subject** ☐ **Object** ☐
4. The woman **who** I used to live next door to has been sent to prison for theft. **Subject** ☐ **Object** ☐
5. The men **who** solved the crime are fraud experts. **Subject** ☐ **Object** ☐

47.2 CROSS OUT THE INCORRECT RELATIVE PRONOUN IN EACH SENTENCE

The cat **that** / ~~who~~ I found belongs to a friend of mine.

1. The dog **who** / **which** is standing outside the police station is a drug-detection dog.
2. The woman **that** / **which** was crying had been robbed by two men on a motorcycle.
3. The man **who** / **which** was sent to prison had stolen hundreds of credit cards.
4. The man **who** / **which** is talking to the police officer had his car stolen.
5. The job **who** / **which** I'd like to do after my graduation is in crime prevention.

47.3 FILL IN THE GAPS WITH A CORRECT RELATIVE PRONOUN

The new sports car *that* I recently bought is extremely expensive.

1. The old man ________ got lost in the city is 98 years old.
2. The lion ________ was born in captivity was released into the wild.
3. The crime ________ we reported is being broadcast on TV!
4. The woman ________ found Samantha's purse is a cleaner.
5. The cat ________ I recently adopted is black and white.
6. The woman ________ I introduced you to last Wednesday is a model.

47.4 MATCH UP THE PARTS OF THE SENTENCES

	The animal	I went to as a little girl	had escaped from the zoo.
1	The rooster	who I liked best at school	is now a hotel.
2	A movie	who won the marathon	is in the main square.
3	The woman	which he saw	was Mr. Jenkins.
4	The runner	that serves the best food	belongs to my neighbor.
5	The jacket	I dated last year	is now falling apart.
6	The restaurant	that crows loudly all day	was running his first race.
7	The school	which won a lot of awards	is now married.
8	The teacher	which I bought 5 years ago	is *Crazy Cuckoo*.

47.5 REWRITE THE SENTENCES, ADDING COMMAS WHERE NECESSARY

My friend Sarah who I met at school is coming to visit.
My friend Sarah, who I met at school, is coming to visit.

1. The stolen goods which were extremely valuable were found by the police.

2. My little brother who is only six is always getting into trouble at school.

3. The robbers who were all from Southampton were caught as they tried to leave the crime scene.

4. My house which I moved into two months ago has been burgled.

47.6 SAY THE SENTENCES OUT LOUD, CORRECTING THE ERRORS

My new car, who I'd only just bought last week, was scratched today.
My new car, which I'd only just bought last week, was scratched today.

1. The robber, which left his fingerprints behind, was easily caught by the police.

2. My wallet, who was in my bag, was stolen while we were in the market.

3. Mr. Townsend, that is a suspect in a murder inquiry, has fled the country.

4. My credit card details, who I'd used for an online purchase, were stolen.

47.7 READ THE ARTICLE AND ANSWER THE QUESTIONS

31 CITY BEAT

LET'S FIGHT CRIME

Exhibition highlights new products that fight crime

Anybody concerned about safety should pay a visit to the Crime Aware Exhibition, which opened yesterday at the Millennium Conference Center.

The companies that are taking part are experts in the field of crime prevention, and many of them are launching new products at the show.

One standout product in the exhibition is the Digital Peephole. This product, which has been in development for two years, attaches to your front door. Usually when you use a peephole, the person who is on the other side of the door is very difficult to see. However, the Digital Peephole links to an LCD screen. The visitor, who you may or may not know, can be clearly seen.

The Crime Aware Exhibition, which is now in its twelfth year, runs from April 2 to April 7.

The Crime Aware Exhibition is only open to police officers. True ☐ False ☑ Not given ☐

1. You have to pay to go into the Millennium Conference Center. True ☐ False ☐ Not given ☐
2. There are crime prevention companies at the exhibition. True ☐ False ☐ Not given ☐
3. You can see brand-new products at the exhibition. True ☐ False ☐ Not given ☐
4. It took three years to make the Digital Peephole. True ☐ False ☐ Not given ☐
5. The Digital Peephole is not expensive. True ☐ False ☐ Not given ☐
6. The Digital Peephole allows you to identify visitors. True ☐ False ☐ Not given ☐
7. The Digital Peephole allows you to talk to visitors via a screen. True ☐ False ☐ Not given ☐
8. The first Crime Aware Exhibition was 20 years ago. True ☐ False ☐ Not given ☐
9. You can visit the exhibition on April 3. True ☐ False ☐ Not given ☐

48 More relative clauses

Relative words define or describe a noun in the main part of the sentence. Different relative words are used depending on the nouns that they relate to.

New language Where, when, whereby, whose
Aa Vocabulary Courtroom phrases
New skill Using relative words

48.1 CROSS OUT THE INCORRECT WORDS IN EACH SENTENCE

Let me tell you about the process ~~when~~ / ~~where~~ / **whereby** the sugar is dissolved in the water.

1  That's the restaurant **when** / **where** / **whereby** we ate that excellent chicken curry.

2  There was an agreement **when** / **where** / **whereby** both sides decided to support each other.

3  This is the church **when** / **where** / **whereby** my parents got married 30 years ago.

4  He's thinking about the time **when** / **where** / **whereby** we went to Barcelona for the weekend.

5  We use an application procedure **when** / **where** / **whereby** everything is done electronically.

6  The director talked about the area **when** / **where** / **whereby** the film was shot.

7  That's the office **when** / **where** / **whereby** my colleagues Jessica and Peter work.

8  We're now in the packing area **when** / **where** / **whereby** all of the items are packed.

9  Heat treatment is a process **when** / **where** / **whereby** heat is applied to metals.

10  This photo is from the semester **when** / **where** / **whereby** we lived in the dorm.

11  We provide a system **when** / **where** / **whereby** companies can find talented people.

48.2 FILL IN THE GAPS USING THE WORDS IN THE PANEL AND "WHERE," "WHEN," OR "WHEREBY"

We've set up *an exchange program whereby* our employees can work abroad for a short time.

1. The kitchen is ______________________ I most enjoy spending my time. I just love cooking.
2. Early morning is ______________________ I'm by myself and can have some peace and quiet.
3. Spring is ______________________ we most enjoy going out for walks in the country.
4. Photosynthesis is ______________________ plants convert sunlight into energy.
5. This is ______________________ the last annual trade fair for construction systems was held.

the time of day	the exhibition hall	the room
~~an exchange program~~	the season	the process

48.3 REWRITE THE SENTENCES, CORRECTING THE ERRORS

That was the hotel when we found those insects in the bed. It was absolutely disgusting!
That was the hotel where we found those insects in the bed. It was absolutely disgusting!

1. The TV program gave us a lot of information about the process where cheese is produced.

____

2. That was the big museum in New York when they have those wonderful Picasso masterpieces.

____

3. That was the time where the car broke down and we had to wait hours before someone came to help.

____

4. I'm just waiting for the moment whereby everyone goes quiet so I can start speaking.

____

5. We're looking at the process where fuel is burned to create the steam that drives the turbine.

____

48.4 LISTEN TO THE AUDIO AND MARK THE CORRECT SUMMARY

1. A woman went to a beauty salon where she had a manicure that she wasn't happy with. ☐
2. A woman went to a beauty salon where she had a skin cleansing treatment she wasn't happy with. ☐
3. A woman went to a beauty salon to have a skin cleansing treatment that made her ill. ☐
4. A woman went to a beauty salon where she had a manicure that made all of her fingers bright red. ☐

48.5 REWRITE THE SENTENCES USING "WHOSE"

Richard is doing as much overtime as he can. His son starts college this year.
Richard, whose son starts college this year, is doing as much overtime as he can.

1. Fiona always walks in the park in the morning. She has a large and energetic dog.

2. ZFF is a company that is starting to work in China. Its CEO gave an interview on TV last night.

3. Jack is learning to play the trumpet. His school has received more money for music classes.

4. Francesca is really stressed out right now. Her computer has just crashed.

5. Mandy took some time off work last week. Her mother has suddenly become ill.

6. The company has innovative HR policies. Its employees now have unlimited time off.

7. The tennis club is expanding every year. Its tennis courts are located on the outskirts of the town.

48.6 READ THE ARTICLE AND ANSWER THE QUESTIONS

SHARE YOUR STORIES

Smoke, smoke everywhere

An apartment building caught fire

Yesterday, there was a fire in the apartment building where I live. Everything was normal when I got home from work that evening, but then after a while I started to notice the smell of smoke.

I didn't think any more of it, but then suddenly, the smell of smoke became much stronger and it was impossible to ignore. I opened the front door to my apartment and saw that the smoke was coming from across the hall where Mr. Jerome lives.

I called the fire department and, just as the smoke was really starting to build up, they arrived. The firefighters organized a procedure whereby some of them entered the apartment from the balcony while some others tried to break down the door and get in that way. Fortunately, nobody was hurt and there wasn't too much damage to the apartment where the fire started.

Where did the fire happen?

The fire happened in the apartment building where the writer lives.

1. Did the writer notice anything unusual when he got home from work that day?

2. Where did the writer find out that the smoke was coming from?

3. Who called the fire department and when did it arrive at the building?

4. What procedure did the firefighters organize to save the person in the apartment?

5. What were the effects on the apartment where the fire started?

6. How many people were hurt in the fire?

49 Modal verbs in the future

Some modal verbs change form when used to talk about the future. Others cannot be used in the future at all, and have to be replaced with other modal verbs or phrases.

New language "Will be able to," "will have to"
Aa Vocabulary Legal terms
New skill Expressing future ability and obligation

49.1 REWRITE THESE SENTENCES, MAKING THEM REFER TO THE FUTURE

We can't go on vacation this year because we don't have enough money.
We won't be able to go on vacation this year because we don't have enough money.

1. Unfortunately, I have to cancel our meeting because I can't make it.

2. Can you pay the fine if you park your car in this restricted zone?

3. I can't get to sleep if my neighbors are making a lot of noise.

4. Do you have to stay in and study for your final exams?

5. We have to get a good night's sleep tonight because we have an early start.

6. Do you have to take all six exams this semester?

7. We cannot meet our deadlines because the company hasn't delivered on time.

8. Can you help me translate this text from Portuguese to English?

9. I can't help you with the translation because I'm really busy at the moment.

49.2 REWRITE THE SENTENCES, PUTTING THE WORDS IN THE CORRECT ORDER

to | he | another | look | job? | for | Will | have

Will he have to look for another job?

1. next | We | have | work | month. | to | will | hard

____

2. visitors | Will | after | have | day? | to | all | the | look | you

____

3. everything | on | do | They | to | won't | their | have | own.

____

4. our | have | We | will | paper. | recycle | more | of | to

____

49.3 FILL IN THE GAPS TO COMPLETE THE SENTENCES, REFERRING TO THE FUTURE

Mr. Denvers has a lot of appointments this afternoon, so he *won't be able to* see you.

1.  Next year we _______________ save more money, so that we'll be able to buy a house soon.
2.  I'm sorry, but I _______________ come to your concert this evening. I have to work late.
3.  _______________ join us for our annual school reunion next week? It would be great to see you.
4.  We _______________ visit the clients in person this Friday, so we will have to call them instead.
5.  _______________ travel a lot in his new job or will he be able to stay at home a little bit more?

49.4 CROSS OUT THE INCORRECT PHRASE IN EACH SENTENCE

Now we've got the boss's approval, we **will be able to** / ~~will have to~~ get started with the project.

1. According to the weather forecast, it will snow tomorrow, so we **will be able to** / **will have to** go skiing.
2. He **won't be able to** / **won't have to** take the course he wanted to do because it's been canceled.
3. I hope that one day every person **will be able to** / **will have to** realize their full potential.
4. When we turn the next corner, you **will be able to** / **will have to** see the beach and the ocean.
5. She's so happy that she **won't be able to** / **won't have to** wear braces on her teeth any more.
6. If you want to come to the party, you **will be able to** / **will have to** let me know by Friday at the latest.
7. If anyone would like a signed copy of the book, you **will be able to** / **will can to** buy one later.
8. You **won't be able to** / **won't have to** do so much paperwork now that you've got a secretary.

49.5 LISTEN TO THE AUDIO AND WRITE ANSWERS TO THE QUESTIONS IN FULL SENTENCES

Mr. Hall is talking to Mrs. Cooper about her son Peter's performance at school.

Why has Peter been having problems at school recently?
Peter's been having problems at school recently because he hasn't been able to concentrate.

1. If Peter continues like this, what grades will he be able to get?

2. According to Mr. Hall, what is Peter able to do?

3. What will Peter have to do if he doesn't pass his exams?

4. Will Peter be able to get some extra support over the next few months?

49.6 READ THE ARTICLE AND ANSWER THE QUESTIONS

45 GOVERNMENT WATCH

PUBLIC SMOKING BANNED

Government passes law banning smoking in public

The government has passed a law which will ban smoking in all public places. The politicians told us they felt they should pass the law because we are all much more aware of the dangers of passive smoking now. They thought they could be doing more to protect the public. Smokers will only be permitted to smoke on private property from next April when we will have to start observing the law. Some have suggested that the law could be difficult to enforce, but law enforcement agencies are hopeful that businesses will cooperate with them. There's no chance of anyone being arrested for smoking in public places, but offenders will be given an on-the-spot fine if someone reports them.

The article tells us about a new law that the police have passed. True ☐ False ☑ Not given ☐

1. Under the new law, people will not be permitted to smoke in public. True ☐ False ☐ Not given ☐
2. The law was passed to protect people from passive smoking. True ☐ False ☐ Not given ☐
3. Smokers will be permitted to smoke in their own homes. True ☐ False ☐ Not given ☐
4. The law will be enforced from April 14 next year. True ☐ False ☐ Not given ☐
5. Everyone thinks it will be easy to enforce the law. True ☐ False ☐ Not given ☐
6. Smokers' groups have complained about the law. True ☐ False ☐ Not given ☐
7. The police think businesses will work with them to enforce the law. True ☐ False ☐ Not given ☐
8. Some people could be arrested for smoking in public places. True ☐ False ☐ Not given ☐
9. You will have to pay money if you're caught smoking in public. True ☐ False ☐ Not given ☐

50 Modal verbs overview

Modal verbs are used to talk about likelihood, ability, permission, and obligation, among other things. They often refer to hypothetical situations.

New language Using modal verbs
Aa Vocabulary Modal verbs
New skill Asking, offering, and predicting

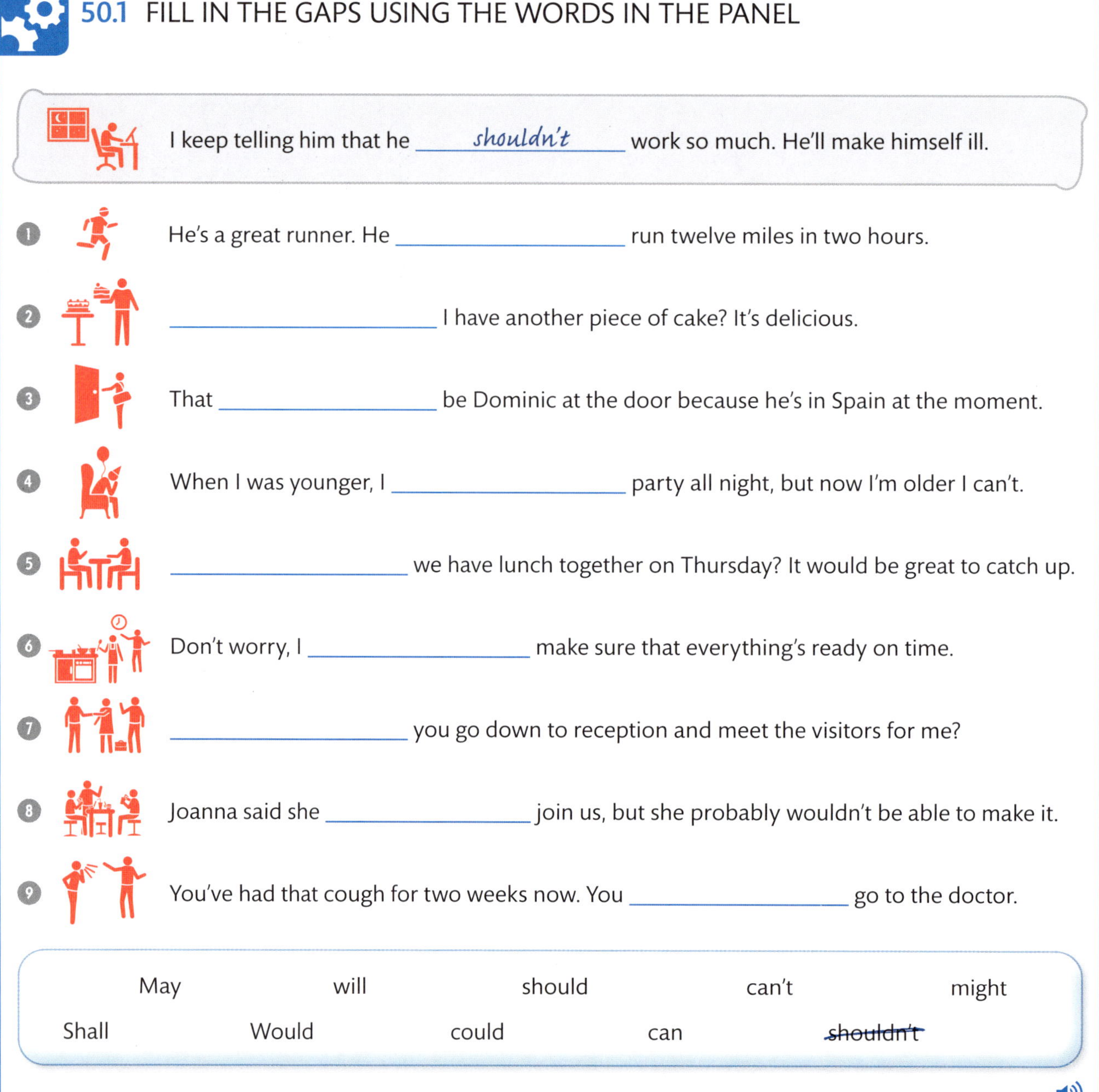

50.1 FILL IN THE GAPS USING THE WORDS IN THE PANEL

I keep telling him that he ___shouldn't___ work so much. He'll make himself ill.

1. He's a great runner. He ________ run twelve miles in two hours.
2. ________ I have another piece of cake? It's delicious.
3. That ________ be Dominic at the door because he's in Spain at the moment.
4. When I was younger, I ________ party all night, but now I'm older I can't.
5. ________ we have lunch together on Thursday? It would be great to catch up.
6. Don't worry, I ________ make sure that everything's ready on time.
7. ________ you go down to reception and meet the visitors for me?
8. Joanna said she ________ join us, but she probably wouldn't be able to make it.
9. You've had that cough for two weeks now. You ________ go to the doctor.

May, will, should, can't, might, Shall, Would, could, can, ~~shouldn't~~

50.2 CROSS OUT THE INCORRECT WORDS IN EACH SENTENCE

You ~~may~~ / ought to / ~~must~~ get a present for her. She would really appreciate that.

1. You can / might / must take your laptop out of your bag before you go through security control.
2. You will / should / may stay here as long as you want. Just remember to lock the door when you leave.
3. Shall / Will / Might I give you a ride home afterward? I'll be in the area at that time anyway.
4. Would / May / Will I help you carry your suitcase up the stairs?
5. When I was a child I couldn't / can't / shouldn't do a handstand, but now I can!
6. Must / Should / Will you help me prepare the training course for our Spanish colleagues?
7. If that doesn't work, you might / could / must call Edward and ask him if he knows what to do.
8. Since he had his operation, he can't / couldn't / won't walk more than 10 steps.

50.3 MATCH THE BEGINNINGS OF THE SENTENCES TO THE CORRECT ENDINGS

	You could fly to Barcelona, → but there's also a good train connection.	so you don't have so much to do?
1	Don't put your fingers so close to the pan.	They taste delicious!
2	Should I help you move those boxes,	get a decent haircut for a change.
3	Will you check that the door	but there's also a good train connection.
4	You must go to reception to register	if it's OK for us to arrive a little later?
5	May I have another cookie?	You could burn yourself.
6	I can't speak French very well,	is locked when you leave?
7	He ought to go to the hairdresser and	but I can understand a lot.
8	Would you call and ask	before you can go to the meeting room.

50.4 MARK THE SENTENCES THAT ARE CORRECT

We had to left early yesterday so we can get the last train home. ☐
We had to leave early yesterday so we could get the last train home. ☑

1. You should have asked your boss to pay you for the overtime you did. ☐
   You should have ask your boss to pay you for the overtime you did. ☐

2. He lost his voice, so he couldn't teach his classes last week. ☐
   He lost his voice, so he can't teach his classes last week. ☐

3. I can't find my keys anywhere. I must left them at home. ☐
   I can't find my keys anywhere. I must have left them at home. ☐

4. She should have asked me for advice. I would have been able to help. ☐
   She should ask me for advice. I would have been able to help. ☐

5. Could you visit the museum when you were on vacation, or was it closed? ☐
   Can you visit the museum when you were on vacation, or was it closed? ☐

50.5 REWRITE THE SENTENCES, CORRECTING THE ERRORS

I'm sure someone must found my wallet and handed it in.
I'm sure someone must have found my wallet and handed it in.

1. You should have bring your laptop to the meeting. Sarah reminded you yesterday.

2. They ought to had more respect for the neighbors when they have a party.

3. Why didn't you ask? I would shared a taxi from the airport to the hotel with you.

4. I know what happened. We must take a wrong turn just after we left the hotel.

51 Vocabulary

Aa 51.1 **CUSTOMS AND CULTURES** WRITE THE PHRASES FROM THE PANEL UNDER THE CORRECT DEFINITIONS

Part of old customs or beliefs

traditional

7 Range or variety

1 The principles and beliefs that somebody holds

8 Get used to an environment, surroundings, or culture

2 Something wrong that you do regularly

9 Polite or accepted social behavior

3 The way a person leads their life

10 Do something that upsets others

4 A fixed, often incorrect, idea about what a person or thing is like

11 People from a nation with a shared culture and language

5 Something that is done locally as part of a tradition

12 The increasing similarity between different cultures across the world

6 Look or seem similar to the surrounding place or people

13 The way that a language is spoken in a certain area

lifestyle	diversity		acclimate	manners
~~traditional~~	cause offence	dialect	bad habit	values
blend in	stereotype	nationality	local custom	globalization

52 Talking about groups

Sometimes you may want to talk generally about groups of people or different nationalities. It is important that you know the correct way to do this.

New language Using adjectives as nouns
Aa Vocabulary Countries and nationalities
New skill Generalizing politely

52.1 WRITE THE CORRECT NAMES FOR THE DIFFERENT GROUPS OF PEOPLE

Chinese = *The Chinese*

1. Dutch = ______
2. Kenyan = ______
3. Swiss = ______
4. Vietnamese = ______
5. Australian = ______
6. Egyptian = ______
7. Argentinian = ______
8. Korean = ______
9. Spanish = ______
10. Greek = ______
11. Japanese = ______
12. Brazilian = ______
13. British = ______

52.2 MATCH THE BEGINNINGS OF THE SENTENCES TO THE CORRECT ENDINGS

Canadians are famous for → their love of winter sports.

1. We're looking for ways of helping
2. The young often have a reputation
3. The British are known for their love of
4. Some people believe that the rich
5. Pets are seen as excellent companions
6. We have started distributing food
7. The injured were airlifted to the hospital

- fish and chips.
- should pay a much higher level of tax.
- to the poor.
- their love of winter sports.
- for being wild and irresponsible.
- immediately after the accident.
- for the elderly.
- the homeless find accommodation.

52.3 FILL IN THE GAPS USING THE WORDS IN THE PANEL

When we went to Beijing last month, we realized how hospitable *the Chinese* are.

1. We've built these ramps and put in these rails to help ________ access the building.
2. I think that ________ should give away more of their money to people who are in need.
3. The emergency services have given ________ all of the medical attention they need.
4. ________ are the group who are likely to spend the most time using social media.
5. In Nairobi, ________ live on the edges of the city in homes they've built themselves.
6. Ancient ________ worshipped cats.
7. We offer accommodation for ________ who can no longer live alone.
8. ________ are known throughout the world for making clocks and chocolate.
9. We don't want ________ to come into contact with infectious diseases.
10. If you'd like to help ________ who live on our streets, come along to our soup kitchen.
11. ________ sometimes aren't offered very much help with finding a new job.
12. He decided to become a doctor because he wanted to help ________ .

the rich · the poor · The young · the elderly · the injured · the homeless · the disabled · the sick · The unemployed · the healthy · The Swiss · Egyptians · ~~the Chinese~~

52.4 MARK THE SENTENCES THAT ARE CORRECT

The government has been spending a lot of money on services for the elderly in recent years. ☑
The government has been spending a lot of money on services for elderly in recent years. ☐

1. The unemployed people are welcome to come and volunteer at the library if they want to. ☐
   Unemployed people are welcome to come and volunteer at the library if they want to. ☐

2. Our charity was set up to help the elderly by organizing a weekly social meet-up for them. ☐
   Our charity was set up to help elderly by organizing a weekly social meet-up for them. ☐

3. The majority of Germans were in support of the decision. ☐
   The majority of German were in support of the decision. ☐

4. Our first priority is to help the injured. Then we can talk to journalists about what's happened. ☐
   Our first priority is to help injured. Then we can talk to journalists about what's happened. ☐

5. This fort was built by the Dutch in the late 1600s. ☐
   This fort was built by Dutch in the late 1600s. ☐

6. The government wants to introduce a new law, which will make the rich pay more in taxes. ☐
   The government wants to introduce a new law, which will make rich pay more in taxes. ☐

7. These parking spaces are only for the disabled. Can you please park somewhere else? ☐
   These parking spaces are only for disabled. Can you please park somewhere else? ☐

8. Most Brazilians are taught English at school. ☐
   Most the Brazilians are taught English at school. ☐

9. Homeless are sometimes seen as dangerous, but this is far from the truth. ☐
   The homeless are sometimes seen as dangerous, but this is far from the truth. ☐

10. The British are coming over here to learn more about our processes and how we do things. ☐
    British are coming over here to learn more about our processes and how we do things. ☐

11. I decided to become a nurse because I really wanted to be able to help the sick. ☐
    I decided to become a nurse because I really wanted to be able to help sick. ☐

12. The French are known for being very relaxed and this is also something I've noticed. ☐
    French are known for being very relaxed and this is also something I've noticed. ☐

52.5 RESPOND TO THE AUDIO, SPEAKING OUT LOUD

What is done in your country to make sure older people are looked after?

The elderly *are given a bus pass so that they can travel easily.*

1. How are people with less money treated in your country?

   The poor ______________________

2. Are people with illnesses comfortable going to see a doctor?

   The sick ______________________

3. Is there good access for people in wheelchairs in your town?

   The disabled ______________________

4. What kind of support is there for people who can't find work?

   The unemployed ______________________

5. How do you think the media portrays young people?

   The young ______________________

6. Is anything done to help homeless people in your country?

   The homeless ______________________

7. What do you and your friends think about rich people?

   The rich ______________________

53 Old and new situations

New situations may seem unusual, but over time they become familiar. You can use phrases that contain "be used to" and "get used to" to talk about this.

New language "Be used to" and "get used to"
Aa Vocabulary Moving and living abroad
New skill Talking about old and new situations

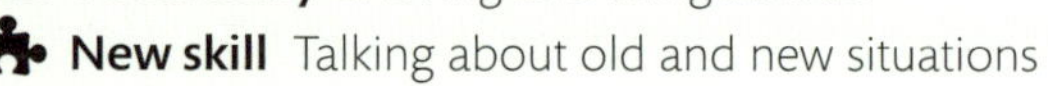

53.1 CROSS OUT THE INCORRECT WORD IN EACH SENTENCE

I **am** / ~~**get**~~ used to running the department on my own, so it's not a problem for me.

1 

It took me a while to **get** / **be** used to the stores being closed on Sundays here.

2 
He's been starting work at 6am for three months now, so he **gets** / **is** used to it.

3 
As we live in the north of Norway, we **get** / **are** used to very cold weather in winter.

4 
I'm still **getting** / **being** used to the fast pace of activity in my new company.

5 
When he first went to live in Australia, he **wasn't** / **didn't get** used to the heat and got burned.

6 
You've been working with us for some time, so you **got** / **are** used to the way we work now.

7 
I just can't **get** / **be** used to working every weekend. I don't think I'll ever like it.

8 
Don't worry about Rachel! She **gets** / **is** used to traveling on her own.

9 
When we had our first child, we had to **get** / **be** used to not having very much sleep.

10 
We've had our new boss for six months now, but I'm still **getting** / **being** used to her style.

11 
Jeremy lives in Los Angeles, so he **gets** / **is** used to living through minor earthquakes.

53.2 FILL IN THE GAPS USING THE CORRECT FORMS OF "BE" AND "GET"

Once Laura ___*gets*___ used to working from home, she'll realize how much better it is for her.

1. Three years after moving, I think we ________ finally used to life in the country and really like it.
2. After a while you'll ________ used to the rhythm of the train and fall asleep.
3. He ________ used to sleeping on a very soft bed at home, so he doesn't like hard beds.
4. I was just ________ used to our old English teacher when she left and we got a new one.
5. He ________ now so used to wearing glasses that he doesn't even notice them anymore.
6. I ________ used to taking the train every day and I knew the timetable by heart.

53.3 REWRITE THE SENTENCES, CORRECTING THE ERRORS

I'm get used to waiting for Simon outside his house because he's always running late.
I'm used to waiting for Simon outside his house because he's always running late.

1. Our customers from other countries get used to getting very high quality products from us.

____

2. I don't think Christina will ever got used to living on her own. She doesn't like it.

____

3. We're get used to being able to communicate with people from all over the world online.

____

4. My friend is not get used to eating spicy food, so it makes him go red in the face.

____

5. He is still being used to the new house he bought last year.

____

6. Our children Joseph and Liz are used to be away from the two of us while we're at work.

____

53.4 MATCH THE BEGINNINGS OF THE SENTENCES TO THE CORRECT ENDINGS

We're not used to getting such bad → service at this restaurant. What has happened?

1. You will have to get used to working
2. We were used to bringing lunch
3. Jack's slowly getting used to living
4. The new shoes were uncomfortable,
5. I'm used to sitting through long and

- in a dorm instead of at home.
- boring lectures. I do it every day.
- long hours if you want to be on this team.
- service at this restaurant. What has happened?
- to work, but now we eat in the canteen.
- but she soon got used to them.

53.5 LISTEN TO THE AUDIO AND ANSWER THE QUESTIONS

A man is talking about moving to a new country and getting used to life there.

How long has the speaker lived in China?
Two weeks ☐
Two months ☐
Two years ☑

1. Where did the speaker live before this?
China ☐
The UK ☐
Japan ☐

2. Who told the speaker that he had to move?
His wife ☐
His boss ☐
His colleague ☐

3. Which other option did the speaker have?
Germany ☐
Japan ☐
India ☐

4. How does he find the people in China?
Direct ☐
Quiet ☐
Rude ☐

5. Who sometimes asks personal questions?
Colleagues ☐
Neighbors ☐
Strangers ☐

6. Where do you not necessarily find the best food?
Nice restaurants ☐
Fast-food outlets ☐
Street markets ☐

7. Where is the speaker now used to going to eat?
Nice restaurants ☐
Fast-food outlets ☐
Street markets ☐

53.6 SAY THE SENTENCES OUT LOUD, FILLING IN THE GAPS

I'm *used to* traveling a lot, so making two trips in one week is OK with me.

1. Our neighbors are so loud, but we'll just have to ______ the noise.
2. I've lived in Tokyo for ten years now, so I'm ______ Japanese food.
3. My boss was pleased about how quickly I ______ giving presentations.
4. We may have to ______ traveling a little farther to get to the shops soon.
5. We were just ______ the new office when we had to move to another one.
6. He's been working in virtual teams for a long time now, so he's ______ it.

53.7 REWRITE THE HIGHLIGHTED PHRASES, CORRECTING THE ERRORS

get used to

1. ______
2. ______
3. ______
4. ______
5. ______
6. ______
7. ______
8. ______
9. ______

To: Kathleen

Subject: Life in London

Dear Kathleen,

It's only my first week in London and there's so much to be used to. I was got used to taking the underground metro in Paris, but now I have to getting used to a new system. I also have to got used to the food. I am used to eating such delicious food in Paris, but now I have to being used to fatty British food. Not all of the food is bad, I suppose, I just need to be used to it. I also have to getting used to speaking English all the time. I don't think I'll ever getting used to that! You be used to living abroad in all different countries. Do you have any tips for me?

Talk to you soon,

Marie

54 Articles

Articles are some of the shortest and yet most common words in the English language. There are several rules stating which article, if any, should be used.

New language Articles
Aa Vocabulary Commonly misspelled words
New skill Saying words with silent letters

54.1 CROSS OUT THE INCORRECT WORDS IN EACH SENTENCE

MOMA is ~~a~~ / an / ~~the~~ excellent art museum that you could visit when you go to New York.

1. A / An / The investors who come to us have a lot of money to invest in companies.
2. We paid for a / an / the audio guide in the palace and it gave us some interesting information.
3. A / An / The CEO of our company is surprisingly young. He's only 30 years old!
4. If you want to travel cheaply in Paris, you should take a / an / the Métro.
5. After dinner, I bought a / an / the ice cream cone and ate it while I was sitting by the fountain.
6. The Eiffel Tower is probably a / an / the most famous landmark in Paris.
7. We were so busy and did so much walking that I need a / an / the early night tonight.
8. The flag is up, so a / an / the Queen must be in the palace today.
9. It's amazing how quickly a / an / the company's share price is going up at the moment.
10. We're thinking about hiring a / an / the boat tomorrow and taking it out on the water.
11. My hotel has a / an / the beautiful view of the harbor and the sea.

54.2 MATCH THE BEGINNINGS OF THE SENTENCES TO THE CORRECT ENDINGS

People who aren't willing to help you → are really irritating, in my opinion.

1. The people who live in our town
2. The restaurant we went to last night
3. I don't know why, but spaghetti
4. A large number of vacationers
5. City tours that are free

- want to stay in an all-inclusive hotel.
- usually aren't as good as ones you pay for.
- is the one where pizza was invented.
- are really irritating, in my opinion.
- don't want the new road to be built.
- always tastes better when you're in Italy.

54.3 REWRITE THE SENTENCES, CORRECTING THE ERRORS

Last year I went on vacation to Kuala Lumpur in Malaysia and had the great time.
Last year I went on vacation to Kuala Lumpur in Malaysia and had a great time.

1. A Petronas Towers are the tallest buildings in Kuala Lumpur and they dominate the skyline.

2. If you go up to the top of the tower, you get a excellent view of the Kuala Lumpur.

3. Street food stands on the side of an road are great places to try Malaysian food.

4. You can also visit Islamic Arts Museum if you go to Kuala Lumpur. It's interesting.

5. Taking the day trip to the nearby Batu Caves is a good idea if you have time.

6. Have you walked through a colorful China Town market in Kuala Lumpur?

54.4 FILL IN THE GAPS USING THE CORRECT ARTICLES, LEAVING A BLANK FOR ZERO ARTICLE

They had __an__ amazing dinner in the restaurant at the top of the tower.

1. This is ________ old typewriter that my mother always used to use.
2. People from Brazil are known for their love of ________ football.
3. I've never seen such ________ wide selection of foods for breakfast as they had there.
4. They love ________ Chinese food, so I'm sure they'll enjoy their trip to China.
5. Our tour guide is ________ older lady who's lived in Dublin all her life.
6. There's ________ university in Bologna which is nearly 1,000 years old.
7. Here's our guide to ________ travel destinations that will be the most popular next year.
8. ________ waitress who served us at that restaurant was very friendly and helpful.
9. Children usually enjoy visiting ________ zoo in Edinburgh. You can even see pandas there.
10. Churros are very popular in ________ Spain. People eat them with chocolate sauce.
11. I wasn't sure whether we should leave ________ tip for the waiter or not.
12. ________ music festival we went to was brilliant. There were a lot of good bands playing.
13. ________ hotel where we stayed is a five-star hotel, so it was very luxurious.

54.5 LISTEN TO THE AUDIO AND ANSWER THE QUESTIONS

George and Carla are talking about the different countries where they have lived.

Germans and Brazilians both love soccer. George thinks Germany has some top class teams.
True ☑ **False** ☐

1. George supports the Bayern Munich team and thinks it's the best team around at the moment.
   True ☐ **False** ☐

2. George says German food is filling and tasty, but it is quite salty for him.
   True ☐ **False** ☐

3. Carla says steak is the most popular food in Brazil. Brazilians love meat, especially barbecued beef.
   True ☐ **False** ☐

4. Carla thinks the famous statue of Christ the Redeemer is the most popular landmark in Brazil.
   True ☐ **False** ☐

5. Carla thinks the Brandenburg Gate is the symbol of Brazil.
   True ☐ **False** ☐

54.6 MARK THE SILENT LETTERS AND SAY THE SENTENCES OUT LOUD

I (k)now you want to go out later.

1. Let's call a plumber to fix the water heater.
2. Foreign visitors think we speak good English.
3. I hurt my knee while we were trekking.
4. I like to listen to music while I'm traveling.
5. To be honest, I don't think I like him.
6. It's so cold. My fingers are numb.
7. He has just trapped his thumb in the door!

55 Abstract ideas

Most abstract nouns are uncountable. Some, however, can be either countable or uncountable, and the two forms often mean slightly different things.

New language Concrete and abstract nouns
Aa Vocabulary Education systems
New skill Talking about abstract ideas

55.1 CROSS OUT THE INCORRECT WORD IN EACH SENTENCE

 Please accept our ~~apology~~ / apologies for the cold soup you were served in our restaurant.

1  We often find that men aren't as good at taking care of their health / healths as women are.

2  She made her anger / angers at the graffiti on the wall clear to everyone in the room.

3  Unfortunately, the funding for all of the library / libraries in our area has been cut this year.

4  He's been having some trouble / troubles getting his computer to start all week.

5  Could you please email me all of the information / informations I need for my trip to Peru?

6  Our company specializes in creating beauty / beauties products for young women.

7  He has a lot of knowledge / knowledges about the history of the Middle Ages.

8  I've made a list of all the deadline / deadlines for the project in this document.

9  We take a lot of pride / prides in our work and always do our very best.

10  It's absolutely freezing today. It must be about minus fifteen degree / degrees outside!

11  We're facing some fierce competition / competitions from companies in South America.

55.2 FILL IN THE GAPS USING THE WORDS IN THE PANEL

There's so much more ___space___ in our new flat than in our old flat in Birmingham.

1. My ______________ are with the families of the victims of the disaster at this terrible time.
2. I come from Nigeria and my ______________ is very important to me. I keep the traditions alive.
3. Our ______________ is that our daughter will go to college and get a good job.
4. Your ______________ is really important to me, and I hope you feel the same.
5. My happiest childhood ______________ are of spending the summer in Sweden with my family.
6. I save some money every month and then at the end of the year I give it to local ______________ .

charities | memories | ~~space~~ | culture | friendship | hope | thoughts

55.3 MATCH THE BEGINNINGS OF THE SENTENCES TO THE CORRECT ENDINGS

Everyone needs some relaxation → after a long week at work.

1. You can now all find out what
2. My car has a top speed
3. The kittens your cat gave
4. I'm going to write the neighbors
5. My cousin Matthew repairs
6. We're here today because we're
7. Nowadays it's more and more
8. I make a living from entering
9. You have to study for six

- birth to are real beauties.
- a letter of apology for all of the noise.
- computers for a living.
- after a long week at work.
- grades you got on the exam.
- competitions. You can win so much!
- of 100 miles per hour.
- semesters before you get your degree.
- important to have good communication skills.
- interested in learning more about other cultures.

55.4 REWRITE THE SENTENCES, CORRECTING THE ERRORS

He's had so much successes as the CEO of this company, but now he wants to move on.
He's had so much success as the CEO of this company, but now he wants to move on.

1. The temperatures this summer are some of the highest in living memories.
2. I work hard on my friendship because friends are an important part of my life.
3. She hopes that she will complete her study and graduate next summer.
4. We're collecting money for charities, but we haven't decided which one we'll give it to yet.
5. There are a lot of free parking space at the front of the building if you're still looking.
6. You will be in our thought while you're away and we'll call you as often as we can.
7. There's always a lot of competitions in the soft drink market. It's hard to break through.
8. He takes so much prides in his garden and he wants other people to enjoy it, too.
9. There are so many time when I wish I had a robot who could do the housework for me.
10. She decided to take all of her knowledges about marketing and put it into a book.
11. The skills he has for soccer is unbelievable for someone of his age.
12. The company is known for the very high qualities of their kitchen products.

56 Vocabulary

Aa 56.1 TECHNOLOGY AND THE FUTURE WRITE THE PHRASES FROM THE PANEL UNDER THE CORRECT DEFINITIONS

The most modern and up-to-date

state-of-the-art

7 The most recent version of a product

1 Say what you think might happen in the future

8 An important discovery or achievement

2 What will happen in the future

9 Plan ahead so that something can happen

3 Something that will happen but it is not possible to say when

10 Have good or positive plans

4 Change or affect something

11 An era based on digital information, when technology is dominant

5 Design something to work in the future, even if technology changes

12 Hope for a successful or positive outcome

6 A huge change in ideas or methods

13 Extremely modern and innovative

have good intentions | digital age | revolution | hope for the best | what the future holds | only a matter of time | breakthrough | make arrangements | the latest model | ~~state-of-the-art~~ | cutting-edge | make predictions | future-proof | have an influence on something

57 Future hopes

To talk about wishes for the future, usually when you want something to change, you use the past tense modals "would" and "could."

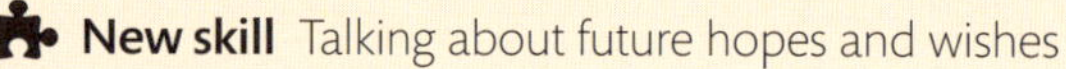

New language "Wish" with "would" or "could"
Aa Vocabulary Hopes for the future
New skill Talking about future hopes and wishes

57.1 REWRITE THE SENTENCES, CORRECTING THE ERRORS

I wish I can go to the movies with you this weekend.
I wish I could go to the movies with you this weekend.

1. My job at the supermarket is so boring, I wish I would find another one.

2. I wish Rosemary is stopping talking about herself all the time. It's so annoying!

3. I wish my teacher will give me more help. I don't understand any of this.

4. They wish they would take some time off work so they could go on vacation.

5. He wishes he can win the first prize in the competition he's entered.

6. She would she could get a leading role in the play, but she never goes to auditions.

7. I wish I would afford to get a new kitchen. This one is so old it's falling apart.

8. Adam wishes his teacher will give him more homework. He doesn't have enough to do.

9. I wish they will make it easier to work out how much tax you have to pay.

57.2 FILL IN THE GAPS USING "COULD" OR "WOULD"

The company wishes its employees *would* take advantage of the training it offers.

1. I wish my boss ______ be a little more polite. He's always rude to everyone.
2. Linda wishes she ______ drive to work, but she still hasn't passed her driving test.
3. They wish their neighbors ______ be a bit quieter. They're always making noise.
4. I wish they ______ tell us what's going to happen now instead of making us wait.
5. Jacob wishes he ______ relax, but he can't because he's having a stressful time at work.
6. I wish we ______ go on a helicopter ride around Manhattan, but we can't afford it.
7. Susanne wishes her daughter ______ call her more often. She only calls once a month.
8. I wish the people on the train ______ move their bags off the seats next to them.
9. They wish they ______ get a good espresso in this town, but they can't find one anywhere.

57.3 MATCH THE BEGINNINGS OF THE SENTENCES TO THE CORRECT ENDINGS

The printer keeps jamming. I wish → I could find one that works.

1. My job is really boring. I wish
2. The snails are eating my plants. I wish
3. The rules are so complicated. I wish
4. I can't type very quickly. I wish
5. They always leave a mess. I wish
6. The bus always takes so long. I wish
7. I'm so sleepy. I wish
8. That machine is very noisy. I wish

they would make them simpler.

someone would turn it off.

I could drive instead.

I could find one that works.

I could go to bed.

I could get rid of them once and for all.

my boss would let me take a course.

they would think about other people.

I could find something more interesting.

57.4 SAY THE SENTENCES OUT LOUD, FILLING IN THE GAPS WITH "COULD" OR "WOULD"

I wish the airline ___would___ make it easier to change flights.

1. The students wish they ______ speak perfect English.
2. He wishes his teacher ______ give him more help.
3. She wishes she ______ go to the party.
4. We wish they ______ let us leave work early.

57.5 LISTEN TO THE AUDIO AND ANSWER THE QUESTIONS

Cheryl is talking to her boss Michael about her job.

Which department does Cheryl work in?

- **Human Resources** ☐
- **Sales** ☑
- **Service** ☐

1. What change does Cheryl want to make to her working life?
   - **She wants to work from home** ☐
   - **She wants to travel more** ☐
   - **She wants to travel less** ☐

2. Where are the customers of Cheryl's company located?
   - **In Cheryl's home town** ☐
   - **Close to headquarters** ☐
   - **Far away from headquarters** ☐

3. According to Cheryl's boss, what does the CEO not want to do?
   - **Move the headquarters to a better place** ☐
   - **Lose the customers the company has** ☐
   - **Keep the head office where it is now** ☐

4. What would be Cheryl's ideal job if she could pick one?
   - **CEO of the company** ☐
   - **Internal sales team leader** ☐
   - **Her boss' job** ☐

5. Why will there be a vacancy within the next two years?
   - **Geoff wants to leave the company** ☐
   - **Geoff is going to retire** ☐
   - **Geoff is going to take a new position** ☐

57.6 READ THE EMAIL AND WRITE ANSWERS TO THE QUESTIONS AS FULL SENTENCES

To: josh.hogan@web.com

Subject: Re: Beach on Monday?

Hi Josh,

How are you? Hope you're well. Everything's good with me. I did my last college exam yesterday, so I'm now free! I wish I could just relax and take it easy this summer, but instead I'm going to do an internship at an accountancy firm. I know it sounds boring, but I really want to become an accountant. I wish that you could just walk into an accountancy job straight after leaving college, but you need to get some work experience and take some more exams. It'll be another five years before I'm fully qualified. I wish they wouldn't make it so difficult, and so long!

I wish I could go to the beach with you on Monday, but that's the first day of my internship. Maybe we could go this weekend instead.

See you soon,

Jessica

When did Jessica do her last exam?

She did her last exam yesterday.

1. What does Jessica wish she could do this summer?

2. What does Jessica wish you could do straight after leaving college?

3. How much longer will it be before Jessica is a qualified accountant?

4. What does Jessica wish she could do on Monday?

58 The future continuous

You can use the future continuous with "will" to make predictions about the future, and also to speculate about what might be happening at the current moment.

New language The future continuous with "will"
Aa Vocabulary Polite requests
New skill Planning your career

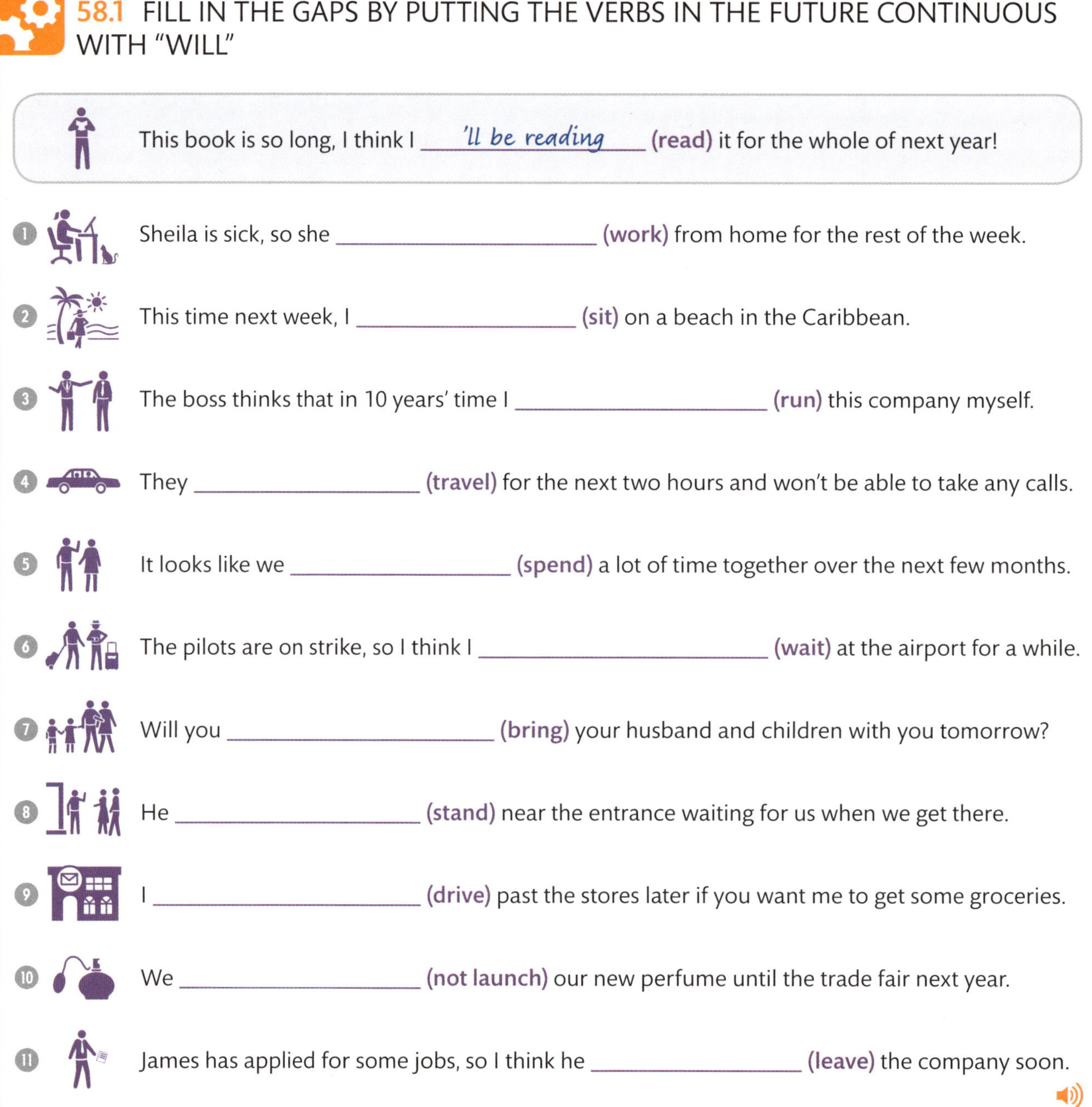

58.1 FILL IN THE GAPS BY PUTTING THE VERBS IN THE FUTURE CONTINUOUS WITH "WILL"

This book is so long, I think I *'ll be reading* (read) it for the whole of next year!

1. Sheila is sick, so she ______________ (work) from home for the rest of the week.
2. This time next week, I ______________ (sit) on a beach in the Caribbean.
3. The boss thinks that in 10 years' time I ______________ (run) this company myself.
4. They ______________ (travel) for the next two hours and won't be able to take any calls.
5. It looks like we ______________ (spend) a lot of time together over the next few months.
6. The pilots are on strike, so I think I ______________ (wait) at the airport for a while.
7. Will you ______________ (bring) your husband and children with you tomorrow?
8. He ______________ (stand) near the entrance waiting for us when we get there.
9. I ______________ (drive) past the stores later if you want me to get some groceries.
10. We ______________ (not launch) our new perfume until the trade fair next year.
11. James has applied for some jobs, so I think he ______________ (leave) the company soon.

58.2 USE THE CHART TO CREATE 12 CORRECT SENTENCES AND SAY THEM OUT LOUD

By this time next week, I'll be working in a big city.

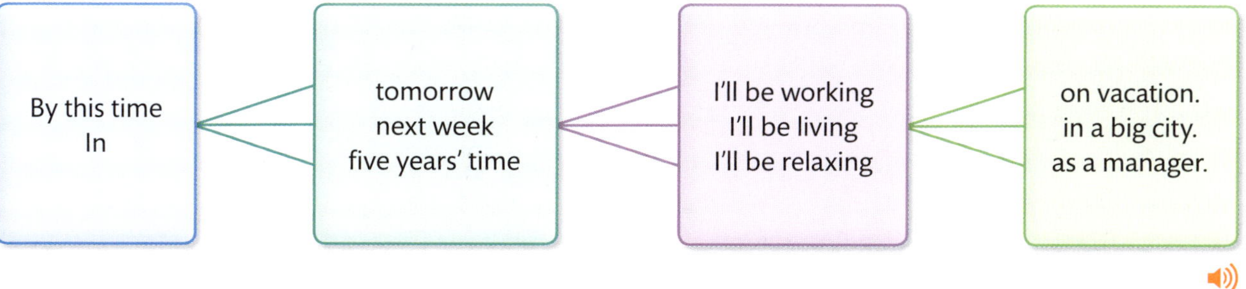

58.3 REWRITE THE SENTENCES, CORRECTING THE ERRORS

We will be fly at 35,000 feet until we start our descent into Vancouver.

We will be flying at 35,000 feet until we start our descent into Vancouver.

1. The next time I go to the mountains, I'll be ski like an expert.

2. In a few years' time, I be playing basketball professionally.

3. We will being hosting some visitors from China next week.

4. This evening they be serving snacks and drinks for everyone.

5. In five years' time, I won't be teach at a primary school any more.

6. Will you asking for input from the audience during your presentation?

58.4 REWRITE THE SENTENCES, PUTTING THE WORDS IN THE CORRECT ORDER

vacation. | I'll | Spain | traveling | to | be | on | my

I'll be traveling to Spain on my vacation.

1. be | in | 10 | time. | software | We'll | this | using | years'

2. will | 6pm | today. | until | be | Lisa | working

3. five | bus | will | leaving | minutes. | The | in | be

4. stopping | Station. | Central | at | This | be | train | will

5. be | I | will | Next | working | from | home. | week,

58.5 LISTEN TO THE AUDIO AND ANSWER THE QUESTIONS

Charles is calling Rachel to find out where Bill is.

Charles wants to find Bill.
True ☑ **False** ☐ **Not given** ☐

1. Bill usually eats his lunch at 12:30pm.
True ☐ **False** ☐ **Not given** ☐

2. Charles is giving a presentation in two weeks.
True ☐ **False** ☐ **Not given** ☐

3. Charles and Bill work in market research.
True ☐ **False** ☐ **Not given** ☐

4. Bill likes to go for a walk around the building.
True ☐ **False** ☐ **Not given** ☐

5. Charles will leave the office at 4pm today.
True ☐ **False** ☐ **Not given** ☐

58.6 READ THE ARTICLE AND ANSWER THE QUESTIONS

DAILY REPORTER

Where are we heading?

The march toward global connectivity

The number of internet users is increasing rapidly and it's predicted that in a few years' time, five billion of us will be shopping online. Around half of these people will be using tablets to access the internet. By 2020, connected devices will be so integrated into our lives that we will see them as "digital assistants."

At this very moment someone, somewhere will be buying something online and it is expected that every retail company will be selling their products on the web in 10 years' time.

Whole cities will become increasingly connected, with free public wi-fi in more and more areas. The internet user of the future will be browsing on the go, wherever they are.

According to the article what is going up very quickly at the moment?

The number of internet users is going up very quickly at the moment.

1. According to the article, how many people will be shopping online in a few years' time?

   ____

2. How many of these people will be using tablets to access the internet?

   ____

3. What will become so integrated into our lives that we'll see them as "digital assistants?"

   ____

4. According to the article, what can we assume that someone, somewhere will be doing right now?

   ____

5. Which retail companies will be selling their products on the web in 10 years' time?

   ____

6. Where will future internet users be able to get online?

   ____

59 The future perfect

You can use the future perfect to talk about events that will overlap with, or finish before, another event in the future.

New language The future perfect
Aa Vocabulary Life plans
New skill Making plans and predictions

59.1 FILL IN THE GAPS BY PUTTING THE VERBS IN THE FUTURE PERFECT

By next March, I *will have bought* **(buy)** my own house.

1. I ______________________ **(finish)** my degree by the time I am 22.
2. You ______________________ **(be)** married for one year in a week's time.
3. We ______________________ **(complete)** all our essays by the end of June.
4. By the time I am 24, I ______________________ **(find)** a good job.
5. I think my son ______________________ **(propose)** to his girlfriend by the end of the year.
6. By the time we are 30, we ______________________ **(have)** our first child.
7. Liza ______________________ **(move)** to London by the end of the month.
8. I ______________________ **(graduate)** from college by this time next year.
9. By the time I am 25, I ______________________ **(leave)** my parents' house.
10. I ______________________ **(make)** one million dollars by the time I'm 40.
11. They ______________________ **(start)** their new business by the end of the month.

59.2 REWRITE THE HIGHLIGHTED PHRASES, CORRECTING THE ERRORS

will have taken

1. ______
2. ______
3. ______
4. ______
5. ______
6. ______
7. ______
8. ______
9. ______

Hot Cakes

HOME | ENTRIES | ABOUT | CONTACT

POSTED AT 8:55PM

MY BUSINESS PLAN

By the end of this month, I **will have take** out a bank loan. I also **will has found** the perfect location for my new cupcake shop, and I **will have perfect** the recipes for my cupcakes. By the end of next month, I **will have open** my new shop and I hope I **will has been** featured in all the local newspapers. By the end of the first week, I hope that I **will have sell** at least 1,500 cupcakes. By the end of the first month, I hope that I **will increased** this number to 8,000 cupcakes. I expect that I **will have make** a profit of $12,000 by the end of the first six months. By the end of the first year, I **have taken** on two members of staff and I **will have launch** my online business. It's an ambitious plan, but I know I can do it!

59.3 SAY THE SENTENCES OUT LOUD, FILLING IN THE GAPS

Ken *will have read* **(read)** all his textbooks before lessons start next week.

1. They ______ **(choose)** the best candidate by the end of the day.
2. Jenny ______ **(buy)** a new dress before the wedding.
3. By the end of the year, I ______ **(complete)** three marathons.
4. I ______ **(open)** all my presents by the end of the party.
5. By the time he starts his new job, Hans ______ **(have)** his hair cut.
6. We ______ **(visit)** 15 countries by the end of this year.

59.4 REWRITE THE SENTENCES USING THE FUTURE PERFECT CONTINUOUS

In a year's time, I **(study)** English for 10 years.
In a year's time, I will have been studying English for 10 years.

1. By the time we arrive in Spain, we **(drive)** for eight hours.

2. Jenna **(run)** her own business for five years in May.

3. In June, I **(work)** as a teacher for 10 years.

4. By the time the cake is decorated, we **(cook)** for six hours.

5. I **(do)** yoga for 10 years by the end of the year.

6. In November, Becky and I **(live)** together for three years.

7. By midday, Jonas **(wait)** to see the doctor for three hours.

8. By the time I have finished, I **(clean)** the house for five hours.

9. By the time the plane lands in Malaysia, we **(travel)** for 13 hours.

10. By December, I **(learn)** to paint for six months.

11. I **(study)** medicine for four years by the end of June.

12. By the end of next month, the police **(look)** for the criminals for a year.

59.5 MARK THE SENTENCES THAT ARE CORRECT

Next week, I will have finished my course at the university. ☑
Next week, I will have been finishing my course at the university. ☐

1. At the end of the week, Lise will have studied in France for three months. ☐
   At the end of the week, Lise will have been studying in France for three months. ☐

2. This time tomorrow, I will have been having my operation. ☐
   This time tomorrow, I will have had my operation. ☐

3. I will have finished this report by the time you get here. ☐
   I will have been finishing this report by the time you get here. ☐

4. Next week, I will have been studying for two years. ☐
   Next week, I will have studied for two years. ☐

5. By the end of January, I will have been finishing my Italian course. ☐
   By the end of January, I will have finished my Italian course. ☐

6. In two hours, I will have written my last report for this client. ☐
   In two hours, I will have been writing my last report for this client. ☐

59.6 REWRITE THE HIGHLIGHTED PHRASES, CORRECTING THE ERRORS

owned

1. ____________________

2. ____________________

3. ____________________

4. ____________________

To: Bill

Subject: Our anniversary

My dearest Bill,

On January 8, we will have **been owning** this house for 10 years. We will have **being** married for 11 years, and we will have **been having** children for six years. What a fantastic 10 years. Thank you! I hope the next 10 years will be just as happy. By then, we will have **been knowing** each other for 25 years, and **being** together almost as long! I can't believe how fast the time flies.

All my love,

Anabel

60 The future in the past

English uses a number of constructions to describe thoughts about the future that we had at some point in the past.

New language "Would" and "was going to"
Aa Vocabulary Changing plans
New skill Saying what you thought

60.1 CROSS OUT THE INCORRECT WORDS IN EACH SENTENCE

I ~~will~~ / would love to see a basketball game in the US. I'm a big basketball fan.

1. I always thought that I will / would go to college, but I then decided to get a job instead.
2. As soon as I get home, I will / would give you a call to let you know I've arrived safely.
3. I'm sure that we will / would still be friends when we're older. There's no doubt about that.
4. He said that he will / would try to get me some tickets for the soccer game if he could.

60.2 MARK THE SENTENCES THAT ARE CORRECT

It's strange that he failed the exam. I thought he's going to get the highest grade. ☐
It's strange that he failed the exam. I thought he was going to get the highest grade. ☑

1. I got up so late, I knew I wasn't going to get to the airport in time. ☐
   I got up so late, I knew I wouldn't going to get to the airport in time. ☐
2. Sarah's an excellent swimmer, so I knew it's going to be hard to beat her. ☐
   Sarah's an excellent swimmer, so I knew it was going to be hard to beat her. ☐
3. My mother promised she won't going to embarrass me by hugging me in public. ☐
   My mother promised she wasn't going to embarrass me by hugging me in public. ☐
4. I found the exam easy, so I believed I was going to get a good grade. ☐
   I found the exam easy, so I believed I will going to get a good grade. ☐
5. He knew he wasn't getting the job, but he wanted to apply for it anyway. ☐
   He knew he wasn't going to get the job, but he wanted to apply for it anyway. ☐

60.3 REWRITE THE SENTENCES, CORRECTING THE ERRORS

I got up at 9 o'clock, so I know I was going to miss my flight at 10 o'clock.
I got up at 9 o'clock, so I knew I was going to miss my flight at 10 o'clock.

1. They couldn't come last week because they are going to a soccer game that evening.

2. She had taken her English exam the next day, so she felt a little nervous.

3. They would meeting with their lawyers that afternoon to decide what to do.

4. Sandra is planning to fly to Tenerife with her daughter yesterday, but the pilots are on strike.

5. Gareth is making a big announcement that afternoon, but then he lost his voice.

6. Camy and Charlie were have a big party to celebrate their anniversary that weekend.

7. Harren is getting married to Jennifer at 2 o'clock that afternoon in New York.

60.4 LISTEN TO THE AUDIO AND MARK WHETHER THE EVENTS REALLY HAPPENED OR NOT

Yes ✓ No ☐

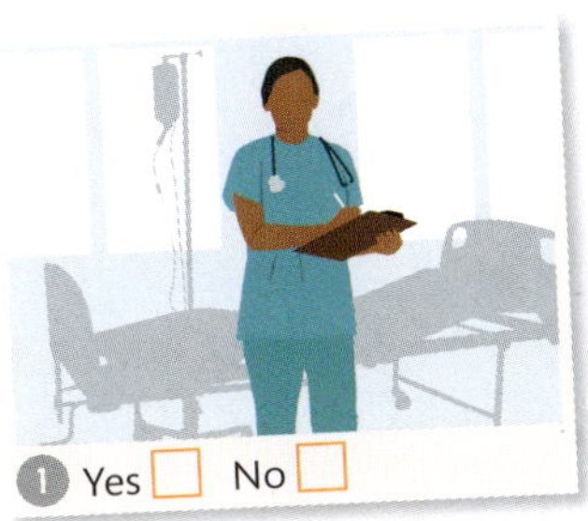

1. Yes ☐ No ☐

2. Yes ☐ No ☐

3. Yes ☐ No ☐

60.5 REWRITE THE SENTENCES USING FUTURE IN THE PAST TENSES

She is nervous as she is taking her English speaking exam this morning.
She was nervous as she was taking her English speaking exam that morning.

1. I know that I will be the marketing head of a leading company one day.

2. When I see him I know that I'm going to marry him and move to another country.

3. I'm taking my last exam in chemistry at college this afternoon.

4. I think I will travel around the world working as a part-time photographer.

5. She believes she will get a recording contract as soon as she finishes her course at college.

6. I know I will be late when I see how much traffic there is on the road.

7. I'm meeting some Chinese customers this morning for a presentation on distribution.

8. I think Shania and Jo will go somewhere warm for their holiday this year.

9. He is building an extension on the back of their house in Germany.

10. I decide I will retire early and spend more time with my family and close friends.

11. I know I'm going to be able to climb to the top of the mountain sooner than the others.

12. The company is interviewing some more people for the marketing job this week.

61 Vocabulary

Aa 61.1 **ART AND CULTURE** WRITE THE PHRASES FROM THE PANEL UNDER THE CORRECT DEFINITIONS

Be extremely absorbed in something

be engrossed in something

❶ Complicated / simple artistic or cultural ideas

❷ Long, written stories that are fictional

❸ Say what you feel, even if it is controversial

❹ Say that something is very good and tell others about it

❺ The fictional people in a book, film, or play

❻ The series of events that makes up the story in a book, film, or play

❼ Say that something is extremely good / bad

❽ Very positive reviews

❾ A feeling or effect that lasts a long time

❿ Alter or change a decision or feeling about something

⓫ Finally make a decision

⓬ The first / last moments of a book, film, or play

⓭ To set a particular mood or tone

glowing reviews | heap praise / criticism on something | ~~be engrossed in something~~ | plot | highly recommend | lasting impression | characters | make up your mind | speak your mind | opening / closing scenes | create an atmosphere | highbrow / lowbrow | change your mind | novels

62 Leaving words out

When you want to communicate clearly, it can be helpful to avoid repetition. One way to do this is to drop any unnecessary words.

New language Ellipsis
Aa Vocabulary Entertainment
New skill Leaving out unnecessary words

62.1 CROSS OUT THE WORDS THAT CAN BE LEFT OUT OF EACH SENTENCE

They could have gone to Spain on vacation, but they didn't want to ~~go to Spain on vacation~~.

1  The ceremony honored firemen and the ceremony honored paramedics.

2  We could go to the session on marketing or we could go to this talk on public relations.

3  It would be nice to go to the theater or to go to a film. You can decide.

4  This process was described by Gutmann and it was also described by Quirke.

5  She could have directed the TV series or she could have directed the film version.

6  They should use paper bags and they should recycle more of their garbage.

7  He might have become a great writer, but he didn't want to become a great writer.

8  The problem is that he wants to leave work early, but she doesn't want to leave work early.

9  He was chosen to play the lead role and he did an excellent job.

10  I could wear this yellow dress for the wedding or I could wear this blue skirt.

11  You could eat at the new Italian restaurant or you could eat at the Mexican restaurant.

62.2 READ THE ARTICLE AND ANSWER THE QUESTIONS

SILVER SCREEN

What to watch

Your one-stop guide to films this week

First Kiss Fans of romantic comedies will go to see *First Kiss* and fall in love with it. You could go to see it with your friends or that special someone in your life.

Starship Ipsilon This is a fun remake of an old science-fiction film and makes fun of the genre of sci-fi. Die-hard sci-fi fans may not like the new actors and storylines, but will go and see it anyway, I imagine.

Dead of Night The plot of this horror film is slightly ridiculous and could have been written by any 10 year old. The director has directed many well-known horror films, but we won't count this one among his best work.

Bobby IV Bobby Johnson is definitely back and shows us why he's the greatest wrestler of all time in this new sequel in the Bobby series. Bobby never gives up and does everything in his power to regain the world championship.

What type of film is *First Kiss*?
- Action ☐
- Horror ☐
- Romantic comedy ☑

1. Who should you not go to see *First Kiss* with?
   - Your friends ☐
   - Your partner ☐
   - Your parents ☐

2. What is wrong with *Dead of Night*?
   - Its plot ☐
   - Its special effects ☐
   - Its music ☐

3. How would you describe *Starship Ipsilon*?
   - Blockbuster ☐
   - Spoof ☐
   - Prequel ☐

4. Who will go to see *Starship Ipsilon*?
   - Dedicated sci-fi fans ☐
   - Those who are new to sci-fi ☐
   - Actors from the original film ☐

5. What kind of film is *Bobby IV*?
   - Remake ☐
   - Sequel ☐
   - Documentary ☐

62.3 FILL IN THE GAPS WITH THE REPEATED WORDS THAT HAVE BEEN DROPPED

It's a shame. I liked the film, but my brother didn't [like the film].

1. I'm so sorry! I broke your television, but I didn't mean to [______________].
2. We can't go to the movies tonight but we can [______________] tomorrow.
3. He told me he could speak French, but I don't think he can [______________].
4. My daughter loves horror films and [______________] thrillers.
5. We went to Venice and [______________] rode in a gondola this summer.
6. She could sit in the kitchen or [______________] the garden.
7. Do we need a new computer? We could get a laptop or [______________] a tablet instead.
8. It's such a beautiful day. We should go to the park or [______________] the beach.
9. The critics loved the latest blockbuster and [______________] said it was worth watching.
10. I need to borrow your car. I will email shortly to explain why [______________].

62.4 LISTEN TO THE AUDIO AND ANSWER THE QUESTIONS

Rachel and Simon are talking in the movie theater, waiting for the film to start.

Simon and Rachel are going to see *Death Kiss*.
True ☑ **False** ☐

1. The film starts at 7:30pm.
   True ☐ **False** ☐
2. Simon has booked the tickets.
   True ☐ **False** ☐
3. Rachel wants a hotdog.
   True ☐ **False** ☐
4. Simon wants buttered popcorn.
   True ☐ **False** ☐
5. The last film Simon saw was very boring.
   True ☐ **False** ☐
6. Rachel went to the film with Gavin.
   True ☐ **False** ☐
7. Gavin is 15 years old.
   True ☐ **False** ☐

62.5 CROSS OUT THE INCORRECT WORD IN EACH SENTENCE

The people I met when I was on vacation were **surprisingly** / ~~**highly**~~ good at speaking English.

1. I worked really hard on my entry, so I was **ridiculously** / **bitterly** disappointed that I didn't win.
2. The line for tickets at the museum was **painfully** / **heavily** slow. I thought we would never get in.
3. I won't go to that restaurant again. The prices were **heavily** / **astronomically** high!
4. The trip was **painfully** / **ridiculously** long because we were stuck in traffic for two hours.
5. I was **deeply** / **bitterly** moved by the poem she read at her mother's funeral.
6. Everyone knows that farmers in this country are **heavily** / **deeply** subsidized.
7. I think you should avoid mentioning any **astronomically** / **highly** controversial topics in your talk.

62.6 MATCH THE BEGINNINGS OF THE SENTENCES TO THE CORRECT ENDINGS

	She always works long hours	she knew who might be able to help.
1	We went for a walk in the woods	a beach or city break?
2	She emailed and called everyone	or go out for dinner tonight?
3	The cathedral is beautiful	and doesn't take very much time off.
4	Do you think we should go on	but not his face. It's been a long time.
5	He went cycling along the Rhine	and took some wonderful photos of the trees.
6	I want to move,	and ask him to confirm the details.
7	Could you call or email him	and is the seat of the Bishop of Rouen.
8	I can remember his name,	stayed at a wonderful resort on the coast.
9	They went to Mauritius and	and visited a lot of vineyards.
10	Do you want to cook	but he doesn't.

63 Substituting words

As well as ellipsis (leaving words out), you can also avoid repeating yourself by replacing some phrases with shorter ones. This is called substitution.

New language Substitution
Aa Vocabulary Books and reading
New skill Replacing phrases

63.1 CROSS OUT THE INCORRECT WORD IN EACH SENTENCE

We saw a lot of dogs at the rescue center, but the **one** / ~~**ones**~~ we adopted was the cutest.

1  I've eaten a lot of pizza in my time, but the **one** / **ones** I ate in Rome last year was the best.

2  I love these high-heeled shoes, but I think it's time I got some new **one** / **ones**.

3  Kirsten did well on both parts of the exam, but she did especially well on the first **one** / **ones**.

4  I really like the movies he's in, especially the earlier **one** / **ones** from the start of his career.

5  Our daughter likes a lot of subjects at school, but the **one** / **ones** she enjoys the most is science.

6  Mike has written a few books, but I think the first thriller he wrote is the best **one** / **ones**.

7  Ann tried on 10 different wedding dresses before she found the **one** / **ones** she wanted.

8  There are many activities for older children and some for younger **one** / **ones**.

9  I love all of the cakes Sam makes, but the **one** / **ones** she made today was really delicious.

10  I've been to a lot of countries, but the **one** / **ones** I enjoyed visiting the most was Japan.

11  Sarah isn't happy with her office assistant, so she wants to get a new **one** / **ones**.

63.2 FILL IN THE GAPS USING "ONE," "ONES," OR "SOME"

We still have *some* issues to resolve before the project is completed.

1. If you need any pens to write with, I have ______ here.
2. If you'd like a copy of my notes, I will print ______ for you.
3. They need some more batteries because the ______ I gave them last time have run out.
4. If you find anywhere selling cups of coffee, could you get me ______ ?
5. There's water here in case you need to use ______ while you're painting.
6. My new computer is slower than the ______ I got rid of when I bought it.
7. This cheeseburger tastes as good as the ______ I ate in the other restaurant.

63.3 REWRITE THE SENTENCES, CORRECTING THE ERRORS

Our car is so old and unreliable these days. We need to get a new ones.
Our car is so old and unreliable these days. We need to get a new one.

1. If you need any more paper to write on, there's one on my desk.

______

2. If you're looking for some new running shoes, I'd recommend the some on the left.

______

3. I have three tickets and I only need two, so I could give you some if you like.

______

4. If you need any information about the building, ask me and I'll give you ones.

______

5. If they like Italian restaurants, there's a great some just down the road.

______

6. I think Jenny and Matthew's wedding was the best ones I've ever been to.

______

63.4 MATCH THE BEGINNINGS OF THE SENTENCES TO THE CORRECT ENDINGS

If you need a pencil, → I have one over here.

1. I know you want a new computer,
2. My sister bought me an album,
3. If you're looking for bookstores,
4. I think my favorite authors
5. We should buy new flowers
6. Please help yourself to tea or coffee
7. I wanted to bring a cake,

- but it wasn't the one I wanted.
- are the ones who write about vampires.
- if you would like some.
- I have one over here.
- but I didn't have time to bake one.
- and get rid of these old ones.
- there are some on Upper Street.
- but we can't afford one.

63.5 MARK THE SENTENCES THAT ARE CORRECT

I like spicy food, but my wife doesn't like. ☐
I like spicy food, but my wife doesn't. ☑

1. I didn't enjoy it, but my friend enjoyed. ☐
   I didn't enjoy it, but my friend did. ☐
2. Did you see the new movie? We did see. ☐
   Did you see the new movie? We did, too. ☐
3. You bought a blue hat! I did, too. ☐
   You bought a blue hat! I do, too. ☐
4. Do I still cycle to work? Yes, I do. ☐
   Do I still cycle to work? Yes, I did. ☐
5. He works downtown, but she doesn't. ☐
   He works downtown, but she isn't. ☐
6. My mom went, but my dad didn't. ☐
   My mom went, but my dad didn't went. ☐
7. Did you bring your camera? I didn't. ☐
   Did you bring your camera? I didn't bring. ☐
8. You baked cookies! I did, too. ☐
   You baked cookies! I do, too. ☐
9. Does she like reading? Yes, she does. ☐
   Does she like reading? Yes, she do. ☐
10. They went skiing last year, but we didn't. ☐
    They went skiing last year, but we don't. ☐
11. My friend found it difficult. I did, too. ☐
    My friend found it difficult. I found, too. ☐

63.6 LISTEN TO THE AUDIO AND ANSWER THE QUESTIONS

Michael is talking to Kristen about an expensive smartwatch he got as a gift.

Michael has a new smartwatch. **True** ☑ **False** ☐

1. Kristen has the same smartwatch as Michael. **True** ☐ **False** ☐
2. You can only use the smartwatch as a smartphone. **True** ☐ **False** ☐
3. Hi-tech watches are on sale at a shop in the mall. **True** ☐ **False** ☐
4. Michael's mother gave him the smartwatch. **True** ☐ **False** ☐
5. Michael and his mother couldn't afford to replace the smartwatch. **True** ☐ **False** ☐
6. Kristen wants Michael to bring her a voucher for the online shop. **True** ☐ **False** ☐

63.7 RESPOND OUT LOUD TO THE AUDIO, USING SUBSTITUTION

Would you like to go to the mall?
[suppose] *Yes, I suppose so.*

1. Is it going to be sunny later?
[hope] ______

2. Did you remember to lock the door?
[think] ______

3. Didn't Tarkovsky direct your favorite movie?
[did] ______

4. Will the drinks be free tonight?
[imagine] ______

5. Will Sarah be at the party tonight?
[assume] ______

64 Shortening infinitives

As well as ellipsis and substitution, you can also shorten (or "reduce") infinitives to prevent repetition. This will help you to sound more natural when speaking.

New language Reduced infinitives
Aa Vocabulary Music and performance
New skill Avoiding repetition

64.1 CROSS OUT ALL THE WORDS THAT YOU CAN LEAVE OUT

I want to get the best tickets for the show but I can't afford to ~~get them.~~

1  I wanted to wake up early today, but I wasn't able to wake up early today.

2  Stefan was enjoying the ballet. At least, he seemed to be enjoying it.

3  I'm so nervous! I'm singing on stage tonight, but I really don't want to sing on stage tonight.

4  Your dog likes chasing people a lot more than he used to like chasing people.

5  I'm so thirsty! I meant to buy a drink before the movie, but I forgot to buy one.

6  Don't be nervous. There's no need to be nervous.

7  Darren said he'd help us unpack, but it seems that he won't be able to help us.

8  I really wanted to go to that concert, but I couldn't afford to go to it.

9  If you want to be promoted, you have to show me that you deserve to be promoted.

10  Helena asked me to join the college choir, but I didn't want to join the choir.

11  I'm sorry I'm so late! I didn't mean to be so late.

64.2 REWRITE THE SENTENCES, CORRECTING THE ERRORS

Richard usually forgets to send me a birthday card but this year he's promised not.
Richard usually forgets to send me a birthday card but this year he's promised not to.

1. I'd really like to go away this year, but I won't able to.

2. Keisha said I should go to her party tonight, but I don't really want.

3. I tried to find out Will's email address, but I wasn't to.

4. Frankie liked the birthday present we bought her. At least, she seemed.

5. I didn't realize that it was necessary to wear a tie, but apparently we have.

6. I'm very concerned about my test results, even though the doctor says there's no need be.

64.3 LISTEN TO THE AUDIO AND ANSWER THE QUESTIONS

Paul and Jess are discussing a concert they would like to go to.

Jess definitely wants to see the horror movie.
True ☐ **False** ☑

1. Paul invites Jess to see a rock band.
True ☐ **False** ☐

2. The musicians' instruments are recycled.
True ☐ **False** ☐

3. The musicians are originally from South Africa.
True ☐ **False** ☐

4. Paul is not sure that he can get the tickets.
True ☐ **False** ☐

5. Paul will call Jess when he has the tickets.
True ☐ **False** ☐

64.4 MATCH THE BEGINNINGS OF THE SENTENCES TO THE CORRECT ENDINGS

	I wasn't planning to go to the concert,	but I wasn't able to.
1	I'd really like to buy a new pair of shoes,	though I don't need to.
2	I'm not sure if I can visit my aunt this weekend,	but he can't afford to.
3	Jonas would really like to buy a car,	but I would love to.
4	I'll watch a movie if all my friends want to,	although I prefer to.
5	I don't insist on going to warm countries for vacations,	but I hope to.
6	I tried to get tickets for the concert,	but I wouldn't choose to.

64.5 FILL IN THE GAPS USING THE WORDS IN THE PANEL

I said we should get coffee first, and she *agreed*.

1. I am always really nervous before I go to the doctor's. It's difficult not ______.
2. It's not certain that I'll do well on my exams, but I ______ to.
3. Marie wants me to go shopping with her, but I really don't ______ to.
4. I've never been to the US. I'd love the ______.
5. You can get a vaccination before your trip, but you don't ______ to.

need ~~agreed~~ chance expect to be want

64.6 REWRITE THE SENTENCES, PUTTING THE WORDS IN THE CORRECT ORDER

can | We | to | movie theater | go | you | want | tonight | the | if | to.

We can go to the movie theater tonight if you want to.

1. but | listening | sister | to. | music, | hates | to | I | loud | love | my

____

2. can | work | to. | early | You | leave | afternoon | if | like | this | you | would

____

3. be | me | to. | I'd | her | Gigi | asked | delighted | and | said | go | wedding | to | I | to

____

4. agree | do | Don't | the | want | don't | fun run | if | you | to. | really | to

____

64.7 RESPOND TO THE AUDIO OUT LOUD, USING THE PROMPTS

Are you going to go to the show?

[decide] No, *I decided not to*.

1. Would you like to come to the gig with me?

   [delighted] Yes, ______________.

2. Do you want to go swimming tonight?

   [want] No, ______________.

3. Should I dress up for the party?

   [need] No, ______________.

4. Did Miranda enjoy the play?

   [seem] Yes, ______________.

5. Are you going on vacation this year?

   [afford] No, ______________.

65 Expressing reactions

Although discourse markers often don't add content in themselves, they can ease the flow of a conversation and add information about the speaker's opinion.

New language Informal discourse markers
Aa Vocabulary Advanced prefixes
New skill Structuring conversation

65.1 CROSS OUT THE LEAST APPROPRIATE WORDS IN EACH SENTENCE

~~Anyway~~ / Actually, the great thing was that everyone in Canada could understand me.

1  Sorry, I had to take that call. So by the way / as I was saying, the gallery opened in 1903.

2  I've been to that museum, too. Hey, I love your shoes, actually / by the way.

3  This gallery is beautiful. Oh, anyway / by the way, did you see there's a new café downstairs?

4  You think he's an expert? Anyway / Actually, he doesn't really know anything about art.

5  Anyway / By the way, I'm afraid I will have to say goodbye now, but thank you for today.

6  No, actually / by the way, it was George who thought we should buy this painting, not me.

7  Mike's very happy because, as I was saying / anyway, he's getting married next September.

8  Yes, I'd like some coffee. So, actually / as I was saying, we've got a lot of paintings at home.

9  Anyway / Actually, I'm sure you'll have a great time in Tokyo. See you when you get back!

10  So, as I was saying / by the way, Jenny and I have known each other for a long time.

11  Yes, by the way / actually, I've already been here a few times, so I know my way around.

65.2 RESPOND TO THE AUDIO, SPEAKING OUT LOUD AND FILLING IN THE GAPS WITH THE WORDS IN THE PANEL

Andy Warhol is your favorite artist, isn't he?

Actually, my favorite artist is David Hockney.

1. Oh, that's right! I think they have a few Warhol pieces upstairs.

   Yes, but ________ before, I prefer Hockney.

2. Did you go to the exhibition of his work last year?

   No, it was sold out. ________, we should get moving!

3. Yes, it's getting late already. Do you want to see the new installation?

   I've already seen it, ________. I came here last month.

4. I'm going to go to the gift shop before it closes.

   ________, I've already been. But you go.

actually

Actually

as I was saying

~~Actually~~

Anyway

65.3 MARK THE SENTENCES THAT ARE CORRECT

He's really **superactive**. He always solves problems before they arise. ☐
He's really **proactive**. He always solves problems before they arise. ☑

1. The fastest aircraft travel through the air at **antisonic** speeds. ☐
   The fastest aircraft travel through the air at **supersonic** speeds. ☐

2. Powerful computers can **prodict** the outcomes of some experiments with amazing accuracy. ☐
   Powerful computers can **predict** the outcomes of some experiments with amazing accuracy. ☐

3. The first farms in human history were established in the **Postlithic**, or New Stone Age. ☐
   The first farms in human history were established in the **Neolithic**, or New Stone Age. ☐

4. The **prewar** period, after the fighting had ended, saw an economic boom. ☐
   The **postwar** period, after the fighting had ended, saw an economic boom. ☐

65.4 READ THE ARTICLE AND ANSWER THE QUESTIONS

The writer visited a school of fashion.
True ☐ False ☑

1. The writer attended a freshman show.
True ☐ False ☐

2. A reception event took place before the show.
True ☐ False ☐

3. Skye Tyler's work is traditional and conservative.
True ☐ False ☐

4. There was no postmodern art in the show.
True ☐ False ☐

5. Neo-Gothic art reinvents and revises Gothic styles.
True ☐ False ☐

Fresh blood

What influences young artists?

Yesterday I attended the graduation show of young artists who've been studying at the Royal College of Art in London.

During the preshow reception, I mingled with some of the artists in an anteroom next to the exhibition hall. I took the opportunity to ask some of them about what had influenced their work. Skye Tyler, 22 from London, told me she tries to be very antiestablishment.

When we went into the exhibition hall, I noticed that a lot of the artists had produced some interesting postmodern pieces. Others were influenced by a style that could only be described as neo-Gothic, as it is a reinvention and updating of Gothic art from the Middle Ages.

Aa 65.5 MATCH THE DEFINITIONS TO THE CORRECT WORDS

a room leading into another room → anteroom	preview
1 see something in advance	antibacterial
2 something built on top of something else	anteroom
3 harmful to bacteria	superstructure
4 made longer	postpone
5 a new interpretation of classical ideas	superhuman
6 do something later than planned	preassigned
7 cure for poison	antidote
8 better than human	prolonged
9 allocated in advance	neoclassical

65.6 FILL IN THE GAPS USING THE PREFIXES IN THE PANEL

I'm afraid you can't come in. All tickets for the exhibition have been __pre__ assigned.

1. He's interested in _______ liberalism. I'm not sure what that is, but it's a new type of liberalism.
2. I've been enjoying the _______ game buildup, but now I just can't wait for the game to start.
3. _______ classical architecture became popular when interest in ancient Greece rose again.
4. We've organized a _______ conference event so people can meet before the meetings start.
5. James must be _______ human! It's amazing how he manages to work and travel so much.
6. She specializes in _______ natal care, so she looks after newborn babies.
7. _______ modern art was a reaction by artists against the modernist art that came before it.
8. Instead of finishing her degree, she's decided to _______ pone her studies and go traveling.
9. You first go into the _______ chamber of the tomb of Tutankhamun and then the main chamber.
10. If I could have any _______ power I wanted, I think it would be the ability to fly.
11. I've had enough of our neighbors' _______ social behavior, they're always making noise!
12. We're celebrating the 50th anniversary of the introduction of _______ discrimination laws.

~~pre~~	post	post	ante	anti	neo	
super	pre	neo	pre	anti	neo	super

66 Getting things done

Sometimes you might want to talk about other people doing things for you, rather than doing things yourself. To do this, you need to use different grammar.

New language "Have / get something done"
Aa Vocabulary Services and repairs
New skill Describing things people do for you

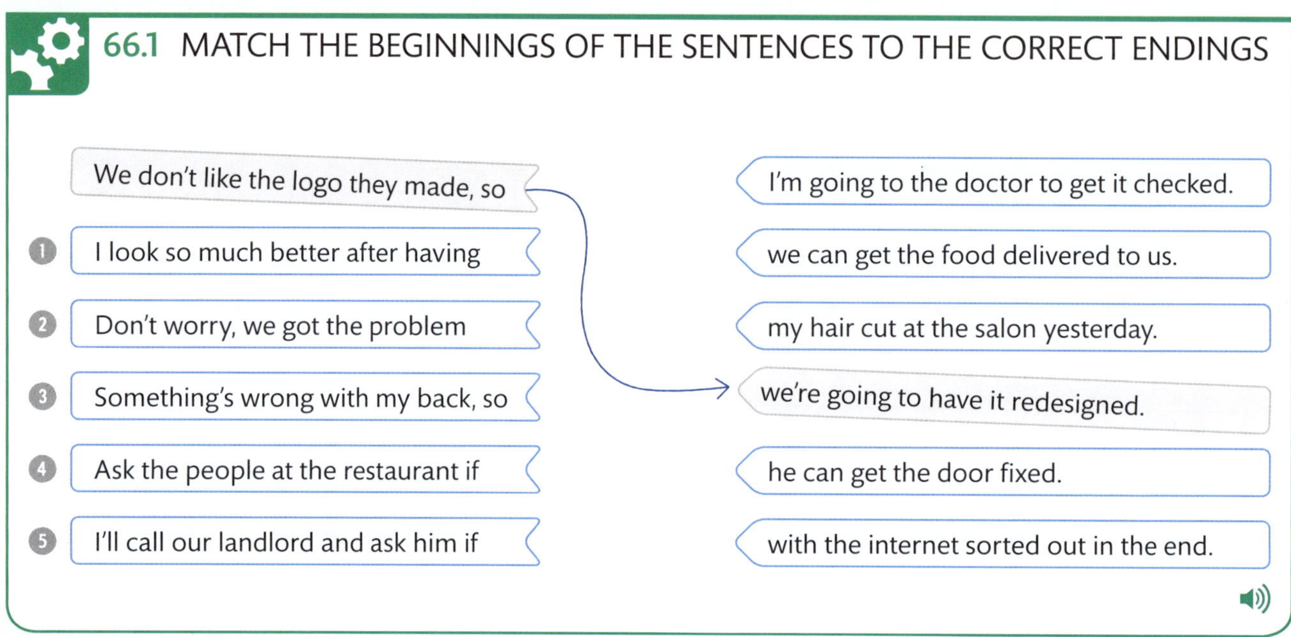

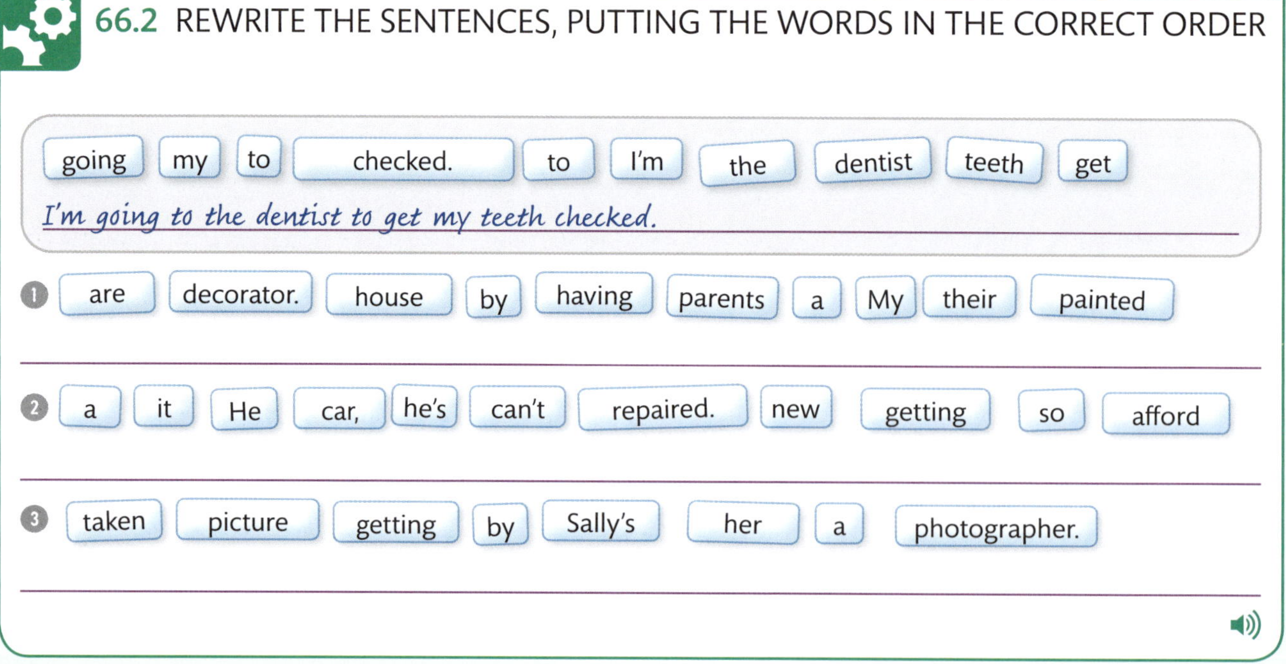

66.3 LISTEN TO THE AUDIO AND ANSWER THE QUESTIONS

Joanne checked her car battery.
True ☑ **False** ☐

1. Joanne changed the spark plugs.
True ☐ **False** ☐

2. Joanne will have to get the car repaired.
True ☐ **False** ☐

3. Lou got oil on Joanne's coat.
True ☐ **False** ☐

4. Joanne will have to get the coat dry cleaned.
True ☐ **False** ☐

5. Romesh will iron his own shirts.
True ☐ **False** ☐

6. Someone is going to cut Romesh's hair.
True ☐ **False** ☐

7. Romesh is interviewing someone for a new job.
True ☐ **False** ☐

66.4 FILL IN THE GAPS USING THE CORRECT FORMS OF THE VERBS

She's been *getting* **(get)** her articles translated by a young German student at the university.

1. Leah needs to go to the dentist as soon as possible ________________ **(have)** her teeth fixed.
2. He's ________________ **(get)** his birth certificate translated into English, so he can get married.
3. They ________________ **(have)** a marquee built in the grounds of the castle for their party last year.
4. She always ________________ **(have)** her essays checked by her mother before she hands them in.
5. My wedding ring ________________ **(get)** stolen when someone broke into our house last week.
6. We've been having problems with our website, but we're ________________ **(get)** them sorted out.
7. Jessica can't come to the phone right now because she's ________________ **(have)** her nails done.
8. We've ________________ **(have)** a lot of changes made to the house since we moved in five years ago.
9. He's been ________________ **(have)** his hair cut at that barber's shop since he was five years old.

66.5 REWRITE THE HIGHLIGHTED PHRASES, CORRECTING THE ERRORS

get

1 ____________

2 ____________

3 ____________

4 ____________

5 ____________

6 ____________

7 ____________

8 ____________

9 ____________

10 ____________

DO IT YOURSELF

Organize a conference

Here's a list of things to keep in mind

If you want to organize a conference, you need to **have** organized. The first thing you need to do is **have** a venue sorted out. You can do this yourself or **get** someone find one for you. Once you've **get** this organized, **get** someone who works at the venue give you an overview of the costs. You can then write a call for papers and **get** colleagues share it with people they know. Make a program and **got** it printed. If you're **have** the programs delivered, make sure the printer knows whether they should deliver them to your home or to the venue. On the day before the conference, get all of the lights and equipment **check** by the venue staff and then **checked** them again yourself! If you've **have** your conference staff trained in how to deal with the delegates at the conference, they'll know exactly what to do on the day.

66.6 REWRITE THE SENTENCES, USING "HAVE" OR "GET"

The hairdresser cut my hair. **(have)**
I had my hair cut.

1 I ordered a pizza delivery for dinner. **(get)**

2 A mechanic fixed my car. **(get)**

3 A decorator is painting our house. **(have)**

4 My shirts are being dry-cleaned. **(get)**

5 A photographer took my picture. **(get)**

6 Someone repaired the oven. **(get)**

7 A dentist checked my teeth. **(get)**

8 Someone is landscaping their garden. **(have)**

9 A student translated my essay. **(have)**

10 My eyesight was tested at the hospital. **(get)**

11 The hotel staff did my laundry. **(get)**

66.7 RESPOND OUT LOUD TO THE AUDIO, USING THE PHRASES IN THE PANEL

Where's Gina?

She's in the bathroom. She's still *getting ready* for the party.

1. Where did you go?

   I'm having problems with my eyes, so I went to the optician to __________ .

2. Where is your purse?

   You won't believe it. I __________ when we were on vacation!

3. I'm really hungry. How can I get a pizza?

   You can either pick the pizza up from the restaurant or you can __________ .

4. When will I get my business cards?

   The business cards are here. Would you like me to __________ to your home address?

5. Is that an old jacket you're wearing?

   No, but I can't believe how filthy it is. I need to __________ as soon as possible.

6. Is your internet up again?

   No, the internet at home still isn't working properly. We need to __________ this week.

7. Are you allowed to have long hair at your new job?

   No, I'm going to the hairdresser's to __________ .

get it sorted out	had it stolen	~~getting ready~~	get them checked
have it dry-cleaned	have it cut	have it delivered	have them sent

67 Complex agreement

One of the basic principles of English is that subjects and verbs must agree. Some subjects, however, can behave as singular or plural nouns depending on their context.

New language Complex agreement
Aa Vocabulary Collective nouns
New skill Using the correct agreement

67.1 FILL IN THE GAPS USING THE COLLECTIVE NOUNS IN THE PANEL

The whole *fleet* is out today and it's sailing across to the other side of the channel.

1. The ____________ was so appreciative of our performance that they gave us three encores.
2. All the ____________ at the hotel where we stayed were extremely friendly and helpful.
3. My son's ____________ is doing a concert at the town hall on Saturday evening.
4. Jake's ____________ is always arguing. His brother and sister are the worst.
5. Next week, all the ____________ in the office are going to do extra training.
6. The ____________ is holding an emergency session to discuss foreign policy issues.
7. Our ____________ is known for being the most environmentally friendly in the company.
8. My ____________ is the market leader in the digital industry and has been for 10 years now.
9. Later this afternoon our ____________ is going to be discussing the issues you mentioned.

family | orchestra | government | staff | ~~fleet~~
teams | department | audience | panel | company

67.2 MARK THE SENTENCES THAT ARE CORRECT

Singing Stars are my favorite TV program. I watch it every Saturday night. ☐
Singing Stars is my favorite TV program. I watch it every Saturday night. ☑

1. Spain have a very long border with Portugal. It's one of the longest in Europe. ☐
   Spain has a very long border with Portugal. It's one of the longest in Europe. ☐

2. The Netherlands are of the best countries to go on vacation if you like cycling. ☐
   The Netherlands is one of the best countries to go on vacation if you like cycling. ☐

3. He's great at soccer, but athletics is the sport that he wants to focus on from now on. ☐
   He's great at soccer, but athletics are the sport that he wants to focus on from now on. ☐

4. Politics were my favorite subject at school, so I decided to study it in college. ☐
   Politics was my favorite subject at school, so I decided to study it in college. ☐

5. The news about the celebrity couple were very hard to believe. ☐
   The news about the celebrity couple was very hard to believe. ☐

67.3 MATCH THE BEGINNINGS OF THE SENTENCES TO THE CORRECT ENDINGS

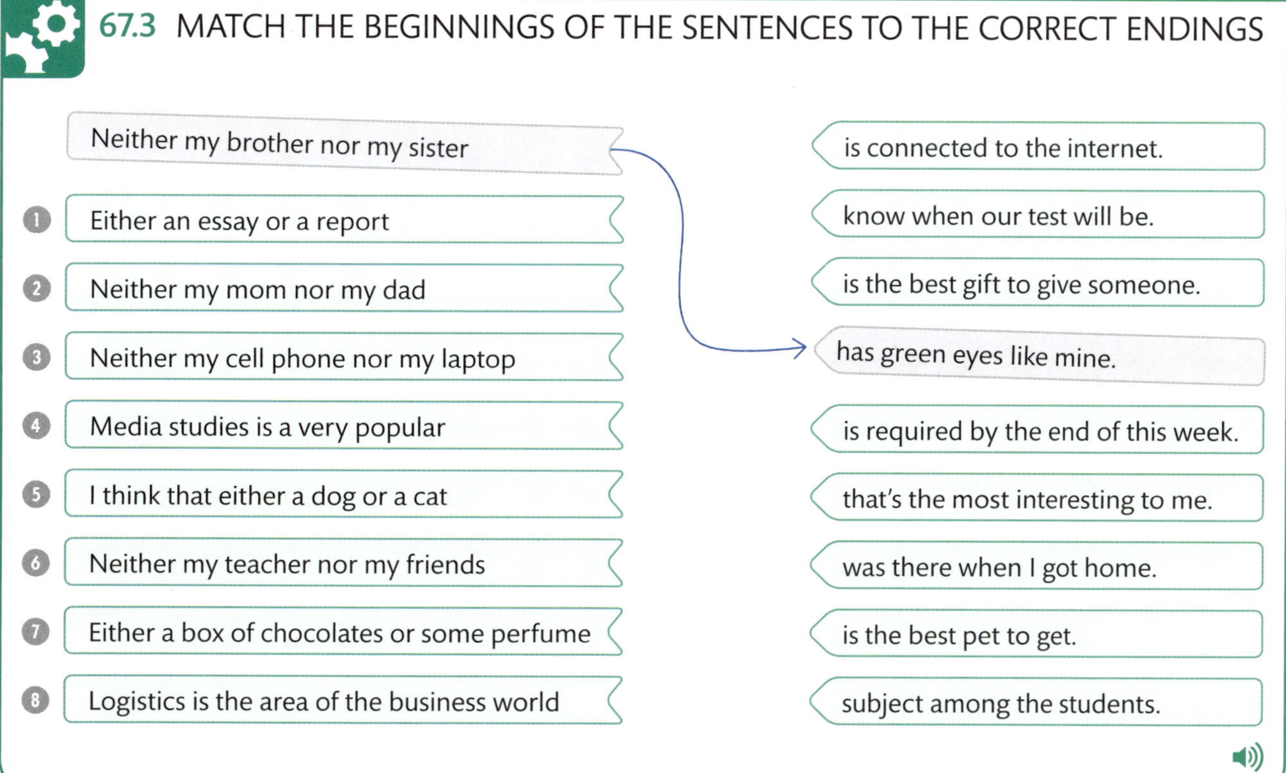

Neither my brother nor my sister → has green eyes like mine.

1. Either an essay or a report
2. Neither my mom nor my dad
3. Neither my cell phone nor my laptop
4. Media studies is a very popular
5. I think that either a dog or a cat
6. Neither my teacher nor my friends
7. Either a box of chocolates or some perfume
8. Logistics is the area of the business world

- is connected to the internet.
- know when our test will be.
- is the best gift to give someone.
- has green eyes like mine.
- is required by the end of this week.
- that's the most interesting to me.
- was there when I got home.
- is the best pet to get.
- subject among the students.

67.4 CROSS OUT THE INCORRECT WORDS IN EACH SENTENCE

The news is / ~~are~~ always depressing. There are so many stories about bad things that are happening.

1. All of the information about this is / are available to you on the college's website.
2. Neither my dad nor my mom was / were very happy when I got suspended from school.
3. Is / Are *The Dragon Leader* a good book or do you not like fantasy novels?
4. Either pop music or rock music is / are what I like to listen to when I'm relaxing.
5. Physics is / are what Charlie studied in college, too.
6. Politics is / are slowly moving to the left in this country at the moment.
7. Is / Are the mathematics you're doing in your class very difficult or can you do it easily?
8. Neither my presentation nor my essay was / were good enough to get me a passing grade.
9. The Bahamas has / have very warm weather at this time of year, so I'd recommend going there.
10. Either English or Spanish is / are the language that people most commonly learn at our school.

67.5 LISTEN TO THE AUDIO AND ANSWER THE QUESTIONS

Neil, a student, is talking about a popular subject in college.

Economics is very popular in college.
True ☑ False ☐ Not given ☐

1. There are 400 new economics students this year.
True ☐ False ☐ Not given ☐

2. Economics with tourism is popular.
True ☐ False ☐ Not given ☐

3. Neil is studying mathematics now.
True ☐ False ☐ Not given ☐

4. Neil thinks mathematics is too difficult for him.
True ☐ False ☐ Not given ☐

5. Both of Neil's parents went to college.
True ☐ False ☐ Not given ☐

6. Neil's parents don't put a lot of pressure on him.
True ☐ False ☐ Not given ☐

7. Neil still lives near his family.
True ☐ False ☐ Not given ☐

67.6 SAY THE SENTENCES OUT LOUD, CHOOSING THE CORRECT WORDS

The Netherlands **is** / ~~are~~ the country where I grew up, but now I live in France.

1. *Jungle Adventures* **is** / **are** the new television show that everyone is talking about.
2. The US **is** / **are** the largest country in North America when it comes to population.
3. This information **need** / **needs** to be shared with everyone else in the team right away.
4. Neither the adults nor the children **was** / **were** interested in the entertainment they provided.
5. I think politics **isn't** / **aren't** a topic that you should discuss when you're making small talk.
6. Neither my black suit nor my dark blue one **is** / **are** clean enough to wear.
7. Neither my phone nor Clark's phone **is** / **are** getting any signal at the moment.
8. Either the lemon or the lime **was** / **were** too strong in the sauce he made.
9. Everyone in Jack's family **is** / **are** interested in birdwatching, so he's going on a trip with them.
10. Neither history nor business **is** / **are** interesting to me.

68 "So" and "such"

You can use "so" and "such" with certain words to add emphasis. They are similar in meaning, but they are used in different structures.

New language "So" and "such" for emphasis
Aa Vocabulary Medical science
New skill Emphasizing descriptions

68.1 CROSS OUT THE INCORRECT WORDS IN EACH SENTENCE

You're so / ~~such~~ amazing! You've had three operations this year and you're still smiling!

1. Last night my mom called me to say that my grandma was very ill. It was so / such a shock.
2. Hong Kong is so / such a fascinating city. You should go there if you get the chance.
3. You've got so / such a difficult job. I don't think I'm patient enough to be a teacher.
4. He carried the baby so / such gently, as if he was scared she might break.
5. I can't believe I've got a job in Paris! It's so / such exciting!
6. That movie was so / such gripping. It was almost three hours long, but the time flew past!
7. You've got so / such a beautiful smile. Has anyone ever told you that?
8. It's always so / such a pleasure to spend time with Tom. He's a lovely man.
9. Keira is so / such generous. Did you know that she gave $250 to charity last month?
10. I'm not surprised the police stopped Mick. He drives so / such dangerously.
11. Thanks for responding so / such quickly. That was really efficient of you.
12. It was so / such a surprise when my cat turned up after being missing for six months!
13. You behaved so / such rudely in front of our guests. I felt quite embarrassed.
14. You learn languages so / such easily! Can you share your secret with me?
15. I think Martin is so / such brave. I couldn't do a bungee jump.
16. Your present job is so / such interesting. Is it also well paid, unlike the previous one?
17. *Back to City Life* was so / such a great book. I want to read it again!
18. It was so / such a relief when the doctor told me the good news. I've been celebrating.
19. I've had so / such a fun evening. Can I see you again tomorrow?

68.2 MATCH THE BEGINNINGS OF THE SENTENCES TO THE CORRECT ENDINGS

The doctor was so tired → that he nearly fell asleep!

1. The medicine works so effectively
2. It was such a bad injury
3. It was such an unexpected result
4. He recovered so quickly
5. Brian is so intelligent
6. The doctor was so reassuring

- that everyone was surprised.
- that she was off work for months.
- that he's sure to go on to college.
- that he nearly fell asleep!
- that I didn't really feel worried.
- that we have a 98 percent cure rate.
- that he was back at work within two weeks.

68.3 FILL IN THE GAPS USING "SO" OR "SUCH"

Elizabeth had *so* little experience in her role as teacher that she was really nervous.

1. It's ____________ a beautiful day. Why don't we go for a walk on the beach?
2. I am ____________ grateful to the doctors that I'm going to send them a thank you card.
3. It was ____________ a thrill to spend time with my grandchildren.
4. The movie was ____________ boring that Pauline and I fell asleep.
5. It was ____________ a surprise that I didn't know what to say.
6. Chantelle is ____________ helpful. She's a lovely young woman.
7. Tom reacted ____________ bravely when the doctor told him he had to go into the hospital.

68.4 REWRITE THE SENTENCES, CORRECTING THE ERRORS

So much surgeons have to work extremely long hours these days.

So many surgeons have to work extremely long hours these days.

1. Such few people eat enough fruit and vegetables every day.

2. Such little funding is available for research into age-related diseases.

3. There are so much medicines to choose from for your condition.

4. Such many wonderful people work in our health service.

5. Charis feels so better since she started doing more exercise.

6. Such few students are bright enough to become doctors and engineers.

7. So many effort goes into making sure the patients are comfortable.

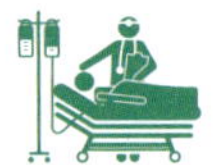

8. Such little money is spent on healthcare services for the disabled.

9. Such many people know someone who has been in the hospital.

10. There has been so many amazing progress in the field of medicine in the last decade.

11. So many time and money has been put into designing this new hospital.

12. It's so easier to play sports since I lost a lot of weight.

68.5 MARK THE SENTENCES THAT ARE CORRECT

Medical treatments today are such much better than they used to be. ☐
Medical treatments today are so much better than they used to be. ☑

1. Lyndsey is so an inspiration to me. I follow everything she posts on her blog. ☐
   Lyndsey is such an inspiration to me. I follow everything she posts on her blog. ☐

2. Jamie made such an effort to find the right present for my birthday. ☐
   Jamie made much an effort to find the right present for my birthday. ☐

3. I have so many free time these days, I've started some new hobbies. ☐
   I have so much free time these days, I've started some new hobbies. ☐

4. The exam was such easy that I wondered whether I had missed something. ☐
   The exam was so easy that I wondered whether I had missed something. ☐

5. You play the piano so beautifully! Can you play it again, please? ☐
   You play the piano such beautifully! Can you play it again, please? ☐

6. There are such few opportunities for people who can't read or write. ☐
   There are so few opportunities for people who can't read or write. ☐

68.6 SAY THE SENTENCES OUT LOUD, PUTTING "SO" OR "SUCH" IN THE CORRECT PLACE

The party was a success. [such]
The party was such a success.

1. These stray cats are a nuisance. [such]

2. I feel much calmer after a walk in the rain. [so]

3. You opened the door quietly last night. [so]

4. *Color* was amazing that I watched it again. [so]

5. There are many shirts to choose from. [so]

6. It's a lovely dress that I'm going to buy it. [such]

7. My dog is always hungry. She eats much. [so]

69 Using articles to generalize

"The" is the most commonly used word in the English language. It can be used in many different situations, as can the indefinite article "a," and the zero article.

New language Generic "the"
Aa Vocabulary Exploration and invention
New skill Using advanced articles

69.1 CROSS OUT THE INCORRECT WORDS IN EACH SENTENCE

~~A~~ / ~~An~~ / The internet is probably the most important invention of the last 50 years.

1  My brother has a / an / the pet spider. I hate it!

2  I'd like a piece of cake and a / an / the orange juice, please.

3  A / An / The airplane was invented by the Wright brothers.

4  Can I ask you a / an / the question?

5  I can see a / an / the man over there with blond hair. But I'm not sure that it's Josh.

6  A / An / The bicycle is a very common form of transportation all over the world.

7  I have a / an / the arrangement with my colleague, where we share the commute to work.

8  There was a / an / the awkward silence when I asked Tami how her job was going.

9  A / An / The hummingbird is one of the smallest birds on the planet.

10  Would you like a / an / the cup of coffee?

11  A / An / The sandwich is named after the Earl of Sandwich, who supposedly invented it.

69.2 FILL IN THE GAPS USING THE CORRECT ARTICLE, LEAVING A GAP FOR ZERO ARTICLE

The telescope was invented in the 16th century.

1. ______ apple a day keeps the doctor away.
2. ______ women are still rarely paid as much as men.
3. ______ human beings are the number-one predator on Earth.
4. There's ______ advertisement for a new smartwatch in today's paper.
5. ______ electric car is now a reality in many countries.
6. ______ students usually don't have very much money.
7. ______ panda is in danger of becoming extinct.

69.3 MARK THE SENTENCES THAT ARE CORRECT

I'd like to introduce my colleague, Sophie Brennan. ☑
I'd like to introduce my colleague, the Sophie Brennan. ☐

1. I'm afraid there isn't a Mark Wilson in this office. Have you got the right name? ☐
   I'm afraid there isn't the Mark Wilson in this office. Have you got the right name? ☐
2. Are you saying you're good friends with a John Smith? ☐
   Are you saying you're good friends with John Smith? ☐
3. This is my sister's best friend, a Kristin Wyatt. ☐
   This is my sister's best friend, Kristin Wyatt. ☐
4. Let me introduce you to the manager of our company, Isaac Myers. ☐
   Let me introduce you to the manager of our company, the Isaac Myers. ☐
5. I don't know of a Lucy Armitage. Is there anyone else you'd like to speak to? ☐
   I don't know of the Lucy Armitage. Is there anyone else you'd like to speak to? ☐
6. You don't mean a Cherry Baldwin, the famous actress, do you? ☐
   You don't mean the Cherry Baldwin, the famous actress, do you? ☐

69.4 REWRITE THE SENTENCES, CORRECTING THE ERRORS

Thomas Edison is widely acknowledged as an inventor of the moving picture.
Thomas Edison is widely acknowledged as the inventor of the moving picture.

1. I can't find the Mikaela Zimmerman in the company directory. Are you sure she works here?

2. Did you manage to get yourself ticket for the concert?

3. Cell phone has become a much smaller and lighter device in recent years.

4. Allow me to introduce you to my fiancé, a Brad Livingstone.

5. I had delicious meal at that new Italian restaurant last night.

6. There's no record of the Thomas Luckett ever having lived here.

7. Dog is often described as man's best friend.

8. Can you believe I was sitting next to an Elizabeth Parker? She's such a huge star!

9. Dress is often the most important thing for a bride at her wedding.

10. This is my boss, a Francesco Coppola.

11. We usually have the breakfast at about 7:15am.

12. Internet has revolutionized our lives since its invention.

69.5 MATCH THE BEGINNINGS OF THE SENTENCES TO THE CORRECT ENDINGS

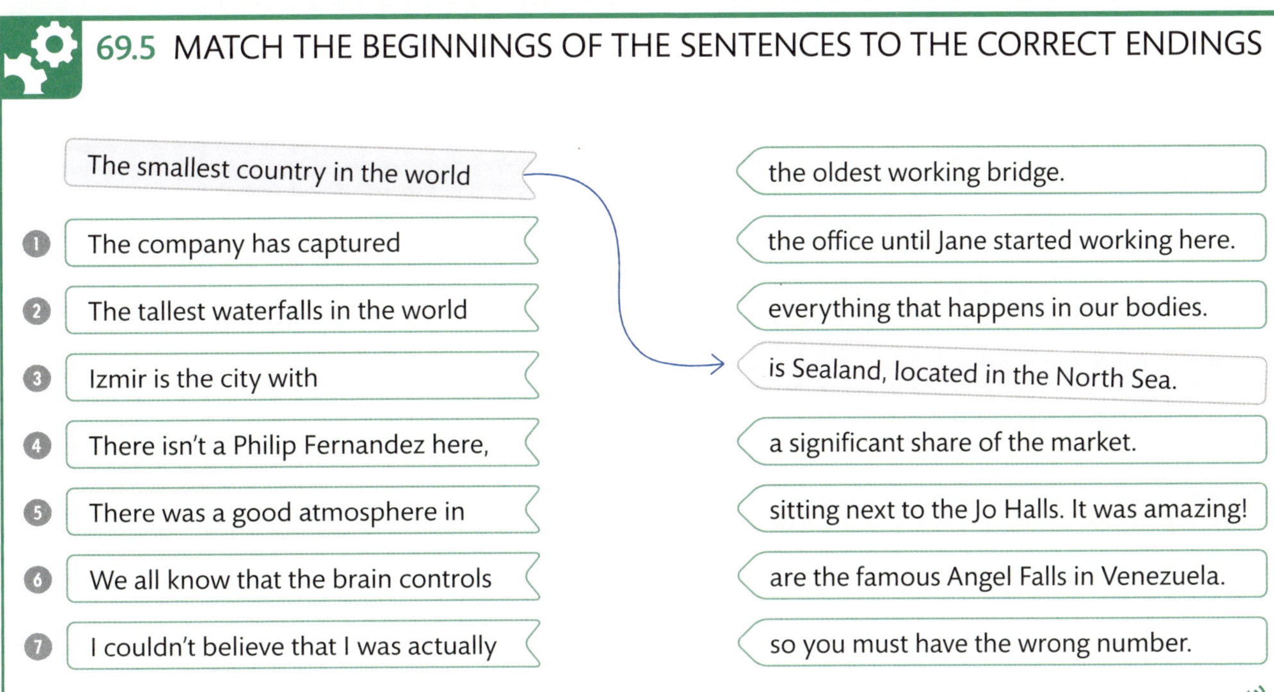

The smallest country in the world → is Sealand, located in the North Sea.

1 The company has captured
2 The tallest waterfalls in the world
3 Izmir is the city with
4 There isn't a Philip Fernandez here,
5 There was a good atmosphere in
6 We all know that the brain controls
7 I couldn't believe that I was actually

the oldest working bridge.
the office until Jane started working here.
everything that happens in our bodies.
is Sealand, located in the North Sea.
a significant share of the market.
sitting next to the Jo Halls. It was amazing!
are the famous Angel Falls in Venezuela.
so you must have the wrong number.

69.6 REWRITE THE SENTENCES, PUTTING THE WORDS IN THE CORRECT ORDER

fastest | peregrine falcon. | The | bird | the | in | world | is | the

The fastest bird in the world is the peregrine falcon.

1 critically | Hawksbill turtle | The | endangered. | a | species | is | that | is

2 Stephen Hawking | scientist | would | me | told | become | day! | a | The | one | I

3 almost | every | are | found | Televisions | the | in | the | home | now | city.

4 afraid | this | list. | that | isn't | on | Susie Fa | there | I'm | a

Transcripciones de los ejercicios de escucha

UNIDAD 1

1.5

Interviewer: I'm here with Heather Miller. Heather is a well-known travel writer from the UK. So, basically, you earn money by traveling all over the world and writing about it, don't you, Heather?

Heather: That's right, yes. Travel writing is my job and it's also something that I love doing.

Interviewer: And how long have you been working as a travel writer?

Heather: I first started about 20 years ago now.

Interviewer: OK, and how many countries have you traveled to during that time?

Heather: I've been to 52 countries so far.

Interviewer: So far? So there are still some more you'd like to visit?

Heather: Yes. I've never been to Central America, for example, so I'd love to go there.

Interviewer: OK, great. What's the most unusual food you've ever tried on your travels?

Heather: Well, I've been writing recipes in a notebook ever since I started traveling and one of the most exciting is one for scorpion soup, which I tried in Cambodia.

Interviewer: Scorpion soup? That doesn't sound very nice.

Heather: It does sound awful, doesn't it? But, in fact, it tastes great. You should try it!

UNIDAD 3

3.4

A funny thing happened to me this morning. I checked my email, as usual, and there was a message from Peter Chivers. Peter's an old friend and we haven't been in touch for years. Reading his email, I was suddenly transported back 25 years, to my school. Peter Chivers and I were best friends. I could see the blackboard and even smell the disinfectant they used on the floor.

Of course, not long after that, in fact two years later, when I was 18, I joined the army. While I was in the army, we didn't really keep in touch. In fact, the next time I saw him was when a mutual friend, Rodney Jones, got married. That was 15 years ago. So I was amazed to find an email from him this morning, but glad to hear that he's OK.

UNIDAD 4

4.5

Richard: Jenni, have you had any thoughts about the best person for the new management position? We really need to choose a new manager as soon as possible.

Jenni: I know, Richard. Well, as far as I'm concerned, we need to choose someone who's resourceful. Someone who can deal with any problems that might arise.

Richard: Yes, I know what you mean. So I think we're really looking for someone with experience, someone with maturity. Would you agree?

Jenni: Yes, definitely. That's why I think Sonia would be a good choice. She's hardworking and she always gets the job done.

Richard: Yes, she's very reliable, that's true. But there's one thing that concerns me about Sonia. I sometimes find her a little arrogant, especially when she's talking to newer employees. She talks like she knows it all. That's why I'd hesitate to promote her to the position of manager.

Jenni: OK, well, who would you suggest instead of Sonia?

Richard: Do you know, I've been thinking about Esther. She's been with the company for seven years now. She could have moved on to different jobs, with better pay, but she stuck with us. I like that... a lot.

Jenni: OK, I've worked with Esther before. She struck me as very likeable. She got along well with everyone, from the cleaners to the team leader. She's got a great personality. I like her, too.

Richard: Well, perhaps we could organize a meeting with her, so we can discuss her work in greater detail.

Jenni: OK, let's do that.

Richard: Great!

UNIDAD 9

9.2

Charlotte: Last month, I went to Venice for a few days to get away from it all with my husband. One evening we saw a beautiful little place where you can sit outside in a garden and have dinner. It looked very welcoming, and one of the waitresses standing at the entrance gave us a menu to look at. They had a good selection of food, so we decided to eat there. But instead of taking us to a table in the garden, the waitress showed us to a table in the dark interior of the building next to it. We couldn't even see the garden from there! We asked to change tables, but the waitress said that wasn't possible. It was quieter inside than it was outside, which was good, but the atmosphere was a little bit strange. We hoped that the food would be good because the prices were quite high. But when our meals came, they didn't look very fresh and I don't think any of the food was homemade, either. The only good thing was that the waitress brought us the bill quickly when we asked for it! We left the restaurant and went outside to sit by the canal in the evening sunshine.

9.4

Victor: In January, I went on a 14-day Caribbean cruise. You must get up early if you want to get a sun bed to lie on. I like to stay in bed until late, so I had to sit on a chair to sunbathe, which wasn't very nice. I can't praise the staff on the cruise enough though. They did everything they could to make me feel comfortable. You really should ask them right away if you need help with anything. They're very happy to help.

If I were you, I'd look at the activities program for the day in the morning and then see what interests you. There are a lot of interesting things to choose from. I did some exercise classes and they were great. But whatever you do, you shouldn't miss the evening entertainment, which was wonderful.

Then there's the food. To be honest, it wasn't as good as I'd expected. Most of the time, it didn't taste like it was fresh, but there was a lot of it!

UNIDAD 10

10.2 ex: We shouldn't have the barbeque on Saturday because there's a hundred percent chance of rain.

10.2.1 There's a good chance that our train will arrive on time. I've taken it many times and it's only been late once.
10.2.2 There's no way that Emma will be able to go a whole week without the internet.
10.2.3 We probably won't go to the karaoke on Friday night. Jessica doesn't like it very much.
10.2.4 I don't think we will win the first prize in the competition, but there's a small chance that we will.

UNIDAD 13

13.4

Jack: What are you doing, Mom?
Mom: Well, I've just ordered all my groceries and bought a birthday present for your dad on the internet. Honestly, I don't know how we used to survive in the days before the internet!
Jack: I can't really imagine it, to be honest!
Mom: No, well, lots of people say that things were better in the old days. But I don't agree with that. Before the internet, if I needed to get someone a birthday present, I would drive the car into town, struggle to find a parking space, pay for parking, then spend half a day wandering around the stores. It would take up half my weekend!
Jack: Now, you can just buy something with a couple of clicks of a mouse.
Mom: Exactly. And it's not only time you save with the internet. Before, I would only be able to buy from the stores I could physically go to. Now, I can search for products from hundreds of websites, literally from all over the world.
Jack: There's more choice.
Mom: A lot more choice. And then there's social networking; things like Facebook. In the past, I used to hear from my cousin in Australia maybe once or twice a year – a birthday card or a Christmas card, with a short note. Now, I can keep up to date on what's happening in her life, simply by being friends with her online. I feel like I'm more a part of her life, even though we never see each other in person.
Jack: That's really interesting!
Mom: I think the internet has made it easier for us to keep in touch with people around the world.

UNIDAD 14

14.2 ex: The coffee at Frank's is nowhere near as good as the coffee at Morello's.

14.2.1 Morello's isn't quite as old as Frank's.

14.2.2 Frank's is just as big as Morello's.

14.2.3 Frank's has half as many employees as Morello's.

14.2.4 Frank's is nearly as popular with customers as Morello's, but not quite.

14.2.5 They don't make the coffee quite as fast at Morello's as they do at Frank's.

14.2.6 Frank's has nowhere near as wide a range of pastries as Morello's does.

14.2.7 Morello's is just as close to downtown as Frank's.

UNIDAD 15

15.4

Linda: Chloe, is that you?
Chloe: Oh, hi, Linda! Wow, it must be, what, two years?
Linda: At least! Time just seems to fly by these days. It just goes quicker and quicker, doesn't it? But how are you? You look really well.
Chloe: Do I? I'm not sure I feel it, to be honest.
Linda: Oh, sorry to hear that, Chloe.
Chloe: Oh, it's nothing serious. I just never get a moment to myself. I seem to be busier and busier these days.
Linda: Because of the kids?
Chloe: Yeah, well, the kids are at school now, so I get a bit of a break during the day. But I always seem to have so much to do. Every day I feel more and more tired.
Linda: I know what you mean.
Chloe: By the time the kids are in bed, I'm exhausted. I usually go to bed about 9:30pm – the earlier the better!
Linda: Oooh yeah, a nice early night! How's Dan doing?
Chloe: He's good, but he's working much harder now because he's been promoted. His job seems to be getting more and more stressful. So he doesn't have much time to help out at home.
Linda: Is he still working for that property development company?
Chloe: Yeah, and they've got a lot of work on at the moment. He's exhausted, too. We have got a vacation booked though, for two weeks, next summer. Pure relaxation. The sooner the better – I can't wait! Anyway, how are you?
Linda: Well, do you remember when I saw you last, I'd met...

UNIDAD 17

17.3

Professor: While you're studying English at this university, there are several things we will expect you to do. First, you must attend class on a regular basis. Second, speak as much as you can during the lessons. This will really help your English to improve. And third, do some self-study in your own time. I will give you some guidance in that. For instance, you can do the extra reading that I will assign at the end of each lesson, such as newspaper and online articles.

Additionally, you will find some grammar and vocabulary worksheets on our online platform, which you can work through. There are, therefore, a lot of options available to you in your self-study. To sum up, self-study is very important and you should all make some time to do it. In conclusion, I would just like to say that if you put the effort in, you will be rewarded.

17.7

Counselor: OK everybody, let's make a start. Today, we're going to be talking about the options you have for your year abroad next year. There are many options available, but first, I'll look at studying at a foreign university. This is a popular option and, therefore, you should get your application in early if you want to do it. You could go to one of our partner universities abroad and continue studying the subject you're currently studying here. Additionally, you could take classes in the language spoken in that country.

Next, I'm going to tell you about another option: working abroad. If you want to get some work experience while you're studying abroad, you'll be able to do that by taking part in our overseas internships program.

Finally, you have the option of combining work and study with one of our dual programs. These are also a popular option because you can study while gaining work experience and earning some money.

Overall, it's up to you to decide which option would work best for you and then make the necessary arrangements with your career advisors. Additionally, you might want to think about your financial situation. Will you need to work to support yourself during your time abroad? So, to sum up, you have three options: studying, working, or studying and working. In conclusion, I would just like to say good luck to all of you.

UNIDAD 18

18.5

Interviewer: Jeremy, you're the student union president. Can you tell us a little bit about the social side of college?
Jeremy: Sure. College isn't just about getting a degree, though of course that's very important, too! There are lots of ways to make friends and meet new people in college.
Interviewer: For example?

Jeremy: Sport is an obvious one. In fact, more than 60 percent of students join one of our clubs. We have all kinds – soccer, hockey, volleyball, swimming, and rugby.
Interviewer: And do you have to have experience to join one of these clubs?
Jeremy: Not necessarily. I would say that in most cases, people have played these sports before. But in a number of cases, students have never played a particular sport before and want to give it a try.
Interviewer: Which is the most popular sports club?
Jeremy: It's the soccer club. It has well over 200 members.
Interviewer: And what about people who aren't athletic? Are there clubs for them?
Jeremy: Oh, definitely. We have all kinds of clubs. You can learn a new skill, like dancing or rock-climbing. Or you can join our gym and get fit. Or you could sing in the college choir.
Interviewer: How much does all this cost?
Jeremy: Not much! The majority of clubs charge as little as $5 per semester to join. And there are as many as 60 clubs to choose from. So in your first year, it's a good idea to join as many clubs as possible, and see which ones you like best.
Interviewer: That's a good tip.
Jeremy: In the majority of cases, when you join a club, you'll meet like-minded people and you might even make friends for life.
Interviewer: Well, thanks for talking to us, Jeremy. That was interesting.
Jeremy: My pleasure.

UNIDAD 23

23.5

Mr. James: Hello, Rose. Good to meet you. Please come in.
Rose: Hello, Mr. James. Good to meet you, too.
Mr. James: So, Rose, you have a very impressive résumé. I imagine you must be getting a lot of job offers right now, aren't you?
Rose: Well, let me see. There was a company in the southwest who contacted me, but I wasn't interested in moving there.
Mr. James: All right. So tell me, what is it exactly that you're looking for in a new position?
Rose: Well, I want to keep living in the same area, so it's important to me that the company I work for is within commuting distance of my home. I'm also looking for a new challenge. I want to push myself and see what I can do in a challenging position.
Mr. James: OK, well, we can definitely offer you a very challenging and interesting position here. What would you say your greatest weaknesses are?
Rose: Let's see. I can be a bit of a control freak at times. I like to keep an eye on everything, you know? But that's only because I want to make sure that everything's going well.
Mr. James: I understand. So, what do you think you would bring to our communications team?
Rose: Well, I think I have a lot of energy – I'm a very driven person – and I think other people who I come into contact with at work are inspired to do their best because of my energy.
Mr. James: Great. That's exactly what a good manager should be doing. To be honest with you, Rose, we've already decided to offer you the position and the board is in agreement.
Rose: Wow, thank you!
Mr. James: We were just wondering what your expectations would be when it comes to salary.
Rose: Salary? Well, I wouldn't want to be earning less than I did in my previous position.
Mr. James: Of course not.
Rose: Do you think I could go away and think about that and then get back to you?
Mr. James: Of course, take all the time you need. When you're ready just drop me an email. We'll have plenty of time to sort this out...

UNIDAD 33

33.5

The Deepwater Horizon oil spill began on April 20th, 2010. High pressure gas rose up onto the oil drilling rig and exploded. Initially, it was just the one rig in the Gulf of Mexico that was contaminated. However, following the original explosion, a large oil leak was discovered and oil started to leak into the sea two days later. It is estimated that oil was flowing into the sea at a rate of 62,000 gallons a day by that time. Oil continued to flow into the ocean at this rate throughout the next six weeks. Efforts were made to stop the flow of oil during that time, but none of them proved successful. Since then, the oil spill has become known as one of the worst manmade disasters in recent history. Despite the clean-up operations, the effect on marine life was devastating and the effects of the oil spill can still be seen in the Gulf of Mexico.

UNIDAD 35

35.4

Stuart Brookes's battle has not been easy – or short. But today, his efforts were finally rewarded.

The environmental campaigner began his fight 15 years ago, when permission was granted for a major new road to be built through the Scottish countryside, less than 200 meters from Stuart's home. It's a beautiful, wild area, where the endangered red squirrel can still be found. Stuart believed that the new road would put further pressure on the red squirrel, which is already struggling to compete with the more successful gray squirrel. To appreciate the size of the problem, it's worth noting that there are 2.5 million gray squirrels in the UK. By comparison, red squirrels number just 140,000.

Stuart set up an action group in 2001, with three like-minded neighbors. Today, the group numbers 590. Over the years, they have organized petitions, attended rallies and protests, and even met the Prime Minister. Today, the Department for Transport announced that the plans for the road had been canceled indefinitely. A day of rejoicing for Stuart, and for the red squirrel.

UNIDAD 38

38.5

Jason: Valerie, do you know where Richard is?

Valerie: No, isn't he at his desk?

Jason: No, he's not there. He might have gone down to the cafeteria, I suppose.

Valerie: Yes, he could have. He sometimes goes down to get a sandwich at about this time.

Jason: Or he may have gotten a call from that client in Brixton and gone down to see them right away.

Valerie: Yes, that's possible.

Jason: He couldn't have decided to just take the rest of the day off, could he?

Valerie: No, I don't think so. That's not the kind of thing Richard would do. Oh, I know, he must have gone shopping to get a present for his wife. It's her birthday today.

Jason: Oh right, OK. Mystery solved, then. I guess he'll be back soon.

Valerie: Have a look on his desk again. He might have left a note for you.

Jason: Yes, he can't have forgotten our meeting at 1. I'll go and have a look.

UNIDAD 42

42.5

Newsreader: It has been announced today that the government will be providing a new series of grants to young people who have started their own companies. This measure was agreed on yesterday. Hundreds of companies have been set up by young people over the last 12 months and will benefit from this new policy. The policy could be introduced as soon as next year according to a source close to the government, but an official starting date hasn't yet been fixed. The announcement was welcomed by entrepreneurs and seems set to have a positive effect on the growth of new businesses in this country.

UNIDAD 43

43.5

Newsreader: He is arguably one of the most stupid thieves on the planet. Alfie Richardson, a 31-year-old painter from South London, has been found guilty of a string of armed robberies across the capital. It would seem that he has committed at least five robberies of banks and post offices, carrying out his raids approximately twice a year. However, last June, Richardson's luck ran out. After robbing a post office in Bethnal Green, it seems that Richardson got greedy. Along with the £25,000 post office staff gave him, Richardson demanded that all the customers in the post office hand over their bags and wallets. One customer, Amanda Lawrence, handed over her bag containing the latest iPhone.

It would appear that Richardson found the phone, and began using it. He didn't bother to erase the phone's ID, or any of its apps. He seems to like taking selfies, as he has taken approximately 120 of them using the phone, all of which were automatically uploaded to Miss Lawrence's online sharing platform.

When Miss Lawrence logged into her online sharing platform, she saw the photos taken on her phone, and immediately contacted the police. They examined the photos, which indicated where Richardson was living and working. Two days later, he was under arrest.

UNIDAD 44

44.6

Newsreader: Last night, the most highly anticipated awards ceremony of the year took place in Los Angeles. Never before had so many people attended because, this year, the ceremony took place in a larger auditorium. Not until 6pm were the guests allowed to enter the auditorium. Hardly had the ceremony begun when a fire broke out in one of the dressing rooms and everyone had to be evacuated. Rarely do you see so many famous and well-dressed people standing around on the side of a road. Only after the fire department had arrived and put the fire out, could everyone go back into the auditorium and the ceremony could continue. It was quite a night!

UNIDAD 48

48.4

Last week, I went to a beauty salon for a special procedure whereby your skin is cleansed by standing in a special cubicle where hot water is sprayed at you from all directions. Just at the moment when I thought I couldn't stand it any more, the beauty therapist turned the water off. I felt great as I walked down the road to the bus stop where I get the bus back to my house, but I noticed that people were looking at me a little bit differently. Twenty minutes later, when I got home, I realized why. My face was bright red! I called the salon where I'd had the treatment, told them what had happened and asked for a refund. Fortunately, they said yes, and we made an agreement whereby I wouldn't make an official complaint and they would give me a free manicure the next time I go to the salon.

UNIDAD 49

49.5

Mr. Hall: Hello, Mrs. Cooper. Nice to see you.
Mrs. Cooper: Nice to see you, too, Mr. Hall. So, what can you tell me about how Peter's doing at school?
Mr. Hall: Well, I'm afraid Peter has been having some problems recently because he hasn't been able to concentrate at school. If he continues like this, he won't be able to get very good grades at the end of the year. He may even fail.
Mrs. Cooper: Oh, no. I had no idea.
Mr. Hall: I know. He's able to make everyone think that he's fine and everything's OK even when it isn't.
Mrs. Cooper: I see. Will he have to repeat the year if he doesn't pass his exams?
Mr. Hall: Yes, that's right.
Mrs. Cooper: But will he be able to get some extra support over the next few months so that doesn't happen?
Mr. Hall: Yes. I will have to ask Mr. Foster if he has time to give Peter and a few other students some extra lessons to help them catch up.
Mrs. Cooper: That sounds good. I hope Mr. Foster will be able to do that. But tell me about maths...

UNIDAD 53

53.5

I moved to China two years ago and before I arrived, I didn't really know what to expect. I've moved around a lot during my life and I had just gotten used to living in the UK, which I really liked. Then my manager told me he wanted me to take a job in the Far East. He offered me either China or Japan, and I chose China. One of the things I had to get used to when I first moved here was how direct some Chinese people can be. They'll tell you exactly what they think, which people in the UK usually don't. But now, I'm used to the fact that people I don't know at all will sometimes ask me very direct, personal questions. Another thing I've had to get used to is the way the Chinese eat, by which I mean: you don't always find the best food in a fancy restaurant. The most delicious food can usually be found in street markets. Now I'm used to that way of eating and I love it.

UNIDAD 54

54.5

Carla: One thing I quickly found out about the Brazilians is that they love soccer.
George: I know. The Germans love soccer, too. They have some top-class teams, especially in the south of Germany.
Carla: Oh yes, I know Bayern Munich. They're the best team around at the moment, aren't they?
George: Well, you could say that, but they're not the team I support.
Carla: All right, but what about German food? I think everyone knows that the Germans love sausage and pretzels, that kind of thing.
George: Yes, that's true. German food is very filling and tasty. Quite salty, too. A bit too salty for me.
Carla: The most popular food in Brazil is probably steak. They absolutely love meat, especially barbecued beef.
George: Yeah, I've seen the big plates of meat they eat!
Carla: Yes.
George: In terms of well-known landmarks, everyone knows the massive statue of Christ the Redeemer in Rio de Janeiro. That's the most famous landmark in Brazil for me.
Carla: Yes, I think it is the most famous landmark for a lot of people. It's a big attraction for tourists. And Germany has the Brandenburg Gate. Everyone knows that, too. It's the symbol of Berlin, I think.

UNIDAD 57

57.5

Michael: Thanks for coming in, Cheryl. I just wanted to find out how things are going with you at the moment and how you see your future with us over the next few years.

Cheryl: Well, as you know, I really enjoy working here and love the sales department, but I do spend a lot of time traveling and a lot of nights away from home. I wish I could be at home more often, you know.
Michael: Sure, I completely understand. Life on the road can be quite hard at times.
Cheryl: Yes. I wish our customers didn't have their branches so far away from our headquarters.
Michael: I know. I sometimes wish that the CEO would let us move to a better location, but he doesn't want to. So, what would you like to do instead?
Cheryl: I wish I could work here at headquarters and manage an internal sales team. That would be my dream job.
Michael: OK. Well, I wish I could tell you that we currently have that kind of vacancy here right now, but we don't. Having said that, I know that Geoff is planning to retire within the next two years, so it may be possible for you to move into his position. We'll have to see if that would be a suitable move...

UNIDAD 58

58.5

Rachel: Hello?
Charles: Hi Rachel, it's Charles. Do you know where Bill is? I need to ask him a few questions.
Rachel: Well, it's 12:30, so I'd say he'll be eating his lunch in the cafeteria right now.
Charles: That's what I thought, but I went to the cafeteria and he isn't there. It's just that in two days' time we'll be presenting the results of our research and I need to check a few things with him.
Rachel: Well, I think that if he isn't eating in the cafeteria, he'll probably be taking a walk around the building. He likes to do that sometimes when he needs to think.
Charles: I checked outside, too, and I couldn't find him.
Rachel: How strange.
Charles: If you see Bill before I do, could you tell him I'll be working in my office until 6 and it would be great if he could give me a call?
Rachel: Sure, I'll do that. I'll only be working until 4pm today, but if I see him before then, I'll let him know.
Charles: OK, thanks a lot, Rachel. Bye for now.
Rachel: Bye.

UNIDAD 60

60.4

When she was 18, Jessica entered a talent competition and won. Everyone told her that she was going to become a pop superstar one day, and she believed them. She was going to train to be a nurse after she finished school, but she decided to concentrate on getting a recording contract instead. Yesterday morning, she was really nervous because she was meeting with a record label that afternoon. But Jessica was so nervous that when she got to the meeting she couldn't speak or sing. She had to apologize to the record label bosses and leave.

UNIDAD 62

62.4

Simon: Hi, Rachel. Which film are we going to see again?
Rachel: Hi, Simon. *Death Kiss*, remember?
Simon: *Death Kiss*? Yes, sure. When does it start?
Rachel: 7:30.
Simon: OK. Have you booked tickets?
Rachel: Yes, of course, two in the back row. I'm getting a hotdog. You?
Simon: Popcorn for me.
Rachel: All right. Buttered or plain?
Simon: Plain.
Rachel: OK. So what was the last film you saw like?
Simon: It was ridiculously long and the pace of the story was painfully slow.
Rachel: Sounds boring.
Simon: Yes, very.
Rachel: Who did you go with?
Simon: Gavin.
Rachel: Oh, OK. How old is he?
Simon: Sixteen, I think. He was excited because this was the first 3D film he'd been to.
Rachel: Oh, no. Was it such a bad film?
Simon: Absolutely terrible.
Rachel: Well, I'm sure this one will be better. Let's go in.

UNIDAD 63

63.6

Kristen: I see you have one of those new smartwatches, Michael. I want one like that!
Michael: Yeah, I'm really happy with it. You can either use it as a normal watch or like a smartphone.
Kristen: Great. It looks like those hi-tech watches, you know the ones in that shop at the mall?
Michael: Yes, I know the ones you mean. I just have to be careful not

to damage it, because it was a gift from my mother and neither she nor I can afford to replace it right now!

Kristen: I know what you mean. By the way, if you see any vouchers for that online shop we talked about yesterday, will you bring me some?

Michael: Sure. I can either bring you some or send you the codes for them.

Kristen: Perfect, thanks!

UNIDAD 64

64.3

Jess: Hi, Paul. What's up?

Paul: Hi, Jess. Listen, what are you doing on Saturday night?

Jess: Hmm, I don't know. I haven't got anything planned for definite at the moment. I was going to go and see that new horror movie, but I'm not sure I really want to. Why?

Paul: Do you want to come to a concert with me? There's this orchestra called the Recycled Orchestra. They take garbage and make it into musical instruments.

Jess: Oh yeah, I've heard about them. Aren't they from South America?

Paul: That's right, but they perform all over the world. They're on a world tour right now, and they're performing live at the Coliseum. I've never seen them live, but I'd love the chance. Are you interested?

Jess: Definitely! How much are the tickets?

Paul: They're 35 dollars each.

Jess: OK, sounds good.

Paul: I'll try to get some tickets today, though I'm not 100 percent sure I'll be able to.

Jess: OK.

Paul: The performance starts at 7:30, so how about we meet at 7 and have a drink first?

Jess: Good idea.

Paul: Perfect! I'll text you to let you know when I've got the tickets, I promise.

Jess: OK, see you Saturday.

Paul: Bye!

UNIDAD 66

66.3

Romesh: Hi, Joanne? What's up?

Joanne: Oh, hi, Romesh. My car won't start. I've checked the battery and the spark plugs, but it still won't go. I think I'll have to get it fixed.

Romesh: Oh no, bad luck! Do you know a good mechanic?

Joanne: Yes, my friend Lou is a mechanic, so I'll get him to take a look. To make matters worse, I got oil from the engine on my coat.

Romesh: Oh, how annoying! Are you going to get it dry cleaned?

Joanne: I checked the label and I think it's OK for me to wash it myself. Anyway, I'll stop complaining. How are you, Romesh? Where are you going?

Romesh: I'm fine, thanks. I'm taking some shirts to the laundry to have them ironed. And I need to get my hair cut today, too. I have an interview for a new job next week.

Joanne: Wow, good luck! Let's have a drink soon and you can tell me all about it.

UNIDAD 67

67.5

Neil: I'm Neil and I'm a student in the UK. I'd say economics is a very popular subject among students at my university. Either economics with logistics or economics with tourism is the most popular course combination. I'm studying economics myself. I started studying mathematics and then I realized that mathematics is much too difficult for me. Fortunately, I have a family who are very supportive. Neither my mother nor my father were very good at school and they didn't go to university, but they've always believed that my studies are important and helped me. The good thing is that neither my mother nor father have put too much pressure on me to do well. They just support me.

Respuestas

01

1.1

1 I'm a sales assistant in a department store that opened recently.
2 Hurry up! The bus is coming. If we miss it, we will be late for work.
3 I'm meeting my new team leader right now to discuss plans for next year.
4 I get up at 7 o'clock every day to get to the office on time.
5 I always have a coffee break at 10 o'clock so I can work faster.
6 Today I'm wearing a new white blouse I bought from the store near my office.
7 She's working in the New York office at the moment, but she's planning to move to California.
8 I think I'm in the wrong building. Cathy lives in building number seven.
9 I'm having lunch in 30 minutes. Would you like to join me?
10 I go home at 5 o'clock every day after I finish work.

1.2

1 **I'm** the new member of the team.
2 **He always** sits at that desk. You'll have to move!
3 The train **arrives** at 7:22am every morning.
4 The bus is **usually on** time, but not today.
5 **I'm talking** to my boss at the moment.
6 **I'm working** on the new project with David today.
7 We **are a** very good team!
8 **I have** a meeting at 9 o'clock every day.
9 **I'm waiting** for you in front of the office.

1.3

1 **I've been trying** to call him all day, but he **hasn't answered** yet.
2 He**'s been working** all day, so he **hasn't had** a break yet.
3 I'm glad I**'ve finished** that project because I**'ve been working** on it for ages.
4 Jo**'s been cooking** all night, but Jim still **hasn't arrived** for dinner.
5 I**'ve been driving** for two hours now and I still **haven't made** it to work.
6 He**'s got** his schedule now and he**'s been meeting** the team all day.

1.4

1 Rebecca is from Australia, **isn't she?**
2 Gary doesn't live far from the office, **does he?**
3 They went to college in the US, **didn't they?**
4 You're working in the Singapore office, **aren't you?**
5 The new employees have their badges, **don't they?**
6 She's been waiting for 20 minutes, **hasn't she?**
7 Angelina worked as an engineer in New York, **didn't she?**
8 Mark has traveled to many countries in Europe, **hasn't he?**
9 They are planning to move out of the city, **aren't they?**
10 Alan should go on the training course next week, **shouldn't he?**
11 You have been to Singapore on a business trip, **haven't you?**

1.5

1 False 2 False 3 False 4 True
5 False

1.6

1 Maxine always takes the 7:45 train to work like Paul, **doesn't she?**
2 Your car is parked on the road in front of the company reception, **isn't it?**
3 Jonathan doesn't work in the sales department anymore, **does he?**
4 She worked for one of our competitors before she started working here, **didn't she?**
5 Nick and Philip have visited a lot of different countries on business trips, **haven't they?**
6 You would like to join us for lunch in the cafeteria today, **wouldn't you?**
7 Jessica didn't go to the strategy meeting we had last Tuesday, **did she?**
8 The boss should be showing the new employees around the office, **shouldn't he?**
9 Katrina and John know each other from their days in college, **don't they?**
10 He's been waiting for some time to talk to the boss about his promotion, **hasn't he?**
11 James isn't going to be the next head of the Human Resources department, **is he?**
12 Daniel should present the results of his research to the rest of the team, **shouldn't he?**
13 You worked with Janet on the project we did in Singapore, **didn't you?**
14 He works from home two days a week so he can spend time with his family, **doesn't he?**
15 Simon and Gregory are working on a prototype for the new product, **aren't they?**

02

2.1

1 Action 2 Action 3 State 4 State
5 State 6 Action 7 State 8 State
9 Action 10 Action

2.2

1 She's concentrating hard at the moment.
2 I hate video games. They're so boring.
3 He wants to move to a bigger place.
4 She seems to be a reliable employee.
5 He's reading a science-fiction novel.
6 I'm just cooking some pasta for dinner.
7 The package weighs four pounds.
8 I can't hear you at all.
9 Laura is appearing in the show this evening.
10 What do you think of me?

2.3

1 The items that the bags **contain** are heavy.
2 **I see** the mountains in the distance.
3 He **is weighing** the boxes on the scales right now.
4 We **spent** two hours doing our work.
5 I **believe** everything you say.
6 I'm sorry, but **I feel** that you're wrong.
7 I **was listening** to the radio when you came in.
8 This milk **smells** bad.
9 Shaun **usually arrives** at work at 8am.

2.4

1 William **wants** to travel around the world when he's older.
2 I **am tasting** the soup to see if it needs more salt or pepper.
3 I **am seeing** my dentist later this afternoon for a consultation.
4 My knees **hurt** when I walk too far or sit for too long.
5 My colleagues **are having** lunch right now in the cafeteria.
6 Michael **is being** all shy and quiet now that you're here to visit.

03

3.1

1 Laura **went into business** straight after school, at the age of 18.
2 The difference between these two cars is **clearly visible**.
3 You've studied so much for the exam. Now all that's left is to **do your best.**
4 I **distinctly remember** asking you to pack the passports. Don't tell me you forgot!

5 I think it's **extremely unlikely** that you'll win the lottery tonight.
6 I don't think Steffi likes me. She seems to have a **low opinion** of me.
7 The smell of fresh bread always **stirs up memories** of my grandma.
8 Bill made a big mistake at work and it has **ruined his career.**
9 I'm very lucky to have a **close family.** We meet up every Sunday for lunch.

3.2
1 True 2 False 3 Not given 4 True
5 Not given 6 True 7 Not given
8 False 9 True

3.3
1 I met my wife while I was in college.
2 When I was young, I loved climbing trees.
3 After I retired, I moved to Florida.
4 During the summer I worked in a café.
5 I worked part-time while I was studying abroad.

3.4
1 25 years ago
2 23 years ago
3 15 years ago

3.5
1 Stephanie **graduated** from college with an honors degree **last** year.
2 Bill **had been running** for many years when he **decided** to run a marathon.
3 Matthew **started** working at the company 33 years **ago**.
4 Leah **had** a baby **last** month. Her name's Sophie and she's beautiful.
5 Peter **arrived** very early **this** morning because he has an important meeting.
6 Jenny **was working** in a bar in London when she **met** Stephen.
7 Jenny and Stephen **got married** this year **on** June 7.
8 Stuart **had been living** in the US **for** 10 years before he moved to the UK.
9 When they **were** five years old, Anna and Jasmine **were** best friends.

3.6
1 Whether too much sleep is bad for you **is a matter of opinion.**
2 There is a popular belief that **the number 13 is unlucky.**
3 Lionel has gone into business, **selling clothes he has designed himself.**
4 There's forecast to be light rain later on, **so take an umbrella.**
5 When I smelled that perfume, it stirred **up memories of my first love.**
6 The airport is still closed, so **it's extremely unlikely we'll fly today.**

7 I'm not sure why Rebecca has **such a low opinion of me.**
8 The scandal over drug-taking ruined **her career in athletics.**

04

4.1
1 She's **an intelligent little** girl. She always does well at school.
2 It's a **horrible, ugly old** car. I'm not going to buy it as I don't like it.
3 We're going on a **fantastic, cheap** train trip across Europe for our vacation.
4 This is such **a comfortable old** sweater. I love wearing it in winter.
5 Gio always wears **stylish Italian** clothes. He is a fashion designer in London.
6 Today we're going to present our **innovative new** tablet to you for the first time.
7 Don't forget to try these **delicious spicy** sauces, which we've created ourselves.
8 I was one of the first to ride in a **unique high-speed** train while I was there.
9 Sometimes a **reliable low-tech** product is a better option than a more hi-tech one.

4.2
GENERAL OPINION:
nice, **lovely**, **bad**, **awful**
SPECIFIC OPINION:
kind, **sad**, **ugly**, **tasty**

4.3
1 My grandma is a **wonderful, generous old** lady.
2 I bought this **awful, ugly expensive** dress on the internet.
3 What a **pleasant, friendly young** man Peter is!
4 Jon's got a **beautiful, stylish new** car.

4.4
1 Lana's **dis**honest. She hides information and never tells the truth.
2 You're so **in**considerate. Think about other people for a change!
3 It was very **un**kind of you to make your sister cry. You should apologize to her.
4 Leon always has a solution for a problem. Unfortunately, he's often **in**correct.
5 Susanne is always being rude to her parents. She's so **dis**respectful.
6 Stop behaving like a five-year-old! You're so **im**mature!

4.5
1 inexperienced 2 arrogant 3 Esther
4 seven years 5 popular

4.6 Model Answers
1 He solved the problem by taking charge of the situation and seeking help from others.
2 He wants to be promoted into management.
3 He might appear rude because he is shy and awkward in social situations.
4 He can go on training programs to help him with his social skills.
5 Jenson needs to improve his social skills before he can be considered for promotion.
6 The review is generally positive.

05

5.1
1 It's **a shame that** some people aren't interested in learning languages.
2 It's **interesting that** you chose that book because it's the book that I chose, too.
3 It's **not important to** win. What you should be focused on is doing your very best.
4 It is **easy to** learn English vocabulary, but it's difficult to learn the grammar.
5 It's **good that** our neighbors are so understanding because we make a lot of noise!
6 When it's so cold outside, it's **important to** wrap yourself up as warmly as possible.
7 It's **essential that** everyone has enough water to drink while we're out walking in the heat.
8 It's **bad to** look at your phone while you're driving. You could have an accident.
9 Joshua has been doing so badly at school that he's **unlikely to** do well in his exams.
10 It is **difficult to** understand people when they speak English very quickly.
11 Look at those black clouds over there. I think it's **likely to** rain sometime soon.
12 Our train is so delayed. I think it's **unlikely that** we'll get home before midnight!
13 It's really **bad that** some people don't care about the environment. They should!
14 It's **important that** our children do their best at school and get a good education.
15 It's **good to** have all of the family here together again. I've missed everyone.

5.2
1 **It** is unlikely that I will finish this assignment on time.
2 It's difficult **to** decide what to order because it all sounds delicious.
3 **To** lose at this point would be very difficult after coming so far.
4 It's easy **to** start writing an essay, but it's not always easy to finish one!
5 It's essential **that** everyone follows the rules and does what they're told.

6 **To** read English is easy, but to write in English is more difficult.
7 It's important **to** choose an interesting topic to give a presentation about.

5.3

1 I have a certain aptitude for **navigating with a map, but I still get lost.**
2 My friend has a complete inability **to plan ahead. He's always late!**
3 It seems like some people have a **natural ability to run long distances.**
4 Dr. Finn had a remarkable capacity **to memorize huge passages of text.**

5.4

1 At a college
2 Surfing the internet
3 Natural
4 Tonal

5.5 Model Answers

1 Because it's important **to be able to communicate with people from all over the world.**
2 I think English is likely **to be a popular language for a long time.**
3 I think I have **a natural ability for learning languages.**
4 It's difficult **to remember all of the words and say them when you need them.**

06

6.1

1 once-in-a-lifetime
2 thirst for adventure
3 check out
4 go sightseeing
5 hopelessly lost
6 see somebody off
7 leg of a journey
8 look around
9 check in
10 feel homesick
11 culture shock
12 get away from it all
13 stop off

07

7.1

1 I usually get up at 7am.
2 I would like to check in early.
3 I need to check out by 9am.
4 He works out for two hours.
5 We always go out on Fridays.
6 Please line up here to go in.
7 Martin showed up at the party.

7.2

1 They want to check in at the hotel.
2 He keeps on complaining about his job.
3 She doesn't like getting up early.
4 She works out in the morning.
5 We're going out for Sheila's birthday.
6 He showed up late to work yesterday.
7 Jo, please come in and join us here.
8 Tim is coming down for my birthday.
9 Cooking is hard, but you should keep at it.
10 He always checks out early.

7.3

1 She really needs to **clean** her desk **up**. It's full of papers and old coffee cups.
2 The sixth grade students are **putting** a show **on** to celebrate the end of their time at this school.
3 Everyone needs to **hand** their forms **in** by Friday. Otherwise you can't go on the trip.
4 I need you to **look** a few words **up** in the dictionary for me. Can you do that?
5 I'll **check** the hotels in Monte Carlo **out** and let you know what the prices are.

7.4

1 It's not a problem. We'll come over and pick **it** up from your place.
2 He was so angry he tore **it** up and threw it around the room.
3 You should put **it** on when you go outside. It's absolutely freezing.
4 If you cut **it** out, you can use it to get two for the price of one at the supermarket.

7.5

1 He's always trying to **live up to** his reputation as a big spender.
2 We're **coming up with** some really good ideas at the moment.
3 I should just **get rid of** the things that I don't need.
4 She's so fast. I can't **keep up with** her.
5 Melissa's great. I really **look up to** her.

7.6

1 We all went to the airport with John and **saw him off**.
2 Her plane **took off** at 9:20am, so she should land at 2:50pm.
3 He always **stops off** to see his mother on his way home from work.
4 Hi Jonathan, it's me again. I'm sorry we were **cut off** just now.
5 The traffic was so bad that we **set off** at 9 o'clock and didn't arrive until 12.
6 I'm worried about my new dog. I don't think he **gets along with** Buster.

7.7

1 True 2 True 3 False 4 Not given
5 False 6 False 7 True 8 False
9 False 10 True

08

8.1

1 I **learned** a lot of Japanese while I **was living** in Japan.
2 While I **was waiting** for the train, I **met** my favorite singer.
3 As we **were walking** home last night, we **saw** a firework display.
4 We **stopped** at the café while we **were visiting** the castle.
5 I **got** off my bike a few times while I **was cycling** to work.
6 I **saw** a lot of cafés when I **was strolling** around town.
7 While I **was wandering** around, I **found** a good bookstore.
8 She **took** so many pictures when she **was traveling**.
9 I **was having** problems with my car until he **helped** me.

8.2

1 We tried a local restaurant because **the hotel receptionist had recommended it (to us).**
2 I went in the sauna after I **had been in the swimming pool (at the hotel).**
3 We rented a bike because **a friend of ours had said it was a good idea.**
4 They gave us a welcome drink just after **we had arrived at the hotel.**
5 We didn't have to wait in line to go in because **we had bought advance tickets.**

8.3

1 The Miller family **had been going** to Croatia for years before it became popular with tourists.
2 We needed to move around after we **had been sitting** on the plane for 14 hours.
3 I **had been waiting** for them at the airport for half an hour before they arrived.
4 Our team **had been losing** in the first half of the game, but they came back in the second.
5 She **had been studying** Spanish for six months before she went to Mexico.
6 It **had been raining** for five days in a row before we had some sunshine.

8.4

1 She **had been planning** to cycle across China, but then she **had** an accident on her bike.

2 When they **got** back home, they discovered that someone **had burgled** their house.
3 After I **had been traveling** around Asia for six months, I **felt** very happy to be back home.
4 Before I **went** to South America, I **hadn't tried** tango dancing.
5 He **wanted** to visit the fjords because he **had heard** they were beautiful.

8.5

1 I had written some practice answers **before the exam, so I was well prepared.**
2 When I got back to the parking lot, **I realized that someone had stolen my car.**
3 Before I started working here, I had **been working in the US for six months.**
4 I had given the matter a lot of thought **before I decided to change jobs.**
5 They were eating at a restaurant when **a famous author came in.**
6 She wanted to go to Spain because **her parents had told her it was fantastic.**
7 They had been planning to go out, **but they decided to go to bed early.**
8 I was feeling extremely tired because **I had not been sleeping very well.**

8.6 Model Answers

1 Jason had moved to New York a few months earlier.
2 Jason had been doing an internship in London before he moved to New York.
3 Jason saw the woman again a few days later.
4 The woman was the first person to write a message.

09

9.1

1 When you're in Berlin, you ought to visit the television tower.
2 I know! You really should take the kids down to the swimming pool.
3 You might want to take a boat trip around the lake while you're here.
4 Jonas could make a reservation. Then he'll definitely get a seat on the train.
5 Yes, it's awesome. You really must do that.

9.2 3

9.3

1 We had some outstanding food at Lionel's restaurant! **You ought to try the pasta.**
2 The room wasn't bad, although ours was a lot smaller than some of the others. **You could ask for a larger room if this is an issue.**
3 We can't praise our tour guide enough. She gave us such a lot of interesting information. **You must ask for Irene if you go there.**
4 I had trouble sleeping because the sheets were very rough. **You might want to bring a sheet!**
5 The staff at the bar had fantastic recommendations for drinks. **You really must try the cocktails.**

9.4

1 Like 2 Like 3 Like 4 Dislike

9.5

1 You **must** put on a lot of sun cream or you'll burn.
2 You **had better** take your walking boots if you're going to go hiking while you're there.
3 The firework display will be absolutely stunning. You **must** go and see it.
4 If I were you, I **would** take the train from Paris to London instead of flying.
5 You **should** ask if they have any vacancies at the Hotel Bennetton.

9.6

1 car 2 photographs 3 car doors
4 dish 5 photographs

9.7 Model Answer

Hi Jake!
How are you? It's been a long time since I sent you a letter, so I thought I would tell you about our family trip to Paris. **We went to** France in August and it was wonderful. **The highlight for me was** all the incredible French food! **I really enjoyed the** museums and galleries too. **You ought to** go when you get the chance. **If I were you, I'd** make it the next family adventure! **You must** come and visit us soon, too.
Look forward to hearing from you. **You'd better** not take a month to reply this time!
Best wishes,
Jaya

10

10.1

1 The plane is two hours late now, **so we will miss our connecting flight.**
2 Sadly, the project won't be finished **by the end of June after all.**
3 We might have time to visit the spa **if we leave now and we hurry up.**
4 Ask the rep from the travel agency, as **she will probably know the answer.**
5 He definitely won't be trying beef **because he's a vegetarian.**
6 It's unlikely that he will call, as **I don't think he has my phone number.**
7 When we arrive at the airport, **we will wait for you in the arrivals hall.**
8 It's very unlikely that it will rain, since **there isn't a cloud in the sky today.**

10.2

1 Likely 2 Unlikely 3 Unlikely
4 Unlikely

10.3

1 The internet has **fundamentally** changed how we book our vacations.
2 **Luckily**, we had nice weather every day when we were on vacation.
3 **Unfortunately**, Emma was sick when we were on vacation.
4 The trip home was **predictably** slow. There are always problems on that route.
5 They make their pancakes in **essentially** the same way that we do.
6 **Interestingly**, Winston Churchill had stayed at our hotel when he was in the region.
7 **Fortunately**, we were fit enough to be able to hike back down the coast.

10.4

1 **Luckily**, we made it to the hotel before the reception closed for the night.
2 Windsurfing is **essentially** sailing with a surfboard.
3 **Unfortunately**, the hotel is completely booked up.
4 **Interestingly**, the café was also an art gallery.
5 **Surprisingly**, Richard actually went in the pool. You know how he normally hates water.
6 **Predictably**, Donald got sunburned again. He never puts any sun tan lotion on.

10.5

1 Not given 2 True 3 True 4 False
5 False 6 True 7 True 8 Not given
9 True

11

11.1

1 grow up
2 run in the family
3 stick up for somebody
4 see eye to eye with somebody
5 make friends with somebody
6 click with somebody
7 give birth
8 drift apart
9 bump into somebody
10 put your foot down
11 look up to somebody
12 close friend
13 break up with somebody

12

12.1

1 I have bright blue eyes **like my mother.**
2 We live in different countries, **but we all get together at Christmas.**
3 My siblings are all very intelligent, **especially my brother, who's a scientist.**
4 My dad loves to play board games, **particularly chess.**
5 They like different TV channels **so they watch them in different rooms.**
6 We can video chat with each other **since we all have smartphones or laptops.**
7 She is interested in my life at college **because she wasn't able to go.**
8 I enjoy going fishing **just as my father does. He's great at it.**
9 My father is a great cook, **so he always makes dinner for us.**
10 We only see each other once a month **because we're all so busy now.**
11 It's hard to buy a present for dad and, **as a result, he always gets socks!**
12 We cook something different for her **as she's a vegetarian.**
13 My relatives all talk a lot, **especially when they all get together.**
14 Ann and I still stay up late chatting **just as we used to do when we were kids.**
15 I love cooking Chinese food, **though my family doesn't eat it often.**

12.2

1 My brother loves sports, **especially** ice hockey.
2 Our family usually goes to Greece on vacation, **though** last year we went to Turkey.
3 My brother got great grades at school, **so** he studied at a good university.
4 My dad works in the garden every day **as** he has a lot of free time after retiring.
5 My mother loves cats **just as** my grandmother did.
6 My sister loves music, **particularly** rock and pop bands.
7 My mother's always wanted to go to Paris, **so** we organized a trip for her 50th birthday.
8 We do sometimes argue with each other, **but** we never stay angry at each other for long.
9 My two younger brothers are very close **as** they shared a room when they were growing up.
10 My family isn't very big **like** my husband's.
11 We will have a big family gathering this year **as** all my cousins will be here.
12 Sonya is a talented painter **just as** her grandmother was.
13 All my relatives are good singers, **particularly** my aunt.

12.3

1 She searched for her mother's last name **online, yet she didn't find anything helpful.**
2 As a result of a friend's recommendation, **she decided to look at family records online.**
3 Her mother had many fascinating ancestors, **notably one who was an army general.**
4 Whereas her mother's side was interesting, **her father's ancestors were all dull.**
5 Therefore, she decided to concentrate on **finding out more about her mother's side.**
6 As well as the army general, **other ancestors of hers were very interesting.**
7 As a result of her research, **she felt more connected to her family.**

12.4

1 **Due to** the delay to our flight from Atlanta, we missed our connecting flight.
2 It was raining heavily, **so** we decided to cancel the barbecue.
3 My mother is always late, **but** my father is always on time.
4 Ronald Tuft received a number of awards, **notably** the Victoria Cross.
5 Her early work is very radical and her later work is **equally** innovative.
6 Hotels have to be careful **since** it's easy for guests to write bad reviews nowadays.

12.5

1 False 2 True 3 Not given 4 True
5 True 6 False 7 False 8 Not given

13

13.1

1 When I was young, we would **visit** our grandparents every weekend.
2 I didn't **use** to like olives. Now I love them!
3 Did they **use** to have a car?
4 In the summer break, we **would spend** all day at the beach if it was sunny.
5 We **used** to live in an apartment in Milwaukee before we moved to Chicago.
6 When I was a student, I **would look** for special offers to save money.
7 In my old job, I **would listen** to customers' complaints all day long.
8 Did **you use** to play soccer?
9 When I was very young, I **would not eat** any vegetables.
10 At school, my best friend was Leo. We **used to do** everything together.
11 My brother didn't **use to like** swimming. Now he loves it.

13.2

1 Did you use to have a computer at home when you were a child?
2 I worked in Paris from 2005 to 2009.
3 Liam has been to Los Angeles twice.
4 We didn't use to have to wear a school uniform at my school.
5 I used to ride a bicycle to school every day, even in the rain.

13.3

1 would get up 2 would cycle
3 used to spend 4 would get
5 used to moan 6 used to complain
7 never used to

13.4

1 Not given 2 False 3 True
4 Not given 5 False

13.5

3

13.6

1 Janine has similar **values** to us. She loves animals and she's a vegetarian.
2 Your dog is so **greedy**! He's eaten a bowl of food and still wants more.
3 I take **honesty** very seriously. I can't employ people who lie to me.
4 These days there is greater **acceptance** of people with differing points of view.
5 The best thing about Philip's **character** is that he is so kind.

13.7

1 Did you **use** to go to dance classes when you were young?
2 I **did** a lot of housework yesterday afternoon.
3 I didn't **use** to enjoy jogging, but now I do.
4 When I was young, my parents would **take** us to the beach every summer.

13.8

1 When I was young, I wouldn't clean up my bedroom. It made my mom really angry!
2 My brother and I would play video games for hours when we were young.
3 I didn't use to drink tea when I was little. Now I drink it all day long!
4 In college, I would often meet my friends for coffee after classes had finished for the day.

14

14.1

1 This train ticket is **half as** expensive as that one because of the 50 percent discount.
2 He is **just as** intelligent as his brother. They both got high grades.

3 Peter is **nearly as** good at soccer as the others. He'll catch up quickly.
4 My new place is **nowhere near as** big as my old one. It only has one bedroom instead of four.
5 The new album is **not quite as** catchy as their old stuff. I liked their first album a little more.
6 My new computer is **not quite as** fast as my old one. It's actually a little slower.
7 This new soft drink tastes **nearly as** good as SodaUp, but it's not quite the same.
8 The car was **nowhere near as** expensive as we'd thought. It was a real bargain.
9 They both worked hard. She deserved to win **just as** much as he did.

14.2

1 Frank's 2 Neither 3 Morello's
4 Morello's 5 Frank's 6 Morello's
7 Neither

14.3

1 This train isn't quite as fast as we'd thought.
2 He can't type as quickly as she can.
3 It was nowhere near as good as I'd hoped.
4 It tasted just as good as it did last time.
5 She doesn't shop as much as she used to.
6 They ran as quickly as they could.
7 The car wasn't nearly as fast as we thought.
8 He told us to do it as efficiently as possible.
9 Cooking took half as long as usual today.
10 I wasn't as confident as I was before.
11 These pastries are just as good as Ann's.

14.4

1 Most people think that if a product has a **high price**, it must be good quality.
2 My friend Robbie is a very **heavy sleeper**. Nothing wakes him up!
3 I was very pleased to hear that my teacher has a **high opinion** of me.
4 After traveling for thirty hours with very little sleep, I needed some **strong coffee**.
5 Discount retailers like this one sell everything at a **low price**.
6 Everyone leaves work at about 5pm, so there's always **heavy traffic** at that time.
7 I like **weak coffee** with lots of milk in it.

14.5

1 I love cakes and candy. You could say **that have a sweet tooth.**
2 Sometimes it's fun to spend money **on a three-course meal.**
3 My brother is a businessman **so he has to wine-and-dine clients.**
4 The dinner party was amazing. My friends **went out of their way to cook for us.**
5 He cooked an interesting **savory dish using tofu and fish.**

14.6 Model Answers

1 Catherine was not quite as enthusiastic about banking as her sister was.
2 Catherine's friends were working about half as many hours as she was.
3 Catherine's mom was just as worried as her dad about how much she was working.
4 Catherine thought her second experience of studying was not quite as scary as her first.
5 The photography major was just as interesting as Catherine had thought it would be.

15

15.1

1 The more I think about the exam, **the more nervous I feel.**
2 The older you are, **the wiser you become.**
3 The more the boat shook, **the more frightened we felt.**
4 The more advanced the course becomes, **the more difficult it gets.**
5 The higher up the mountain you go, **the colder it gets.**

15.2

1 The more I earn, the more I save.
2 The more time we spend outdoors, the happier we feel.
3 The harder Joel works, the unhappier he becomes.

15.3

1 The **more** difficult a challenge is, the **more** I enjoy it.
2 The **earlier** you start working on the project, **the** sooner you'll finish.
3 **The longer** an action film is, **the** less I want to watch it.
4 The **hotter** it is, **the thirstier** I become in the summer months.
5 The **angrier** Peter gets, **the less** sure I become of how to react.
6 **The** more successful my sister becomes, **the** more stressed she gets.
7 The **friendlier** a person is, the more popular they are at work.
8 The more I study, the less **certain** I become of what I know.
9 The **more** dangerous an adventure sport is, the more I like it.
10 **The** further you swim in the mornings and evenings, **the** fitter you'll become.
11 The **less** junk food you eat in the day, the **slimmer** you'll get.
12 **The** more interviews with successful people I read, **the** more I realize success is down to hard work.

15.4

1 busier and busier 2 and more tired
3 the earlier the better 4 and more stressful
5 the sooner the better

15.5

1 Because of climate change, temperatures on Earth are getting **hotter and hotter**.
2 In developed countries, people are getting **richer and richer**. Is this fair?
3 Ben practices the piano every day so he's getting **better and better**.
4 Every time I look at my baby daughter she seems **more and more beautiful** to me.
5 I waved as the boat got **farther and farther** away, and a tear slid down my cheek.

16

16.1

1 enrol in
2 attend classes
3 strikingly different
4 take a test / take an exam
5 contrast differences
6 undergraduate
7 meet a deadline
8 a world of difference
9 miss a deadline
10 continuous assessment
11 postgraduate
12 give someone feedback on something
13 clear distinction

17

17.1

1 such as = **for example**
2 additionally = **in addition**
3 furthermore = **moreover**
4 therefore = **as a result**
5 to conclude = **in conclusion**

17.2

1 It is, therefore, easier to study **in a place where you know the language.**
2 There are a lot of possibilities. For **example, studying at a university.**
3 First, you have to think about **what the benefits would be.**
4 In conclusion, I think studying **abroad is something everyone should try.**
5 Moreover, you also have the chance **to meet people from other countries.**
6 If you know Spanish, for instance, **go to a Spanish-speaking country.**

17.3
1 False 2 False 3 True 4 False
5 True 6 False

17.4
SEQUENCING: **first**, **second**, **third**
EXAMPLES: **for example**, **for instance**, **such as**
ADDING: **additionally**, **moreover**
CONCLUDING: **overall**, **in conclusion**

17.5
1 If **they want** to go on the trip, they'll need to sign up today.
2 Unless **we get** three more registrations, we won't be able to run the class.
3 If he wants to join the Spanish class, he **will need** to email me this evening.
4 If **you join** the committee, you will have to give up a lot of your free time.
5 If you want to meet up for coffee later, I **will be** in the library.
6 I **will have** to cancel Tuesday's class unless we can find another room.
7 If **they want** to find out more about our club, we **will be** at the fair tomorrow.
8 Unless **we hear** from them in the next five minutes, we will start without them.
9 If **you are** a biology student, you will need to buy a lab coat by Friday.
10 If **you need** a study partner next semester, I might be available.
11 If **they are able** to come to the film night, it will be a great evening.

17.6
1 If you sign up for this study group, **you have to come to weekly meetings.**
2 When you are a student ambassador, **you are a representative of the university.**
3 You will fail the exam **unless you work a lot harder.**
4 When I give you homework, **I expect you to do it.**
5 Send me an email **if you have any further questions.**
6 If you want to find a part-time job, **you can go to our career center.**
7 If you're interested in hiking, **you can join the Expeditions Society.**
8 Unless you can pay a big fine, **don't take your library books back late.**
9 When you go into the second year, **you can apply to study abroad.**
10 I am always ready to listen **if you need someone to talk to.**
11 If you want to study French, **you should visit the language center.**
12 Unless you attend classes regularly, **you will not understand this subject.**

17.7
3

18

18.1
1 approximately half 2 a small minority
3 the vast majority 4 just under a third

18.2
1 In **a few** cases students are asked to retake the year.
2 In **a number** of cases students drop out and leave college.
3 In **some** cases students can ask to defer and start college a year later.
4 In **a majority** of cases students make friends for life while in college.
5 In **most** cases students live on campus in their first year.
6 **Just under** a quarter of students have part-time jobs.

18.3
1 False 2 True 3 True 4 Not given
5 True 6 False 7 Not given 8 True
9 True 10 Not given 11 False

18.4
1 In a **few** cases, the company will hire candidates who do not have a degree
2 Approximately **two-thirds** of students regularly buy fast food.
3 I'm not prepared to pay as **much** as $180 to go to a music festival.
4 In **some** cases, patients are asked to stay at home so they don't infect others.
5 The plane tickets are really cheap. They cost as **little** as $30.
6 Can you believe it? Out of 120 professors, as **many** as 90 can speak three languages.
7 **Well over** 90 percent of students complete their studies.
8 In a **minority** of cases, students will have to find their own accommodation.
9 In **most** cases, you'll feel much better within a week.
10 The yoga class isn't very popular. There are as **few** as three people at most classes.
11 **Just under** a quarter of students take more than a year to find a job.
12 **Just over** half of students meet their future partner in college.

18.5
1 False 2 Not given 3 True 4 False
5 False 6 Not given

18.6
1 Really? I heard that the class sizes are **really small**.
2 Is that so? My experience is very **different** from that.
3 Is that right? I heard that it is **clean and comfortable**.

19

19.1
2

19.2
1 Money for setting up a new business **can be raised** through these websites.
2 Rachel **had been selling** at local events before she decided to get serious.
3 Rachel found out that social media **was being used** by other entrepreneurs.
4 Rachel **set up** her own website by using a simple web platform.
5 Within a week, Rachel **had been offered** funding by eight investors online.
6 Rachel **took on** someone to work for her as her business grew.
7 Later Rachel **found** another crowdfunding website.
8 Rachel's new tea shop **will be located** in London.

19.3
1 Their products **were being sold at the baseball club last weekend.**
2 Social media **can easily be used by entrepreneurs to promote their businesses.**
3 Our detailed business plan **for the next 12 months will be written this weekend.**
4 His old catering business **had already been sold when he bought the hairdressing business.**
5 All of the cooking equipment **was delivered to our new shop yesterday.**

19.4
1 **Check-in** time at this hotel is 2pm. Your room won't be free until then.
2 Just put the **leftovers** in the fridge. We'll have them for lunch tomorrow.
3 Don't forget to make a **backup** of your files.
4 The police are looking for an **onlooker** who may have seen the bank robbers.
5 Let me make it clear from the **outset** what I expect from you.
6 In the first part of the lesson I'll give you a lot of **input** and then you'll be able to use it.
7 Getting angry with the boss in the boardroom was his **downfall**. He'll never work here again.
8 The police have announced a **crackdown** on bicycle thieves.

19.5

1 True 2 False 3 True 4 False

19.6

1 When my dad cooks, **there are never any leftovers.**
2 After losing my data, I know **it's essential to have a backup.**
3 Never share your login **with anyone for security reasons.**
4 There has been a crackdown **on social media use during class.**
5 I always prefer an early check-in **to make the journey easier.**
6 The police put up a line **to hold back onlookers.**

20

20.1

1 I'm taking my dictionary **in case I need to look some words up.**
2 What if I run out of time? **Then I won't finish the exam.**
3 Suppose I don't understand a question. **I will ask the examiner to repeat it.**
4 What if catch a cold? **That would make it difficult to concentrate.**
5 Suppose I forget to turn my phone off. **I would fail the exam if someone calls me.**
6 I'm going to set two alarms **in case I don't hear the first one.**

20.2

1 Likely 2 Unlikely 3 Likely 4 Unlikely
5 Unlikely 6 Likely

20.3

1 I know it's not likely, but suppose I **had** an accident on the way to school.
2 What if I **help** you review and you help me with my essay?
3 Suppose we **found** a rat in our classroom and the test was delayed.
4 You should ask if you can have more time just in case they **say** yes.
5 Suppose another fire alarm **goes** off during the exam. Will they give us more time?
6 What if we **didn't** know the answers to any of the questions? What would we do?

20.4

1 If you **got** 100 percent in the biology exam on Monday, I would be amazed.
2 We **will learn** much more quickly if we use an app to help us learn the words.
3 What if it **snowed** and we couldn't get to school on the day of the exam?
4 If my brother **won** the prize for the best student, I would be shocked.
5 My parents will be happy if I **pass** the chemistry exam.
6 If we bought a new car, we **would not be** late so often!
7 She **will not finish** in time if she doesn't start her project soon.
8 It would be so much less stressful if the teachers **gave** us some help.

20.5 Model Answers

1 If I could decide how long the weekend was, I would make it four days long.
2 If I have time, I will watch a crime show.
3 If I could go anywhere for six months, I'd go to Peru.
4 If I could have dinner with anyone, I'd choose Orson Welles.
5 If I had the chance to study abroad, I would go to the Sorbonne in Paris.
6 If I won the lottery, the first thing I'd buy would be a house for my parents.
7 If I won tickets to a concert, I'd go with my brother.

21

21.1

1 dead-end job
2 set your sights on something
3 hands-on experience
4 get ahead
5 be fired
6 be snowed under
7 tackle something head-on
8 take off
9 bottom of the career ladder
10 nine-to-five
11 laid off
12 give and take
13 working environment

22

22.1

1 After **completing** my studies I decided to take a year off and go traveling.
2 **Developing** original and innovative products is something I'm particularly interested in.
3 **Instead of** spending the summer having fun, I want to get a job and earn some money.
4 **Since** attending a workshop on project management, I have a deeper understanding of this area.
5 I've applied **for** so many jobs, but I haven't had a single interview.
6 **Before** starting my studies, I had earned very high grades at school.
7 While **volunteering** at a school in Peru, I realized how much I enjoy helping other people.
8 **As well as** giving me a strong theoretical grounding, my degree also gave me practical skills.
9 **Starting** work at your company immediately would be perfect for me.
10 They're **not only** doing interviews for the job, they're also asking people to take a test.
11 **After** completing my studies, I have gained some work experience in marketing.
12 After **seeing** the job ad, I knew this job was the one for me and I applied for it.
13 **Without** working in human resources for 10 years, I wouldn't be able to take on this role.
14 Since **qualifying** as a doctor, I've started working at a local hospital.
15 **Going** out into the community to work with people has been very valuable.

22.2 Model Answers

1 Experience of the logistics industry would be particularly desirable.
2 The candidate will be responsible for growing the number of visitors to the company's website.
3 The ideal candidate would stay in the company for a long time.
4 You need to have a Bachelor's degree or higher to apply for this job.
5 You need to be able to speak and write English perfectly.
6 You have to send your résumé and a cover letter to the company if you want to apply for this job.

22.3

1 I have recently **completed** a degree in mechanical engineering.
2 This has prepared me very **well** for working in the area of product management.
3 One course I **did** on brand design is particularly relevant to this position.
4 I have a keen interest in **following** developments in the food industry.
5 Thank you for taking the time to consider my application and I look forward to **hearing** from you.

22.4

1 The contents of my degree course have prepared me very well for **this position**.
2 I have a **strong interest** in the energy sector and have work experience in this area.
3 You will find that I'm a fast and accurate writer with a keen **eye for detail**.
4 I would be able to **take on** the responsibility that this position involves.
5 The experience I have gained in my previous jobs is **particularly relevant** to this position.

22.5

1 I think I would make an excellent office supervisor at some point in the future.
2 In my old job I experienced some conflict with colleagues.
3 I've organized a lot of events such as trade fairs and product launches.
4 Since graduating from college, I've gained a lot of experience in public relations.
5 I may look to move into a managerial job in a few years' time.
6 I would like to be involved with the organization of marketing campaigns.
7 As you can see, I have extensive work experience in the area of retail.
8 My skills are significantly superior to those of the average candidate.
9 Thank you for taking the time to consider my application.
10 My work experience is particularly relevant to this position.
11 I have an in-depth knowledge of product development processes.
12 I've wanted to be an electrician for a very long time.
13 I very much look forward to hearing from you.

23

23.1

1 Could you tell me if **you have any relevant experience in this area**?
2 I was wondering whether **your studies are relevant to this area**.
3 We'd like to know whether **you've applied for any other jobs**.
4 I was wondering if **you like working on a team**.
5 We'd like to know if **you're a good team player**.
6 Do you have any idea what **you would like to be doing in 10 years' time**?
7 Could you tell me what **your weaknesses are**?
8 I was wondering where **you worked after completing your studies**.
9 I'm curious to know where **in China you studied**.
10 Could you tell us which **area of our activities you're particularly interested in**?
11 I'd like to know if **you've ever worked abroad**.

23.2

1 Could you tell us which projects you've worked on?
2 I'd like to know how long you plan to work for us.
3 I was wondering where you studied abroad.
4 We'd like to know if you'd like to do further training.

23.3

1 Could you tell us **how you got along with your last boss**?
2 Do you have any idea **where you want to be in five years' time**?
3 I'm curious to know if **you've ever worked with children before**.
4 I was wondering whether **you've ever managed a website before**.
5 Could you tell us **why we should employ you**?

23.4

1 Would you be prepared to travel a lot? **Let's see. It would depend where you wanted me to go.**
2 Would you like to lead a team one day? **Well, I don't know. Managing a team is something I might be interested in.**
3 Could you come in for an interview? **Let me see. I'll check my schedule and let you know.**
4 Could you send us references from your previous employers? **Well, yes, that should be possible. I'll check with them.**
5 Can we count on you to stay with us long-term? **Maybe we should wait and see how I settle in here first.**

23.5

1 How many people are on her team
2 She likes to control everything
3 Her energy inspires the people on her team
4 She wouldn't want to earn less than before
5 Rose will think about what she would expect

23.6 Model Answers

1 **Yes, where to start?** I'm a dedicated worker and a great communicator.
2 **Oh, let me see.** I'd like to have a position in management.
3 **Well,** it's something that I enjoy and would like to continue doing.
4 **Good question, let me see.** I have a keen eye for detail and I always give 100 percent.
5 **Let me see.** I did once take over from my boss while he was on vacation.
6 **I'm not sure.** It would depend how much you needed me to do.
7 **Let's see. I suppose** I could start next month.

24

24.1

1 She finally managed **to cut** down the number of hours she works from 40 to 35.
2 I think our manager should allow us **to leave** work a bit earlier on Friday afternoon.
3 This new piece of software enables me **to make** updates very quickly.
4 Sam threatened **to leave** if the boss doesn't find a new employee to help him.
5 I'm the person in my office who always **volunteers** to stay late.
6 This is the first time that a colleague has invited me **to have** dinner at their home.
7 The merger deal we completed last month has caused our profits **to** increase.
8 He doesn't like people **telling** him what to do while he's at work.
9 The boss has offered **to send** me on a training course to improve my computer skills.
10 He enjoys **playing** the role of the hot-shot manager when visitors come.

24.2

1 My colleague enjoys **hearing** from satisfied customers.
2 My new smartphone **enables** me to stay connected with my office wherever I am.
3 She hates her colleagues **telling** her what she should do in her department.
4 We like our customers **to give** us feedback on the services we provide them.
5 My boss **offered to** give me an office of my own next year.

24.3

1 False 2 True 3 Not given
4 True 5 False

24.4

1 She always stops **to look** at what's on at the movie theater when we walk past it.
2 I remember **watching** that movie with Brian Owen, but it was a very long time ago.
3 She reminded him **to go** to the supermarket after work, but he still forgot!
4 I wish they would stop **looking** at us like that. They're making me nervous.
5 He finally remembered **to buy** me some flowers for my birthday. He usually forgets.
6 When I was a child, my mother always encouraged me **to eat** fruit and vegetables.
7 The turbulence caused the airplane **to move** from side to side for about 10 minutes.
8 He knew that we weren't interested in what he had to say, but he still went on **talking**.
9 I would advise you **to take** an aspirin for your headache.

10 Did you see Donald volunteering **to organize** the office party this year?
11 He tried **to push** the table through the door of our new living room, but it was too big.
12 The boss threatened **to make** us work all weekend if we didn't finish the project by Friday.

24.5

1 Jade remembered giving me that doll as a birthday present when I was a child.
2 The inspector advised us to change our safety procedures in the factory.
3 She likes people talking about how great she is. She has a very big ego!
4 The loan we got from the bank enabled us to build an extension on our house.
5 I'll write a note to remind myself to bring that book with me next week.

24.6 Model Answers

1 Jackie advises Lynn to talk to her boss.
2 Jackie suggests Lynn's boss could allow her to do a training course.
3 Jackie says that Lynn should leave her job and look for something else.
4 Jackie believes that Lynn is very talented.
5 Jackie thinks Lynn shouldn't accept people telling her she's not good enough to become a manager.

25

25.1

1 Jake lent me a pencil.
2 The teacher offered me some help.
3 She borrowed a book from Liz.
4 Susanne sent me a postcard from her vacation.
5 We donated some old clothes to the families.
6 They paid 20 dollars for the book.
7 John sent me an email yesterday.
8 I'm sure she told you the truth.
9 We gave the dog some biscuits.
10 He brought his computer to her house.
11 Joanne gave him her notes.
12 She lent her car to her son.
13 They bought the teacher some chocolates.
14 Brian passed the message on to Fiona for me.
15 Richard lent me his pen.
16 She always gives me a ride to work.
17 The teacher gave bad grades to those students.
18 Jason passed a note to me in class.
19 Kathryn lent her son some money.
20 They brought a lot of energy to the discussion.
21 He sold his old car to the neighbor.
22 They gave her some candy.
23 She gave some books she didn't need to them.

25.2

1 Robert gave me a lot of help.
2 Emma gave that book to me.
3 He lent his bike to a friend.
4 They passed the message on to me.
5 He gave his wife a great birthday present.

25.3

1 He sold his books to another student.
2 She bought a car for her daughter.
3 He passed the message on to her.
4 They donated money to the charity.
5 He lent some money to his son.
6 I sent him an email.

25.4

1 True 2 Not given 3 True 4 True
5 True 6 Not given

25.5

1 However, I thought **nothing ventured, nothing gained** and I decided to just go for it anyway.
2 Things really took off when I met an angel investor who basically wrote me a **blank check**.
3 Her faith in my abilities was the **ace up my sleeve** that gave me an edge over the competition.
4 As a result, I was able to **hit the ground running** and everyone was coming to me.
5 I had really **cornered the market** there.

26

26.1

1 take minutes
2 give a presentation
3 take questions
4 get down to business
5 sum up
6 show of hands
7 set a date
8 run out of time
9 on the agenda
10 board of directors
11 attend a meeting
12 conference call
13 absent

27

27.1

1 Anna, you're welcome to help **yourself** to tea or coffee and cookies.
2 I taught **myself** to use this computer program.
3 He is very proud of **himself** for getting the highest grade in his class.
4 You can all sit **yourselves** down anywhere you like.
5 We helped **ourselves** to the free food at the staff party.
6 I'm annoyed with **myself** for not thinking about that.
7 She accidentally cut **herself** while she was cooking.
8 The members of the team argued among **themselves** for about half an hour.
9 They're very pleased with **themselves** because their boss praised their work.
10 I often ask **myself** why I decided to leave the country and move to the city.
11 He felt that he had let **himself** down.

27.2

1 My grandparents are 90 years old, but they can still do everything for **themselves.**
2 He prides **himself** on his honesty and integrity.
3 Ramona is really busy today. Could you take this package to the post office for **her**?
4 You don't need to translate that for me. I can do it for **myself**.
5 They got the contract because they worked much harder than **us**.
6 You are all very welcome. Please make **yourselves** at home here.
7 Our neighbors were shouting at **each other** until 10 o'clock last night.

27.3

1 We want you to prepare the presentations **yourselves**.
2 The CEO **himself** mentioned me during his annual speech.
3 I am very proud! I repaired the bike **myself**.
4 We should be proud that we've achieved all of this by **ourselves**.
5 Food **itself** is changing and so are our eating habits.
6 They congratulated **themselves** on a job well done.
7 The shop manager **herself** came down to apologize to me for her mistake.

27.4

1 I'm glad that we were able to do it **ourselves** without asking the boss for help.
2 The presentation **itself** went well, but the meeting afterwards went badly.

3 All of the children behaved **themselves** really well during the flight.
4 The president's wife **herself** came to shake my hand and give me the award.
5 I felt very pleased with **myself** when I found out that my painting had won the prize.
6 This is the first time that he's been able to walk by **himself** since the accident.
7 I'm looking forward to having the house to **myself** while my parents are away.
8 You should all help **yourselves** to any books on my bookcase that you're interested in.
9 Your mother isn't going to wash your clothes anymore. You'll have to do it **yourself.**

27.5

1 I can't come to the English lesson as **I'm completely snowed under at work.**
2 The boss has asked her to **stay behind this evening.**
3 Customer service is something we **need to work on this year.**
4 My computer is not working. Can **you sort it out?**
5 On Fridays we usually **knock off at 12 o'clock.**

27.6

1 Sometimes, I'm so snowed **under** at work that I don't have time to eat my lunch.
2 I need to sort **out** these customer queries.
3 She allowed **herself** enough time to drive to the bank and park her car before the meeting.
4 Our project manager has given **us** more responsibility.
5 I'm still trying to catch **up** with the work I should have done last week.
6 We can't tear him **away** from the video game he's playing for more than ten minutes.
7 I think I have taken **on** too much work. I'm absolutely exhausted!
8 I always ask for challenging projects, but my boss never lets **me** do them.
9 Here's the safety information for working in this building. Could you all familiarize **yourselves** with it?
10 I'm sorry, but I'll have to ask Jason to deal with this. I'm completely snowed **under** at the moment.
11 When students fail their exams, they usually don't blame **themselves**.
12 When I take my children on the train, I bring some toys that they can occupy **themselves** with.

28

28.1

1 He can't stand **waiting** for people. He doesn't understand why people can't be on time.
2 I have to say that I prefer **cooking** for myself to eating out. I can eat whatever I want then.
3 I hate **moving**, but fresh flowers make a new house feel more like home.
4 How would you propose **solving** the big problems that we have?
5 Your flight had such a long delay that I began **to wonder** if you would ever make it back home.
6 He likes **to go** to a concert or the opera once a month or even more frequently if he can.
7 You continued **to ignore** my concerns even after you had seen the negative effects yourself.
8 I love **swimming** outdoors in a lake or in the ocean, even if the water's quite cold.
9 We started **to plan** our wedding last year as we knew it would take a long time.

28.2

1 In our family we usually prefer **beach vacations to city breaks.**
2 The design department proposed **making some changes to the sizes.**
3 Despite being tired, he continued **to run for the last six miles.**
4 We've always really loved **walking in the countryside.**
5 When I was younger I hated **getting up early, but now I like it.**
6 I have to say I can't stand **hearing music from people's phones.**
7 The music was so good that I started **dancing along to it.**
8 Ten years ago he began **saving money so he could buy a house.**
9 Marjorie proposed **putting more time between our meetings.**

28.3

1 Now I regret **asking** him about his family. I had no idea what had happened to them.
2 He graduated at the top of his class and we think that he will go on **to be** a successful lawyer.
3 We regret **to inform** you that on this occasion your application was not successful.
4 I remember **putting** my car keys on the table, but then someone must have moved them.
5 Don't worry, he won't forget **to call** you when he arrives in Australia.
6 After our success this season, we're sure the hotel will go on **being** popular next season.
7 Please remember **to write** to catering and ask if they can cater for 80 instead of 60.
8 Can we stop **to buy** some snacks and get coffee at the next service station we get to?

28.4

1 We stopped to get coffee.
2 I remembered to buy her a present.
3 I regret telling him that.
4 Did you forget going to Paris with me?
5 They went on celebrating until 2am.
6 I stopped going to the gym in February.
7 Sometimes I forget to charge my phone.
8 I regret to inform you about the changes.
9 I remember visiting you when I was a child.

28.5

1 I forgot to ask Valerie if she wanted to join us for dinner this evening.
2 I always remember to close all of the windows when I leave the house.
3 Who would have thought he would go on to be such a successful ballet dancer in the future?
4 The views along the coast road were so beautiful we decided to stop to take photos.
5 I regret saying that he doesn't work as hard as everyone else. He hasn't spoken to me since.

28.6

1 She had to go on working into her sixties.
2 We regret to inform you about the flight cancelations.
3 They stopped accepting paper applications two years ago.
4 Please remember to turn your computer off.

28.7

1 Why do you always forget **to buy** milk when you go to the supermarket on your own?
2 When are you going to stop **working** there and do something you really want to do?
3 Do you regret **getting** that tattoo of a dolphin on your neck now?
4 Do you think you would like **to run** the whole company one day?
5 Can we stop **to have** dinner at that nice restaurant in town on our way home?

29

29.1

1 She's a **brilliant** scientist. I'm sure she'll win the Nobel Prize for physics one day.
2 The fact that smoking can damage your health was **unknown** to most people until the 1970s.
3 It's amazing that such a **tiny** chip can contain so much data.
4 This scarf was handmade in Malaysia and the design is completely **unique.**

5 Could you please send me this document in a **digital** format? I can then upload it to our site.
6 The weather was **awful** last weekend. It wouldn't stop raining and it was really cold, too.
7 I think it's **disgusting** that there's so much bacteria on our phones.
8 She tries to avoid using cosmetic products that have too many **chemical** ingredients in them.
9 We're very proud of our **industrial** heritage, such as these 19th-century factory buildings.

29.2

1 They had an absolutely fantastic trip to South Africa. They're already planning their next trip.
2 He's absolutely fascinated by trains so we decided to buy him a train set for his birthday.
3 The delegates at the conference were largely European with a few North Americans.
4 We wanted to create a completely digital product for today's young people.
5 It's completely impossible to put this table together. I'll never be able to do it.

29.3

1 It's **hugely** important that as many people as possible see these billboards.
2 This product is **extremely** useful if you don't have very much time to spend on housework.
3 We think that our customer base will be **rather** interested in this new feature.
4 Our competitors' products are **wholly** inadequate to deal with these challenges.
5 The first design was **absolutely** awful, so we had to get rid of it and create a new one.
6 The coffee machine has a **totally** unique feature that enables you to make hot or cold milk.
7 I'm **utterly** exhausted after putting so much effort into the product launch last week.
8 The CEO can speak **quite** good English, but he's much better at Spanish or Portuguese.
9 Have you noticed that our new packaging designer is **really** talented?

29.4

1 I loved it! I thought it was **thoroughly enjoyable** and very funny.
2 I'm shy, so I'd feel **absolutely terrified** if I had to do that.
3 It would be so inconvenient! I'd be **utterly miserable**.

29.5

1 I thought the test was fairly **difficult, but my friend found it easy.**
2 Our product will be really **popular with consumers everywhere.**
3 The presentation was pretty **interesting and I learned a lot from it.**
4 My boss sometimes gets quite **annoyed if we fall behind schedule.**

29.6

1 False 2 True 3 Not given 4 True
5 True 6 True 7 Not given
8 Not given 9 False 10 Not given

30

30.1

1 He wrote a bad review of the movie **to let everyone know it's terrible.**
2 She took the toaster back **not to get a new one, but to get a refund.**
3 I looked everywhere in the store **in order to find the items I needed.**
4 The store gave them a voucher **so as to keep their business.**
5 He called the restaurant manager **to complain about a rude waiter.**
6 She raised her voice **so that everyone would hear her.**
7 We called the airline **to ask them to cancel our flights.**
8 You need to fill in this form **in order to get your money back.**
9 I called our internet provider **to find out when they will connect us.**
10 I talked to our neighbors **to let them know they're being too noisy.**
11 Now we check all of the pallets **to ensure the goods in them aren't broken.**
12 He looked for the company online **to find out what others think about it.**
13 I called the HR department **to find out about vacancies.**
14 He asked to speak to the chef **to compliment his cooking.**
15 She talked to the salon manager **in order to complain about her haircut.**
16 I covered the goods in shrink wrap **in order to protect them.**

30.2

1 She took her car to the garage so that the mechanics could fix it.
2 We use RFID technology so that we can track the goods.
3 He wrote a positive review of the hotel so that other people would know how good it was.
4 I usually get up 5am so that I can go running before I go to work.
5 She spent a lot of time planning her presentation so that she would be well-prepared.

30.3

1 Our products are made **to** withstand all temperatures.
2 Our career website is **for** busy professional people.
3 You can use this little USB stick **to** connect to the internet in any location.
4 This headset is **for** video-chatting and web-conferencing.
5 This hi-fi system is only **for** serious music fans, as it's very expensive.

30.4

1 Can we offer you a voucher **to show** we are sorry for the inconvenience caused.
2 I will be making a **complaint** about your airline as soon as I get home.
3 I'm not very satisfied **with** the product I received from the company two days ago.
4 Could you **let** me know when the basket of fruit that I ordered last week will arrive?
5 These workers are employed **to** pick and pack the goods in the factory outside the city.
6 Thank you for your prompt **assistance** with the ongoing matter of delayed product delivery.
7 You can use this device **for** cleaning the windows in your house quickly and effectively.
8 I recently **ordered** a pair of running shoes from you as a gift for my sister.
9 I need a **replacement** for this kettle as soon as possible, or else I will require a refund.
10 I look forward **to hearing** from you about the meeting next week.

31

31.1

1 extinct
2 harmful to the environment
3 wind farm
4 consume
5 fossil fuels
6 renewable energy
7 endangered
8 solar panel
9 destruction
10 climate change
11 reduce your carbon footprint
12 global warming
13 alternative energy

32

32.1

1 If I **had known** it was raining, I **would have brought** my umbrella.
2 I **would not have known** the party was canceled if he **had not told** me.

3 If I **had arrived** at the train station earlier, I **would not have missed** the train.
4 If they **had studied** more, they **might have passed** the exam.
5 If I **had known** you didn't like onions, I **would not have used** them.
6 If I **had not gone** to college, I **might have taken** a gap year.
7 We **would not have put** the box there if we **had known** that it would fall.
8 If I **had realized** he was unhappy, I **could have talked** to him about it.
9 I **would have worn** a suit if I **had known** the CEO was coming to visit us.
10 If we **had given** out more samples, we **would have sold** more products.
11 If she **had known** there was a test, she **would have prepared**.

32.2

1 If we'd known there was a train strike on, we would've driven there. 2 If I hadn't gone to that party, I wouldn't have met my husband.
3 If I'd worked harder, I might've been promoted last year.

32.3

1 I would have called you if I had **known** you were in town.
2 If we had taken a taxi, we **wouldn't** have missed our flight.
3 If I **had** left the house at nine, I would not have been late for the interview.
4 I would **have** made it home by 7 o'clock if my train had left on time
5 If we had known the movie was that good, we **would** have gone to see it.

32.4

1 False 2 Not given 3 False
4 False 5 True 6 False 7 True

32.5

1 If only we **had asked** for a room on the second or third floor. It wouldn't have been so noisy.
2 I wish we had been able to spend more time at that museum. It **was** really interesting.
3 If only we had been there in summer. We **could have taken** a boat trip on the river.
4 I wish we **had gone** to the Eiffel Tower earlier. We might not have had to wait so long.
5 I wish we **had read** the reviews of that restaurant before we decided to eat there.
6 I love that band. If only we **had known** they were doing a concert down the road from the hotel.
7 If only we had taken the train to the airport. We **would have arrived** there faster.

32.6

1 My brother always makes fun of me. If only **I had a sister instead**!
2 Why didn't I take your advice? I wish **I'd listened to you.**
3 I left my wallet on the train. I wish **I hadn't forgotten it**.
4 My presentation was awful. If only **I'd practiced more**.
5 I got soaked outside. If only **I'd brought my umbrella**.
6 I'm so bored at work. I wish **I'd taken time off**.
7 I hate walking. If only **I hadn't crashed my car**.

33

33.1

1 You **should** have separated your waste for recycling.
2 We **ought** to have bought fair trade chocolate.
3 She **should not** have wasted so much paper.
4 The company **should not** have dumped their waste in the river.
5 They **should** have used wood from sustainable forests.
6 We **should** have found out about the risks beforehand.
7 You **should** have changed to energy-saving light bulbs.
8 He **should** have turned the lights off when he left.
9 They **ought** to have reduced the amount of traveling their employees do.
10 We **should not** have cut down so much of the rainforest.
11 You **ought** to have drunk tap water instead of bottled water.
12 She **should not** have showered for so long. She's wasting water!
13 They **should not** have flown the goods halfway across the world.
14 We **ought** to have talked to the local community about this.
15 Governments **should** have made a law to stop this happening.
16 We **should not** have buried the waste in that landfill.
17 He **ought** to have turned his computer off at night.
18 You **should** have stopped using new plastic bags every time you go shopping.

33.2

1 We should not have dumped the waste in the river.
2 We should not have used so many pesticides in these fields.
3 We should not have overfished the oceans.
4 We ought to have switched to greener cars sooner.
5 We should have thought about the effects of the mine on the river.
6 We should have protected the wildlife from the oil spill.

33.3

1 We should not have built the dam there.
2 We ought to have started using renewable energy earlier.
3 They should have recycled all their waste materials.
4 We ought to have left the island as it was.
5 We should not have destroyed the orangutans' habitat.
6 They should have thought about the impact on fish supplies.
7 We should not have ignored what the protesters said.
8 We ought to have stored those chemicals more carefully.
9 We should have had more controls at the power plant.

33.4

1 overconfident 2 overloaded
3 overcrowded 4 overworked
5 overcautious

33.5

1 However, **following** the original explosion, a large oil leak was discovered.
2 It is estimated that oil was flowing into the sea at a rate of 62,000 gallons a day **by that time.**
3 Oil continued to flow into the ocean at this rate **throughout** the next six weeks.
4 Efforts were made to stop the flow of oil **during** that time, but none of them proved successful.
5 **Since then**, the oil spill has become known as one of the worst manmade disasters in recent history.

34

34.1

1 I'm **afraid of** getting trapped in an elevator, so I always take the stairs.
2 In recent years, there's been a huge **increase in** smartphone ownership.
3 My children sometimes **argue about** who gets to watch TV.
4 I always **ask for** a window seat when I fly so I can look out the window.
5 We'll never **agree about** how to raise children.
6 I think he'll win. All of the signs **point in** his direction.
7 There's been a **decline in** the number of letters people have written in the last decade.

8 The economic situation had the **effect of** pushing house prices down.
9 There's a **lack of** interest in the project among the people in my team.
10 I'm afraid I'm going to be **late for** our appointment this morning.
11 They're really **grateful for** all of the opportunities they've been given.
12 We **talked about** my previous work experience and career goals.
13 There's been a **decline in** the number of people watching live television in recent years.
14 When I call my sister, we **talk about** absolutely everything that's been going on in my life.

34.2

1 My husband and I sometimes argue **about** whose turn it is to do the dishes.
2 Frank is never late **for** any meetings in the office.
3 The course was canceled due to a lack **of** interest by students.
4 I know a lot of people who are afraid **of** spiders and snakes.
5 She's very grateful **for** the chance to study medicine in the US.
6 Marlon will talk **about** his travels in the Amazon rainforest this evening.
7 I'm so grateful **for** the opportunity you have given me.

34.3

1 True 2 False 3 Not given
4 Not given 5 True 6 Not given

34.4

1 We are currently searching **for** a suitable location for a new offshore wind farm.
2 The Prime Minister apologized **to** the public for not giving them all of the facts.
3 I'm so bored **with** news stories about how the Earth is getting hotter. It's freezing today!
4 If we reduce the amount of packaging we use, that will result **in** us having less waste.

34.5

1 **Environmentally-friendly** farming practices help farmers grow more food.
2 **This** government isn't going to stand by and do nothing about climate change.
3 What changes can **you** make in **your** everyday life to make it a healthier one?
4 There **isn't** a future for the nuclear power industry in this country.

34.6

1 talk about 2 suitable for 3 grateful for
4 leads to 5 effect of 6 agree about
7 points in 8 increase in 9 lack of
10 ask for 11 afraid of 12 decline in
13 argued about

35

35.1

1 I'm not rich, but I try to donate **a little** money to charity every month.
2 Sadly, there are **few** Sumatran tigers left in the world today.
3 I have **little** patience for people who are always late. I'm always on time!
4 There are very **few** people I would lend money to. But my brother is one of them.
5 **Little** can be done to completely stop climate change in our time.
6 Do you need some help to finish that report? I have **a little** time I can spare.
7 There are **a few** paintings in the museum I haven't seen. Can we stay a bit longer?
8 There's **little** point in explaining it to Jen. She never listens to what I say.
9 I know you're on a diet, but would you like **a little** bit of chocolate?
10 There are very **few** old buildings left in this city. It's sad that we've lost so much history.
11 I don't have lots of friends, but I've got **a few** that I'm really close to.

35.2

1 There are fewer job opportunities **than there used to be.**
2 People have less time for **hobbies and sports these days.**
3 Fewer people are interested **in local history these days.**
4 Our university offers fewer **courses than it did 10 years ago.**
5 I wish I'd brought less **luggage with me on vacation.**
6 Kelly changed jobs, but she's now **earning less money than before.**

35.3

1 Less money is spent on care for the elderly.
2 We all need to use less electricity.
3 Fewer people are worried about pollution.
4 I wish I had less work to do.
5 People are having fewer children.
6 Fewer people enjoy gardening nowadays.

35.4

1 False 2 False 3 True
4 True 5 True

35.5

1 She has been working for quite a **few** years.
2 I've earned quite a **bit** of money.
3 Amal has quite a **bit** of work experience.
4 There are quite a **few** students in this class.
5 I've spent quite a **bit** of time on this report.
6 Jo has made quite a **few** friends at university.
7 There's quite a **bit** of rice left over.
8 There are quite a **few** things I have to do.
9 It took quite a **bit** of effort to finish the race.
10 I've got quite a **few** pairs of sneakers.
11 We've got quite a **few** vacations planned.
12 She gave me quite a **bit** of useful advice.
13 There's quite a **bit** of garbage on the floor.

35.6

1 The park is empty. There must be **fewer than** 10 people here.
2 My daughter's school is tiny. It has **fewer than** five teachers.
3 Seattle is **less than** 20 miles from here. It won't take long to drive there.
4 Applicants should supply no **fewer than** two references.
5 The plane leaves in **less than** half an hour. We'd better hurry!
6 I've got **less than** $2 in cash. Could you lend me some money, please?
7 The company had to cut some jobs, so we now have **fewer than** 15 employees.
8 It's **less than** 10 minutes until the game starts. I'm so excited!
9 I'm afraid the course is canceled because **fewer than** 10 people signed up.
10 Jeremy is being paid **less than** all his friends. He wants a new job.
11 I always pack light. My suitcase weighs **less than** 12 pounds.
12 It's very disappointing that **fewer than** eight countries signed the agreement.

36

36.1

1 make a wish
2 set of beliefs
3 have serious misgivings / doubts
4 good / bad omen
5 gossip
6 word of mouth
7 drop a hint
8 pure luck
9 folklore
10 urban myth
11 beginner's luck
12 start / spread a rumor
13 believe in something

37

37.1

1 Chris hasn't turned up for training. He **might not** have realized it was today.
2 Your phone **might not** have been stolen. Have you checked in your desk?

3 I found a wallet. It **might** have been dropped by someone walking to the station.
4 Liz isn't answering her emails. She **may** have gone away.
5 I **may** have forgotten to send Lola a birthday card. I'm not sure.
6 That strange noise **could** have been a fox outside. There are a lot of them in this area.
7 I'm sure Les **could not** have sent such a rude message. He's usually such a gentleman.
8 Jen and Will are late. They **might** have missed the train.
9 Helena **could not** have grown 20 inches last year. That's too much in 12 months!
10 That bag is a fake. You **could not** have bought a real one. It was far too cheap.
11 You **might not** have caught the flu. It might just be a bad cold.
12 I **may** have left my glasses at work. I can't find them.
13 You **might not** need an operation. You might just need to take some medicine.
14 You **could not** have seen Sally in town yesterday. She's in China.
15 It **might not** have been Sally I saw in town. But it was someone who looks like her.
16 Your purse **could** have been stolen when you were waiting in line at the market.
17 We **may not** have bought the right ingredients for the cake. I'm not sure. Let's check.

37.2

1 She couldn't have gone out. All her clothes are dirty!
2 Anyone could have left the freezer door open.
3 They may not have remembered to close the window.
4 They may have had a party.
5 They may have forgotten to turn down the hob.
6 They might have made a big dinner for lots of people.

37.3

1 My car has a scratch on it. Someone could have reversed into it in the parking lot.
2 Your email could have gone into my junk folder. I'll check again.
3 You could not have visited my old school. It was turned into an office in 2012.
4 You could not have spoken to Jill on the phone. She's flying to Brazil right now.
5 I might not have said the right thing to Annabel. She looked a bit upset.

37.4

1 They **said they couldn't believe what they were seeing.**
2 She **said she wasn't lying.**
3 She **told me she didn't believe in things like ghosts.**
4 He **said he had heard a terrible scream the night before.**
5 She **said that she would never stay in a castle ever again.**
6 She **said she took a photo and there was a ghost in it.**
7 He **told me that they had had a lot of fun on Halloween.**
8 They **told me they were so scared that they couldn't move.**

37.5

1 I asked him how much his new jacket was.
2 I asked him if / whether he felt tired.
3 I asked her if / whether they were going to get married.
4 I asked him what he had done last weekend.
5 I asked her if / whether Carina was good enough to play for the team.
6 I asked him if / whether he was busy right then.
7 I asked him where he had gone on vacation.
8 I asked her if / whether she would call me back when she was free.
9 I asked her if / whether Robert was the new office manager.

37.6

1 I asked her what her favorite food was.
2 I asked him if / whether he was nervous about the exam.
3 I asked him where he played tennis.
4 I asked him if / whether she was easy to talk to.
5 I asked her if / whether they were a difficult team to play.
6 I asked them when they were going away.
7 I asked him why he was so sad.

38

38.1

1 Someone could have **taken** my coat because they thought it was theirs.
2 They **must** have already left. That's the only explanation.
3 He couldn't have **written** such a good essay without any help from his teachers.
4 There **may / might** have been an accident, but I'm not really sure.
5 I know it's unlikely, but someone **may/ might** have found the money and handed it in.
6 He might have **given** me the wrong directions. He doesn't know this town very well.
7 He couldn't **have** known that they would ask him a question about that. That's unfair.
8 It can't have **been** a ghost. They don't really exist!
9 She must have **been** imagining it. There's nobody upstairs.

38.2

1 Have you checked your phone? **She could have tried to call you.**
2 He's not answering the door. **He might have left already.**
3 I still can't get through to her. **She might have left her phone at home.**
4 They must have changed their address. **That's why our letters keep being returned.**
5 Have you looked in the top drawer? **He might have left the keys there.**
6 Their plane might have been delayed. **Is there anything on the arrivals board?**
7 You must have dialled the wrong number. **Nobody called Sheila lives here.**
8 We may have lost James and Katie. **They're no longer following behind us.**
9 He can't have thrown the tickets away! **They must be here somewhere.**

38.3

1 I **might** have won the competition if my entry had arrived in time.
2 They **can't** have lost their way. They know this area very well.
3 I **must** have done something to upset her. She's not speaking to me.
4 She **couldn't** have opened that door. She doesn't have a key for it.
5 They **may** have destroyed those documents. We haven't found them.

38.4

1 You must **have dealt with** a lot of customers over the last 20 years.
2 Mom and Dad might **have hidden** our presents in this cupboard.
3 He can't **have left** without saying goodbye. He must still be here.
4 The children might **have outgrown** these toys. They prefer video games now.
5 They must **have run** very fast to finish the race in such good time.
6 They can't **have told** you everything. There's a lot more that you need to know.
7 The students might **have gone** to the classroom we were in last semester instead.

38.5

1 True 2 False 3 True 4 False 5 False

39

39.1

1 If he **were** more organized, he wouldn't have been late for work again today.
2 If I had lost my job, **I would be** living with my parents again now.
3 If he had kept on learning English, he **would be** fluent by now.

4 If they **had known** how stormy it would be, they wouldn't be outside today.
5 If your aunt hadn't lent you money, you **wouldn't be able to** buy a house now.
6 If he **were** more confident, he wouldn't have failed his driving test.
7 If you had gone to college, you might **have** a good job by now.
8 If they had finished painting the bedroom, we **wouldn't have to** sleep in the loft tonight.

39.2

1 I would wear my coat **if I hadn't forgotten it**.
2 If we had saved more money, **we wouldn't have to be so thrifty now**.
3 If you had believed what they said, **you would not be where you are today**.
4 He wouldn't be so bad at cooking **if his Dad had shown him how to do it**.
5 He might be more patient **if he hadn't already been waiting so long.**
6 If he had reserved a seat on the train, **he wouldn't have to stand for two hours**.
7 She wouldn't always be late **if she had bought herself a new watch**.
8 If you had read all of the questions, **you wouldn't think that the test was easy**.

39.3

1 He would feel better if he had **slept** a little more last night.
2 If you had **prepared** for the interview properly, you wouldn't be so nervous now.
3 You wouldn't be stuck here if you had **told** the hotel staff about the problem.
4 If you had **set** off earlier, you wouldn't have to rush so much now.
5 He would be less stressed if he had **taken** more time out to relax.
6 If they hadn't **sent** our luggage to the wrong terminal, we would be home by now.
7 She might not be such a good typist if she hadn't **spent** so much time at the computer.

39.4

1 If he **had told** me how upset he was, I would still be there comforting him.
2 If I were a good cook, I **would have invited** you to lunch at our place by now.
3 He **would have stroked** Fido if he wasn't so scared of dogs.
4 If they weren't going to France tomorrow, they **would have gone** to your party.
5 We **could have gone** to the theater if we weren't busy tonight.
6 I would be surprised if Katherine **had wanted** me to go to the ball with her.
7 If the teacher were here, she **would have told** you all to be quiet.
8 If I **had moved** to America, I might be rich and happy now.
9 I would be happy to help you if I **hadn't already agreed** to help Jack.
10 If they **had learned** to ski, they could go on a skiing vacation next year.
11 If we **had looked** at the map earlier, we wouldn't be so lost!
12 If I had taken that job, I **would be** earning a lot more money now.

40

40.1

1 I can't remember what we decided about the color, but I'm sure it'll be bright, **whatever** it is.
2 **Whenever** I go on vacation abroad, I always try the dishes that are typical for that country.
3 I'm sure the new boss will do a good job and treat everyone fairly, **whoever** he or she is.
4 They always believe that they will win the lottery one day, **however** small the chances are.
5 She always ignores any criticism she gets, **whatever** anyone says about her.
6 **Whenever** I fly, I always make sure that I get to the airport two hours before my flight time.
7 I don't think I'll be able to find the answer to this math problem, **however** hard I try.
8 We could talk about this on the phone or I could arrange a meeting, **whichever** you prefer.
9 He always finds the time to call and say goodnight to me **wherever** he is in the world.

40.2

1 **Whoever** completes the questionnaire first will win an exciting prize.
2 We always stay in touch by text message or email **whenever** we're apart.
3 I won't give up until I reach the top of the mountain, **however** hard it gets.
4 I can pick you up at the airport or you can take the train, **whichever** you prefer.
5 I'm not going to put up with this kind of behavior from him, **whoever** he is.
6 We can have Chinese or Italian food or something else, **whatever** you want to do.
7 I always take a little first aid kit with me **whenever** I go on vacation.
8 I'm sure she'll look beautiful in her dress, **whichever** one she chooses.
9 She's determined to change his mind about the Nigeria project, **however** long it takes.

40.3

1 I always fear I'm going to have a bad day **whenever I walk under a ladder.**
2 Whatever happens in my life, **my superstitions bring me comfort.**
3 Whoever told you that **must be very superstitious.**
4 My mother believes in superstitions, **however often they prove to be false.**
5 Whenever a family member gets married, **I give them something blue for luck.**
6 This horse shoe will bring me luck, **however difficult life gets.**
7 She always wears that ring, **however strange it looks.**
8 Whenever she sees a black cat, **she thinks that it'll bring her bad luck.**

40.4

1 come rain or shine 2 throw caution to the wind 3 on cloud nine 4 a bolt from the blue 5 steal someone's thunder
6 right as rain

40.5

1 That's a bolt **from** the blue. I had no idea she was planning to leave the country.
2 I'm going to **throw** caution to the wind and just buy that expensive car!
3 My daughter was ill with the flu last week, but she's right **as** rain now.
4 I'm afraid I'll have to **take** a rain check on that. I'm really busy this week.
5 Whenever I give a sales presentation, Maureen always tries to **steal** my thunder.

41

41.1

1 be a household name
2 attention-grabbing
3 opening night
4 red carpet
5 paparazzi
6 talent show
7 become a celebrity
8 reality show
9 meteoric rise
10 sensationalize
11 celebrity culture
12 headline news
13 newspaper headline

42

42.1

1 These items have been **produced** in our new factory.
2 It has been **reported** that a hurricane will hit the coast this evening.
3 Those tests have been **carried** out in our new laboratory next door.
4 Following the meeting, it has been **decided** that we will increase our prices.

5 He has been **named** by the pharmaceutical company as their new CEO.
6 Our products have been **exported** all over the world since 1995.
7 The proposal has been **rejected** by all the members of the board.
8 There are **alleged** to have been a series of crimes committed by this gang.
9 It has long been **believed** that money isn't his main motivation.

42.2

1 It is understood that there **have been many flight cancelations.**
2 Our organization is thought to **be a trailblazer in the area we work in.**
3 It has been reported that **there will be massive jobs cuts.**
4 It was announced that the company **would recall its latest products.**
5 He is thought to have been **the most successful CEO we ever had.**
6 There are said to be **some nice walking trails around here.**
7 It is hoped that the next generation **will continue the work we've been doing.**
8 Norway is believed to be **among the most beautiful countries.**

42.3

1 This essay **should have been** handed in two weeks ago!
2 Unfortunately, the project couldn't **be completed** on time.
3 It must **have taken** us four hours to get here because of all the traffic jams.
4 She must **have thought** that the meeting started at 11am instead of 10am.
5 Any feedback you may have should **be sent** to our administrator.
6 The machine may **have broken down** because there was some dust in it.
7 Traffic could **be redirected** here during the festival.
8 Free samples can **be obtained** from our store on the first floor.
9 The booking should **have been made** earlier. Then we would have better seats.

42.4

1 The bell must have rung 10 times, but he still didn't come to the door.
2 There is understood to have been a car accident on Station Road this evening.
3 All of the books we sent should have been delivered to the venue by now.
4 It was announced yesterday that students can now apply for scholarships for next year.
5 The driver is thought to have lost his way while driving from the airport back to the city.

42.5

1 Yesterday 2 Young people 3 This isn't clear yet 4 They welcome it
5 Positively

42.6

1 A million gallons of water **were bottled at this plant last year.**
2 Our cars **are rented by business travelers at the airport.**
3 Another conference **could be organized for next September.**
4 All of our dishes **are made by hand by our chefs.**
5 It is hoped **that the supplier will accept the new terms and conditions.**
6 It is reported **that the traffic laws will be changed by the government this year.**
7 All of the company cars **are serviced in this garage.**
8 The solar panels on our roof **were installed by a Spanish company last month.**
9 It is agreed **that he would make an excellent team leader.**
10 The trucks **could have been unloaded in half the time that they actually took.**
11 It was announced **that she would be stepping down from the committee.**
12 It was claimed **that some students didn't get enough help from their teachers.**

43

43.1

1 **Approximately** 40,000 spectators watched the game at the national stadium.
2 The figures **indicate** that our population is aging rapidly.
3 Harris Mode is **arguably** the most handsome man alive today.
4 To **some extent**, we can all do more to improve the state of our health.
5 **It has been said** that unless we stop climate change, the ice caps will melt.
6 It has been **suggested** that the witness lied during the trial.
7 People who purchase violent video games **tend** to be young men.
8 **It looks** like we've missed the bus. We're going to be late again.
9 It **appeared** that the jewelry had been stolen in the early hours of the morning.

43.2

1 The teacher suggested that **Lilian should expect good exam results.**
2 If I don't have coffee in the morning, **I tend to get a headache.**
3 There are approximately 15,000 **people in the town where I live.**
4 It appears that the company **is going to make a loss this year.**
5 The soccer players allegedly **accepted money to lose games.**
6 It has been said that **there's no fool like an old fool.**
7 People often say **they don't have the time to exercise.**

43.3

1 The test results **suggest** that this is a new kind of bacteria.
2 **To some extent**, I'm glad Gina canceled her party. I don't feel very well.
3 Jess **seems** to have gone home early.
4 Carren Lake is **arguably** the most successful British tennis player ever.
5 It **appears** that we have no food left in the fridge.
6 It would **seem** that Clarissa is not answering my text messages.

43.4 Model Answers

1 The incident took place in Banff General Hospital.
2 The medical staff was surprised to see a deer walking into the Emergency Room.
3 The deer seemed to have been injured in an accident on the roads.
4 The deer must have walked approximately 10 kilometers to get to the hospital.
5 The medical staff took the deer to a nearby vet.
6 The vet said that it looked like the animal would make a full recovery.

43.5

1 True 2 False 3 Not given
4 False 5 True 6 True

43.6

1 To some **extent**, the project we worked on last month was a waste of time.
2 It would seem **that** someone has hacked into our database.
3 He has **allegedly** stolen $2 million from his employer.
4 It has been **said** that absence makes the heart grow fonder.
5 It **appears** that you have forgotten to pay your bill.

44

44.1

1 Only after trying to reach the summit three times **did he** give up.
2 Little **does she** know that we're planning a surprise party for her.
3 Only **when** it starts to snow do I stop gardening.

4 Not since the 1980s **has the team** won a major trophy.

44.2

1 Only after living there for five years **did he master the Spanish language.**
2 Not only is she a great mother, **but she's also a top business executive.**
3 Little did they realize **that they were in for a big surprise.**
4 Only when she read their stories **did she realize how well they can write.**
5 Not since his childhood **had he ridden a skateboard.**
6 Only after studying the instructions **did he understand how it worked.**

44.3

1 Little did I know that I would meet my future husband that evening.
2 Not only is he a talented pianist, he is also a writer.
3 Only when he came on stage did the fans start to scream.
4 Only after living there for six months did they talk to the neighbors.
5 Not only was the movie informative, but it was also entertaining.

44.4

1 No sooner had I arrived home than my son asked me to help him with his homework.
2 Little did she know that she would stay for 40 years when she started working there.
3 Never before have people from both communities worked together.
4 Not since I went to see *Sally's Song* have I cried this much at a film.
5 Rarely do you see a dog and cat that get along with each other so well.

44.5

1 **Rarely** have I seen so many people running together.
2 Little **did we** know that we would end up living in Italy.
3 **No sooner** had I reached the station than the train arrived.
4 Not since 1988 **have we** had such a hot summer.
5 **Little** did she know that she would win an award that evening.
6 Never before **have I seen** a child who loves reading as much as she does.
7 Only when I'd had time to recover **did I** realize what a lucky escape I'd had.
8 Only after experiencing it ourselves **could we** understand how difficult it is.
9 **Only after** preparing for six months did they feel ready to take the exam.
10 **Not since** my teenage years have I been so excited about a concert.
11 **Hardly** had he started to speak when someone interrupted him.
12 **Not only** do we produce these dolls here, but we make them all by hand.

44.6

1 True 2 False 3 Not given 4 True
5 True

44.7

1 Hardly had we pitched our tent when it began to rain.
2 Rarely do I feel as happy as when I'm alone.
3 Not since I was a young girl have I danced.
4 Only after calling him five times did he pick up.

45

45.1

1 What I would prefer is to take the train to the international airport.
2 What I really want is to hike the Inca Trail in Peru with my friends this year.
3 What I would really appreciate is some help with using the software to sort data.
4 What she was most surprised by was the party they threw for her birthday yesterday.
5 What we really need is some more time to get the booth ready for the annual fair.
6 What I hate is when people play music on their phones without using headphones.
7 What I really enjoyed was the day we spent at the local spa last weekend.
8 What he realized was that he didn't want to do that boring job for the rest of his life.
9 What I understood was that they aren't very happy about the sudden changes we're making.

45.2

1 The **time** I'd most like to go back to is Ancient Rome so I could visit the Colosseum.
2 The **meal** that I enjoy making the most is spaghetti carbonara. It's quick and easy.
3 The **subject** I liked the most at school was science, so I became a science teacher.
4 The **birthday** that I'll always remember is my twenty-first, when I had a huge party.
5 The **season** that I like the most is winter. I love walking in the snow.
6 The **famous person** I'd most like to have met is Alasdair Rove. I love his music and his style.
7 The **teacher** who influenced me the most is probably Mr. Lucas, my English teacher.
8 The **movie** that reminds me the most of my childhood is *Little Tim*. I loved it!
9 The **song** that always gets me up and dancing at a party is *Dancing Bells* by Claude Robert.

45.3

1 **Why** do you always take on more than you can actually do in a day?
2 **The place** that I would most like to be right now is a Caribbean beach.
3 **The person** I most admire and look up to is probably Shakespeare.
4 **The thing** he absolutely hates is people who talk while they're eating.
5 **Where** is Jonathan doing his Master's degree?
6 **The time of day** I like the most is first thing in the morning when I'm alone.

45.4

1 You went to France last year, didn't you? **No, it was Slovakia where we went.**
2 Didn't we meet for the first time in 2005? **No, it was 2006 when we first met.**
3 You met Sam at the party, didn't you? **No, it was Rosemary that I met.**
4 Wasn't it in Paris that he proposed? **No, actually it was in New York.**
5 Weren't we 10 when we went to Peru? **No, it was when we were 11.**
6 Wasn't it Mrs. Kins who taught us French? **No, it was Mrs. Bond who took that class.**
7 Didn't John go running with Philip? **No, it was David he did that with.**
8 Did you make this cake here? **No, it was Joanne who made that one.**
9 He majored in history in college, didn't he? **No, it was physics that he majored in.**

45.5

1 It was the young man at the visitor center that helped us a lot in New York.
2 It was an old lady that helped us find the way when we were lost in that Greek village.
3 It was your colleague Charles that I met at the Christmas party last year.
4 It was a restaurant in Florence where we ate the delicious steak by the river.
5 I think it was our second year in college when the two of us first met.

46

46.1

1 (beyond) reasonable doubt 2 convict a criminal 3 crime wave 4 deny all knowledge 5 arrest 6 jury
7 street crime 8 commit a crime
9 pass sentence 10 criminal record
11 reach a verdict 12 make a claim
13 be insured

47

47.1

1 Subject 2 Object 3 Subject
4 Object 5 Subject

47.2

1 The dog **which** is standing outside the police station is a drug-detection dog.
2 The woman **that** was crying had been robbed by two men on a motorcycle.
3 The man **who** was sent to prison had stolen hundreds of credit cards.
4 The man **who** is talking to the police officer had his car stolen.
5 The job **which** I'd like to do after my graduation is in crime prevention.

47.3

1 The old man **who / that** got lost in the city is 98 years old.
2 The lion **which / that** was born in captivity was released into the wild.
3 The crime **which / that** we reported is being broadcast on TV!
4 The woman **who / that** found Samantha's purse is a cleaner.
5 The cat **which / that** I recently adopted is black and white.
6 The woman **who / that** I introduced you to last Wednesday is a model.

47.4

1 The rooster **that crows loudly all day** belongs to my neighbor.
2 A movie **which won a lot of awards** is *Crazy Cuckoo*.
3 The woman **I dated last year** is now married.
4 The runner **who won the marathon** was running his first race.
5 The jacket **which I bought five years ago** is now falling apart.
6 The restaurant **that serves the best food** is in the main square.
7 The school **I went to as a little girl** is now a hotel.
8 The teacher **who I liked best at school** was Mr. Jenkins.

47.5

1 The stolen goods**,** which were extremely valuable**,** were found by the police.
2 My little brother**,** who is only six**,** is always getting into trouble at school.
3 The robbers**,** who were all from Southampton**,** were caught as they tried to leave the crime scene.
4 My house**,** which I moved into two months ago**,** has been burgled.

47.6

1 The robber, **who** left his fingerprints behind, was easily caught by the police.
2 My wallet, **which** was in my bag, was stolen while we were in the market.
3 Mr. Townsend, **who** is a suspect in a murder inquiry, has fled the country.
4 My credit card details, **which** I'd used for an online purchase, were stolen.

47.7

1 Not given 2 True 3 True
4 False 5 Not given 6 True
7 Not given 8 False 9 True

48

48.1

1 That's the restaurant **where** we ate that excellent chicken curry.
2 There was an agreement **whereby** both sides decided to support each other.
3 This is the church **where** my parents got married 30 years ago.
4 He's thinking about the time **when** we went to Barcelona for the weekend.
5 We use an application procedure **whereby** everything is done electronically.
6 The director talked about the area **where** the film was shot.
7 That's the office **where** my colleagues Jessica and Peter work.
8 We're now in the packing area **where** all of the items are packed.
9 Heat treatment is a process **whereby** heat is applied to metals.
10 This photo is from the semester **when** we lived in the dorm.
11 We provide a system **whereby** companies can find talented people.

48.2

1 The kitchen is **the room where** I most enjoy spending my time. I just love cooking.
2 Early morning is **the time of day when** I'm by myself and can have some peace and quiet.
3 Spring is **the season when** we most enjoy going out for walks in the country.
4 Photosynthesis is **the process whereby** plants convert sunlight into energy.
5 This is **the exhibition hall where** the last annual trade fair for construction systems was held.

48.3

1 The TV program gave us a lot of information about the process **whereby** cheese is produced.
2 That was the big museum in New York **where** they have those wonderful Picasso masterpieces.
3 That was the time **when** the car broke down and we had to wait hours before someone came to help.
4 I'm just waiting for the moment **when** everyone goes quiet so I can start speaking.
5 We're looking at the process **whereby** fuel is burned to create the steam that drives the turbine.

48.4

2

48.5

1 Fiona, whose dog is large and energetic, always walks in the park in the morning.
2 ZFF, whose CEO gave an interview on TV last night, is a company that is starting to work in China.
3 Jack, whose school has received more money for music classes, is learning to play the trumpet.
4 Francesca, whose computer has just crashed, is really stressed out right now.
5 Mandy, whose mother has suddenly become ill, took some time off work last week.
6 The company, whose employees now have unlimited time off, has innovative HR policies.
7 The tennis club, whose tennis courts are located on the outskirts of the town, is expanding every year.

48.6 Model Answers

1 The writer didn't notice anything unusual when he got home from work that day.
2 The writer found out that the smoke was actually coming from across the hall where Mr. Jerome lives.
3 The writer called the fire department. It arrived at the apartment building when the smoke was really starting to build up.
4 The firefighters organized a procedure whereby some of them tried to enter from the balcony and others tried to break down the door.
5 There wasn't too much damage to the apartment where the fire started.
6 Nobody was hurt in the fire.

49

49.1

1 Unfortunately, I will have to cancel our meeting because I won't be able to make it.
2 Will you be able to pay the fine if you park your car in this restricted zone?
3 I won't be able to get to sleep if my neighbors are making a lot of noise.

4 Will you have to stay in and study for your final exams?
5 We will have to get a good night's sleep tonight because we have an early start.
6 Will you have to take all six exams this semester?
7 We will not be able to meet our deadlines because the company hasn't delivered on time.
8 Will you be able to help me translate this text from Portuguese to English?
9 I won't be able to help you with the translation because I'm really busy at the moment.

49.2

1 We will have to work hard next month.
2 Will you have to look after the visitors all day?
3 They won't have to do everything on their own.
4 We will have to recycle more of our paper.

49.3

1 Next year we **will have to** save more money, so that we'll be able to buy a house soon.
2 I'm sorry, but I **will not be able to** come to your concert this evening. I have to work late.
3 **Will you be able to** join us for our annual school reunion next week? It would be great to see you.
4 We **will not be able to** visit the clients in person this Friday, so we will have to call them instead.
5 **Will he have to** travel a lot in his new job or will he be able to stay at home a little bit more?

49.4

1 According to the weather forecast, it will snow tomorrow, so we **will be able to** go skiing.
2 He **won't be able to** take the course he wanted to do because it's been canceled.
3 I hope that one day every person **will be able to** realize their full potential.
4 When we turn the next corner, you **will be able to** see the beach and the ocean.
5 She's so happy that she **won't have to** wear braces on her teeth any more.
6 If you want to come to the party, you **will have to** let me know by Friday at the latest.
7 If anyone would like a signed copy of the book, you **will be able to** buy one later.
8 You **won't have to** do so much paperwork now that you've got a secretary.

49.5 Model Answers

1 He won't be able to get very good grades and he may even fail.
2 Peter is able to make everyone think that everything's OK, even when it isn't.
3 If Peter doesn't pass his exams, he'll have to repeat the year.
4 Peter will be able to get some extra support over the next few months if Mr. Foster is able to give it to him.

49.6

1 True 2 True 3 True 4 Not given
5 False 6 Not given 7 True
8 False 9 True

50

50.1

1 He's a great runner. He **can** run twelve miles in two hours.
2 **May** I have another piece of cake? It's delicious.
3 That **can't** be Dominic at the door because he's in Spain at the moment.
4 When I was younger, I **could** party all night, but now I'm older I can't.
5 **Shall** we have lunch together on Thursday? It would be great to catch up.
6 Don't worry, I **will** make sure that everything's ready on time.
7 **Would** you go down to reception and meet the visitors for me?
8 Joanna said she **might** join us, but she probably wouldn't be able to make it.
9 You've had that cough for two weeks now. You **should** go to the doctor.

50.2

1 You **must** take your laptop out of your bag before you go through security control.
2 You **may** stay here as long as you want. Just remember to lock the door when you leave.
3 **Shall** I give you a ride home afterward? I'll be in the area at that time anyway.
4 **May** I help you carry your suitcase up the stairs?
5 When I was a child I **couldn't** do a handstand, but now I can!
6 **Will** you help me prepare the training course for our Spanish colleagues?
7 If that doesn't work, you **could** call Edward and ask him if he knows what to do.
8 Since he had his operation, he **can't** walk more than 10 steps.

50.3

1 Don't put your fingers so close to the pan. **You could burn yourself.**
2 Should I help you move those boxes, **so you don't have so much to do?**
3 Will you check that the door **is locked when you leave?**
4 You must go to reception to register **before you can go to the meeting room.**
5 May I have another cookie? **They taste delicious!**
6 I can't speak French very well, **but I can understand a lot.**
7 He ought to go to the hairdresser and **get a decent haircut for a change.**
8 Would you call and ask **if it's OK for us to arrive a little later?**

50.4

1 You should have asked your boss to pay you for the overtime you did.
2 He lost his voice, so he couldn't teach his classes last week.
3 I can't find my keys anywhere. I must have left them at home.
4 She should have asked me for advice. I would have been able to help.
5 Could you visit the museum when you were on vacation, or was it closed?

50.5

1 You should have **brought** your laptop to the meeting. Sarah reminded you yesterday.
2 They ought to **have** more respect for the neighbors when they have a party.
3 Why didn't you ask? I would **have** shared a taxi from the airport to the hotel with you.
4 I know what happened. We must **have taken** a wrong turn just after we left the hotel.

51

51.1

1 values
2 bad habit
3 lifestyle
4 stereotype
5 local custom
6 blend in
7 diversity
8 acclimate
9 manners
10 cause offense
11 nationality
12 globalization
13 dialect

52

52.1

1 The Dutch 2 Kenyans 3 The Swiss
4 The Vietnamese 5 Australians
6 Egyptians 7 Argentinians
8 Koreans 9 The Spanish 10 Greeks
11 The Japanese 12 Brazilians 13 The British

52.2

1 We're looking for ways of helping **the homeless find accommodation.**
2 The young often have a reputation **for being wild and irresponsible.**
3 The British are known for their love of **fish and chips.**
4 Some people believe that the rich **should pay a much higher level of tax.**
5 Pets are seen as excellent companions f**or the elderly.**
6 We have started distributing food **to the poor.**
7 The injured were airlifted to the hospital **immediately after the accident.**

52.3

1 We've built these ramps and put in these rails to help **the disabled** access the building.
2 I think that **the rich** should give away more of their money to people who are in need.
3 The emergency services have given **the injured** all of the medical attention they need.
4 **The young** are the group who are likely to spend the most time using social media.
5 In Nairobi, **the poor** live on the edges of the city in homes they've built themselves.
6 Ancient **Egyptians** worshipped cats.
7 We offer accomodation for **the elderly** who can no longer live alone.
8 **The Swiss** are known throughout the world for making clocks and chocolate.
9 We don't want **the healthy** to come into contact with infectious diseases.
10 If you'd like to help **the homeless** who live on our streets, come along to our soup kitchen.
11 **The unemployed** sometimes aren't offered very much help with finding a new job.
12 He decided to become a doctor because he wanted to help **the sick**.

52.4

1 Unemployed people are welcome to come and volunteer at the library if they want to.
2 Our charity was set up to help the elderly by organizing a weekly social meet-up for them.
3 The majority of Germans were in support of the decision.
4 Our first priority is to help the injured. Then we can talk to journalists about what's happened.
5 This fort was built by the Dutch in the late 1600s.
6 The government wants to introduce a new law, which will make the rich pay more in taxes.
7 These parking spaces are only for the disabled. Can you please park somewhere else?
8 Most Brazilians are taught English at school.
9 The homeless are sometimes seen as dangerous, but this is far from the truth.
10 The British are coming over here to learn more about our processes and how we do things.
11 I decided to become a nurse because I really wanted to be able to help the sick.
12 The French are known for being very relaxed and this is also something I've noticed.

52.5 Model Answers

1 The poor **are supported by the government and by charities.**
2 The sick **are often reluctant to see a doctor as healthcare can be expensive.**
3 The disabled **are considered every time a new building is constructed.**
4 The unemployed **are encouraged to volunteer in a field that interests them.**
5 The young **are always portrayed as loud and lazy.**
6 The homeless **have to rely on donations from strangers.**
7 The rich **are seen as a very lucky group of people.**

53

53.1

1 It took me a while to **get** used to the stores being closed on Sundays here.
2 He's been starting work at 6am for three months now, so he **is** used to it.
3 As we live in the north of Norway, we **are** used to very cold weather in winter.
4 I'm still **getting** used to the fast pace of activity in my new company.
5 When he first went to live in Australia, he **wasn't** used to the heat and got burned.
6 You've been working with us for some time, so you **are** used to the way we work now.
7 I just can't **get** used to working every weekend. I don't think I'll ever like it.
8 Don't worry about Rachel! She **is** used to traveling on her own.
9 When we had our first child, we had to **get** used to not having very much sleep.
10 We've had our new boss for six months now, but I'm still **getting** used to her style.
11 Jeremy lives in Los Angeles, so he **is** used to living through minor earthquakes.

53.2

1 Three years after moving, I think we **are** finally used to life in the country and really like it.
2 After a while you'll **get** used to the rhythm of the train and fall asleep.
3 He **is** used to sleeping on a very soft bed at home, so he doesn't like hard beds.
4 I was just **getting** used to our old English teacher when she left and we got a new one.
5 He **is** now so used to wearing glasses that he doesn't even notice them anymore.
6 I **was** used to taking the train every day and I knew the timetable by heart.

53.3

1 Our customers from other countries **are** used to getting very high quality products from us.
2 I don't think Christina will ever **get** used to living on her own. She doesn't like it.
3 **We're** used to being able to communicate with people from all over the world online.
4 My friend is **not used** to eating spicy food, so it makes him go red in the face.
5 He is still **getting** used to the new house he bought last year.
6 Our children Joseph and Liz are used to **being** away from the two of us while we're at work.

53.4

1 You will have to get used to working **long hours if you want to be on this team.**
2 We were used to bringing lunch **to work, but now we eat in the canteen.**
3 Jack's slowly getting used to living **in a dorm instead of at home.**
4 The new shoes were uncomfortable, **but she soon got used to them.**
5 I'm used to sitting through long and **boring lectures. I do it every day.**

53.5

1 The UK 2 His boss 3 Japan 4 Direct
5 Strangers 6 Nice restaurants
7 Street markets

53.6

1 Our neighbors are so loud, but we'll just have to **get used to** the noise.
2 I've lived in Tokyo for 10 years now, so I'm **used to** Japanese food.
3 My boss was pleased about how quickly I **got used to** giving presentations.
4 We may have to **get used to** traveling a little farther to get to the shops soon.
5 We were just **getting used to** the new office when we had to move to another one.
6 He's been working in virtual teams for a long time now, so he's **used to** it.

53.7

1 was used to 2 get used to
3 get used to 4 was used to
5 get used to 6 get used to
7 get used to 8 get used to
9 are used to

54

54.1

1 **The** investors who come to us have a lot of money to invest in companies.
2 We paid for **an** audio guide in the palace and it gave us some interesting information.
3 **The** CEO of our company is surprisingly young. He's only 30 years old!
4 If you want to travel cheaply in Paris, you should take **the** Métro.
5 After dinner, I bought **an** ice cream cone and ate it while I was sitting by the fountain.
6 The Eiffel Tower is probably **the** most famous landmark in Paris.
7 We were so busy and did so much walking that I need **an** early night tonight.
8 The flag is up, so **the** Queen must be in the palace today.
9 It's amazing how quickly **the** company's share price is going up at the moment.
10 We're thinking about hiring **a** boat tomorrow and taking it out on the water.
11 My hotel has **a** beautiful view of the harbor and the sea.

54.2

1 The people who live in our town **don't want the new road to be built.**
2 The restaurant we went to last night **is the one where pizza was invented.**
3 I don't know why, but spaghetti **always tastes better when you're in Italy.**
4 A large number of vacationers **want to stay in an all-inclusive hotel.**
5 City tours that are free **usually aren't as good as ones you pay for.**

54.3

1 **The** Petronas Towers are the tallest buildings in Kuala Lumpur and they dominate the skyline.
2 If you go up to the top of the tower, you get **an** excellent view of Kuala Lumpur.
3 Street food stands on the side of **the** road are great places to try Malaysian food.
4 You can also visit **the** Islamic Arts Museum if you go to Kuala Lumpur. It's interesting.
5 Taking **a** day trip to the nearby Batu Caves is a good idea if you have time.
6 Have you walked through **the** colorful China Town market in Kuala Lumpur?

54.4

1 This is **the** old typewriter that my mother always used to use.
2 People from Brazil are known for their love of **[-]** football.
3 I've never seen such **a** wide selection of foods for breakfast as they had there.
4 They love **[-]** Chinese food, so I'm sure they'll enjoy their trip to China.
5 Our tour guide is **an** older lady who's lived in Dublin all her life.
6 There's **a** university in Bologna which is nearly 1,000 years old.
7 Here's our guide to **the** travel destinations that will be the most popular next year.
8 **The** waitress who served us at that restaurant was very friendly and helpful.
9 Children usually enjoy visiting **the** zoo in Edinburgh. You can even see pandas there.
10 Churros are very popular in **[-]** Spain. People eat them with chocolate sauce.
11 I wasn't sure whether we should leave **a** tip for the waiter or not.
12 **The** music festival we went to was brilliant. There were a lot of good bands playing.
13 **The** hotel where we stayed is a five-star hotel, so it was very luxurious.

54.5

1 False 2 True 3 True 4 True 5 False

54.6

1 Let's call a plum**b**er to fix the water heater.
2 Forei**g**n visitors think we speak good English.
3 I hurt my **k**nee while we were trekking.
4 I like to lis**t**en to music while I'm traveling.
5 To be **h**onest, I don't think I like him.
6 It's so cold. My fingers are num**b**.
7 He has just trapped his thum**b** in the door!

55

55.1

1 We often find that men aren't as good at taking care of their **health** as women are.
2 She made her **anger** at the graffiti on the wall clear to everyone in the room.
3 Unfortunately, the funding for all of the **libraries** in our area has been cut this year.
4 He's been having some **trouble** getting his computer to start all week.
5 Could you please email me all of the **information** I need for my trip to Peru?
6 Our company specializes in creating **beauty** products for young women.
7 He has a lot of **knowledge** about the history of the Middle Ages.
8 I've made a list of all the **deadlines** for the project in this document.
9 We take a lot of **pride** in our work and always do our very best.
10 It's absolutely freezing today. It must be about minus fifteen **degrees** outside!
11 We're facing some fierce **competition** from companies in South America.

55.2

1 My **thoughts** are with the families of the victims of the disaster at this terrible time.
2 I come from Nigeria and my **culture** is very important to me. I keep the traditions alive.
3 Our **hope** is that our daughter will go to college and get a good job.
4 Your **friendship** is really important to me, and I hope you feel the same.
5 My happiest childhood **memories** are of spending the summer in Sweden with my family.
6 I save some money every month and then at the end of the year I give it to local **charities**.

55.3

1 You can now all find out what **grades you got on the exam.**
2 My car has a top speed **of 100 miles per hour.**
3 The kittens your cat gave **birth to are real beauties.**
4 I'm going to write the neighbors **a letter of apology for all of the noise.**
5 My cousin Matthew repairs **computers for a living.**
6 We're here today because we're **interested in learning more about other cultures.**
7 Nowadays it's more and more **important to have good communication skills.**
8 I make a living from entering **competitions. You can win so much!**
9 You have to study for six **semesters before you get your degree.**

55.4

1 The temperatures this summer are some of the highest in living **memory**.
2 I work hard on my **friendships** because friends are an important part of my life.
3 She hopes that she will complete her **studies** and graduate next summer.
4 We're collecting money for **charity**, but we haven't decided which one we'll give it to yet.
5 There are a lot of free parking **spaces** at the front of the building if you're still looking.
6 You will be in our **thoughts** while you're away and we'll call you as often as we can.
7 There's always a lot of **competition** in the soft drink market. It's hard to break through.
8 He takes so much **pride** in his garden and he wants other people to enjoy it, too.
9 There are so many **times** when I wish I had a robot who could do the housework for me.
10 She decided to take all of her **knowledge** about marketing and put it into a book.
11 The **skill** he has for soccer is unbelievable for someone of his age.
12 The company is known for the very high **quality** of their kitchen products.

56

56.1

1. make predictions
2. what the future holds
3. only a matter of time
4. have an influence on something
5. future-proof
6. revolution
7. the latest model
8. breakthrough
9. make arrangements
10. have good intentions
11. digital age
12. hope for the best
13. cutting-edge

57

57.1

1. My job at the supermarket is so boring, I wish I **could** find another one.
2. I wish Rosemary **would stop** talking about herself all the time. It's so annoying!
3. I wish my teacher **would** give me more help. I don't understand any of this.
4. They wish they **could** take some time off work so they could go on vacation.
5. He wishes he **could** win the first prize in the competition he's entered.
6. She **wishes** she could get a leading role in the play, but she never goes to auditions.
7. I wish I **could** afford to get a new kitchen. This one is so old it's falling apart.
8. Adam wishes his teacher **would** give him more homework. He doesn't have enough to do.
9. I wish they **would** make it easier to work out how much tax you have to pay.

57.2

1. I wish my boss **would** be a little more polite. He's always rude to everyone.
2. Linda wishes she **could** drive to work, but she still hasn't passed her driving test.
3. They wish their neighbors **would** be a bit quieter. They're always making noise.
4. I wish they **would** tell us what's going to happen now instead of making us wait.
5. Jacob wishes he **could** relax, but he can't because he's having a stressful time at work.
6. I wish we **could** go on a helicopter ride around Manhattan, but we can't afford it.
7. Susanne wishes her daughter **would** call her more often. She only calls once a month.
8. I wish the people on the train **would** move their bags off the seats next to them.
9. They wish they **could** get a good espresso in this town, but they can't find one anywhere.

57.3

1. My job is really boring. I wish **I could find something more interesting.**
2. The snails are eating my plants. I wish **I could get rid of them once and for all.**
3. The rules are so complicated. I wish **they would make them simpler.**
4. I can't type very quickly. I wish **my boss would let me take a course.**
5. They always leave a mess. I wish **they would think about other people.**
6. The bus always takes so long. I wish **I could drive instead.**
7. I'm so sleepy. I wish **I could go to bed.**
8. That machine is very noisy. I wish **someone would turn it off.**

57.4

1. The students wish they **could** speak perfect English.
2. He wishes his teacher **would** give him more help.
3. She wishes she **could** go to the party.
4. We wish they **would** let us leave work early.

57.5

1. She wants to travel less
2. Far away from headquarters
3. Move the headquarters to a better place
4. Internal sales team leader
5. Geoff is going to retire

57.6

1. Jessica wishes she could relax and take it easy this summer.
2. Jessica wishes you could get an accountancy job straight after leaving college.
3. It will be another five years before Jessica is a qualified accountant.
4. Jessica wishes she could go to the beach with Josh on Monday.

58

58.1

1. Sheila is sick, so she**'ll be working** from home for the rest of the week.
2. This time next week, I**'ll be sitting** on a beach in the Caribbean.
3. The boss thinks that in 10 years' time I**'ll be running** this company myself.
4. They**'ll be traveling** for the next two hours and won't be able to take any calls.
5. It looks like we**'ll be spending** a lot of time together over the next few months.
6. The pilots are on strike, so I think I**'ll be waiting** at the airport for a while.
7. Will you **be bringing** your husband and children with you tomorrow?
8. He**'ll be standing** near the entrance waiting for us when we get there.
9. I**'ll be driving** past the stores later if you want me to get some groceries.
10. We **won't be launching** our new perfume until the trade fair next year.
11. James has applied for some jobs, so I think he**'ll be leaving** the company soon.

58.2

1. By this time next week, I'll be working in a big city.
2. By this time tomorrow, I'll be working in a big city.
3. By this time tomorrow, I'll be working as a manager.
4. By this time tomorrow, I'll be living in a big city.
5. By this time tomorrow, I'll be relaxing on vacation.
6. By this time next week, I'll be working as a manager.
7. By this time next week, I'll be living in a big city.
8. By this time next week, I'll be relaxing on vacation.
9. In five years' time, I'll be working in a big city.
10. In five years' time, I'll be working as a manager.
11. In five years' time, I'll be living in a big city.
12. In five years' time, I'll be relaxing on vacation.

58.3

1. The next time I go to the mountains, I'll be **skiing** like an expert.
2. In a few years' time, **I'll be** playing basketball professionally.
3. We will **be** hosting some visitors from China next week.
4. This evening **they'll** be serving snacks and drinks for everyone.
5. In five years' time, I won't be **teaching** at a primary school any more.
6. Will you **be** asking for input from the audience during your presentation?

58.4

1. We'll be using this software in 10 years' time.
2. Lisa will be working until 6pm today.
3. The bus will be leaving in five minutes.
4. This train will be stopping at Central Station.
5. Next week, I will be working from home.

58.5

1 True 2 False 3 Not given
4 True 5 False

58.6 Model Answers

1 In a few years' time, five billion people will be shopping online.
2 Around half of these people will be using tablets to access the internet.
3 Connected devices will become so integrated into our lives that we'll see them as "digital assistants."
4 We can assume that someone, somewhere will be buying something online right now.
5 Every retail company will be selling their products on the web in 10 years' time.
6 Future internet users will be able to get online wherever they are.

59

59.1

1 I **will have finished** my degree by the time I am 22.
2 You **will have been** married for one year in a week's time.
3 We **will have completed** all our essays by the end of June.
4 By the time I am 24, I **will have found** a good job.
5 I think my son **will have proposed** to his girlfriend by the end of the year.
6 By the time we are 30, we **will have had** our first child.
7 Liza **will have moved** to London by the end of the month.
8 I **will have graduated** from college by this time next year.
9 By the time I am 25, I **will have left** my parents' house.
10 I **will have made** one million dollars by the time I'm 40.
11 They **will have started** their new business by the end of the month.

59.2

1 will have found 2 will have perfected
3 will have opened 4 will have been
5 will have sold 6 will have increased
7 will have made 8 will have taken
9 will have launched

59.3

1 They **will have chosen** the best candidate by the end of the day.
2 Jenny **will have bought** a new dress before the wedding.
3 By the end of the year, I **will have completed** three marathons.
4 I **will have opened** all my presents by the end of the party.
5 By the time he starts his new job, Hans **will have had** his hair cut.
6 We **will have visited** 15 countries by the end of this year.

59.4

1 By the time we arrive in Spain, we **will have been driving** for eight hours.
2 Jenna **will have been running** her own business for five years in May.
3 In June, I **will have been working** as a teacher for 10 years.
4 By the time the cake is decorated, we **will have been cooking** for six hours.
5 I **will have been doing** yoga for 10 years by the end of the year.
6 In November, Becky and I **will have been living** together for three years.
7 By midday, Jonas **will have been waiting** to see the doctor for three hours.
8 By the time I have finished, I **will have been cleaning** the house for five hours.
9 By the time the plane lands in Malaysia, we **will have been traveling** for 13 hours.
10 By December, I **will have been learning** to paint for six months.
11 I **will have been studying** medicine for four years by the end of June.
12 By the end of next month, the police **will have been looking** for the criminals for a year.

59.5

1 At the end of the week, Lise will have been studying in France for three months.
2 This time tomorrow, I will have had my operation.
3 I will have finished this report by the time you get here.
4 Next week, I will have been studying for two years.
5 By the end of January, I will have finished my Italian course.
6 In two hours, I will have written my last report for this client.

59.6

1 been 2 had 3 known 4 been

60

60.1

1 I always thought that I **would** go to college, but I then decided to get a job instead.
2 As soon as I get home, I **will** give you a call to let you know I've arrived safely.
3 I'm sure that we **will** still be friends when we're older. There's no doubt about that.
4 He said that he **would** try to get me some tickets for the soccer game if he could.

60.2

1 I got up so late, I knew I wasn't going to get to the airport in time.
2 Sarah's an excellent swimmer, so I knew it was going to be hard to beat her.
3 My mother promised she wasn't going to embarrass me by hugging me in public.
4 I found the exam easy, so I believed I was going to get a good grade.
5 He knew he wasn't going to get the job, but he wanted to apply for it anyway.

60.3

1 They couldn't come last week because they **were** going to a soccer game that evening.
2 She **was taking** her English exam the next day, so she felt a little nervous.
3 They **were** meeting with their lawyers that afternoon to decide what to do.
4 Sandra **was** planning to fly to Tenerife with her daughter yesterday, but the pilots are on strike.
5 Gareth **was** making a big announcement that afternoon, but then he lost his voice.
6 Camy and Charlie **were** having a big party to celebrate their anniversary that weekend.
7 Harren **was** getting married to Jennifer at 2 o'clock that afternoon in New York.

60.4

1 No 2 Yes 3 No

60.5

1 I knew that I would be the marketing head of a leading company one day.
2 When I saw him I knew that I was going to marry him and move to another country.
3 I was taking my last exam in chemistry at college that afternoon.
4 I thought I would travel around the world working as a part-time photographer.
5 She believed she would get a recording contract as soon as she finished her course at college.
6 I knew I would be late when I saw how much traffic there was on the road.
7 I was meeting some Chinese customers that morning for a presentation on distribution.
8 I thought Shania and Jo would go somewhere warm for their holiday that year.
9 He was building an extension on the back of their house in Germany.
10 I decided I would retire early and spend more time with my family and close friends.
11 I knew I was going to be able to climb to the top of the mountain sooner than the others.
12 The company was interviewing some more people for the marketing job that week.

61

61.1

1 highbrow / lowbrow
2 novels
3 speak your mind
4 highly recommend
5 characters
6 plot
7 heap praise / criticism on something
8 glowing reviews
9 lasting impression
10 change your mind
11 make up your mind
12 opening / closing scenes
13 create an atmosphere

62

62.1

1 The ceremony honored firemen and paramedics.
2 We could go to the session on marketing or this talk on public relations.
3 It would be nice to go the theater or a film. You can decide.
4 This process was described by Gutmann and Quirke.
5 She could have directed the TV series or the film version.
6 They should use paper bags and recycle more of their garbage.
7 He might have become a great writer, but he didn't want to.
8 The problem is that he wants to leave work early, but she doesn't.
9 He was chosen to play the lead role and did an excellent job.
10 I could wear this yellow dress for the wedding or this blue skirt.
11 You could eat at the new Italian restaurant or the Mexican restaurant.

62.2

1 Your parents 2 Its plot 3 Spoof
4 Dedicated sci-fi fans 5 Sequel

62.3

1 I'm so sorry! I broke your television, but I didn't mean to [**break your television**].
2 We can't go to the movies tonight but we can [**go to the movies**] tomorrow.
3 He told me he could speak French, but I don't think he can [**speak French**].
4 My daughter loves horror films and [**my daughter loves**] thrillers.
5 We went to Venice and [**we**] rode in a gondola this summer.
6 She could sit in the kitchen or [**she could sit in**] the garden.
7 Do we need a new computer? We could get a laptop or [**we could get**] a tablet instead.
8 It's such a beautiful day. We should go to the park or [**we should go to**] the beach.
9 The critics loved the latest blockbuster and [**the critics**] said it was worth watching.
10 I need to borrow your car. I will email shortly to explain why [**I need to borrow your car**].

62.4

1 True 2 False 3 True 4 False
5 True 6 False 7 False

62.5

1 I worked really hard on my entry, so I was **bitterly** disappointed that I didn't win.
2 The line for tickets at the museum was **painfully** slow. I thought we would never get in.
3 I won't go to that restaurant again. The prices were **astronomically** high!
4 The trip was **ridiculously** long because we were stuck in traffic for two hours.
5 I was **deeply** moved by the poem she read at her mother's funeral.
6 Everyone knows that farmers in this country are **heavily** subsidized.
7 I think you should avoid mentioning any **highly** controversial topics in your talk.

62.6

1 We went for a walk in the woods **and took some wonderful photos of the trees.**
2 She emailed and called everyone **she knew who might be able to help.**
3 The cathedral is beautiful **and is the seat of the Bishop of Rouen.**
4 Do you think we should go on **a beach or city break?**
5 He went cycling along the Rhine **and visited a lot of vineyards.**
6 I want to move, **but he doesn't.**
7 Could you call or email him **and ask him to confirm the details.**
8 I can remember his name, **but not his face. It's been a long time.**
9 They went to Mauritius and **stayed at a wonderful resort on the coast.**
10 Do you want to cook **or go out for dinner tonight?**

63

63.1

1 I've eaten a lot of pizza in my time, but the **one** I ate in Rome last year was the best.
2 I love these high-heeled shoes, but I think it's time I got some new **ones**.
3 Kirsten did well on both parts of the exam, but she did especially well on the first **one**.
4 I really like the movies he's in, especially the earlier **ones** from the start of his career.
5 Our daughter likes a lot of subjects at school, but the **one** she enjoys the most is science.
6 Mike has written a few books, but I think the first thriller he wrote is the best **one**.
7 Ann tried on 10 different wedding dresses before she found the **one** she wanted.
8 There are many activities for older children and some for younger **ones.**
9 I love all of the cakes Sam makes, but the **one** she made today was really delicious.
10 I've been to a lot of countries, but the **one** I enjoyed visiting the most was Japan.
11 Sarah isn't happy with her office assistant, so she wants to get a new **one.**

63.2

1 If you need any pens to write with, I have **some** here.
2 If you'd like a copy of my notes, I will print **one** for you.
3 They need some more batteries because the **ones** I gave them last time have run out.
4 If you find anywhere selling cups of coffee, could you get me **one**?
5 There's water here in case you need to use **some** while you're painting.
6 My new computer is slower than the **one** I got rid of when I bought it.
7 This cheeseburger tastes as good as the **one** I ate in the other restaurant.

63.3

1 If you need any more paper to write on, there's **some** on my desk.
2 If you're looking for some new running shoes, I'd recommend the **ones** on the left.
3 I have three tickets and I only need two, so I could give you **one** if you like.
4 If you need any information about the building, ask me and I'll give you **some**.
5 If they like Italian restaurants, there's a great **one** just down the road.
6 I think Jenny and Matthew's wedding was the best **one** I've ever been to.

63.4

1 I know you want a new computer, **but we can't afford one.**

2 My sister bought me an album, **but it wasn't the one I wanted.**
3 If you're looking for bookstores, **there are some on Upper Street.**
4 I think my favorite authors **are the ones who write about vampires.**
5 We should buy new flowers **and get rid of these old ones.**
6 Please help yourself to tea or coffee **if you would like some.**
7 I wanted to bring a cake, **but I didn't have time to bake one.**

63.5

1 I didn't enjoy it, but my friend did.
2 Did you see the new movie? We did, too.
3 You bought a blue hat! I did, too.
4 Do I still cycle to work? Yes, I do.
5 He works downtown, but she doesn't.
6 My mom went, but my dad didn't.
7 Did you bring your camera? I didn't.
8 You baked cookies! I did, too.
9 Does she like reading? Yes, she does.
10 They went skiing last year, but we didn't.
11 My friend found it difficult. I did, too.

63.6

1 False 2 False 3 True 4 True
5 True 6 True

63.7 Model Answers

1 I hope so!
2 I think so.
3 No, Steven Spielberg did.
4 I don't imagine so.
5 I assume so.

64

64.1

1 I wanted to wake up early today, but I wasn't able to.
2 Stefan was enjoying the ballet. At least, he seemed to be.
3 I'm so nervous! I'm singing on stage tonight, but I really don't want to.
4 Your dog likes chasing people a lot more than he used to.
5 I'm so thirsty! I meant to buy a drink before the movie, but I forgot.
6 Don't be nervous. There's no need to be.
7 Darren said he'd help us unpack, but it seems that he won't be able to.
8 I really wanted to go to that concert, but I couldn't afford to.
9 If you want to be promoted, you have to show me that you deserve to be.
10 Helena asked me to join the college choir, but I didn't want to.
11 I'm sorry I'm so late! I didn't mean to be.

64.2

1 I'd really like to go away this year, but I won't **be** able to.
2 Keisha said I should go to her party tonight, but I don't really want **to**.
3 I tried to find out Will's email address, but I wasn't **able** to.
4 Frankie liked the birthday present we bought her. At least, she seemed **to**.
5 I didn't realize that it was necessary to wear a tie, but apparently we have **to**.
6 I'm very concerned about my test results, even though the doctor says there's no need **to** be.

64.3

1 False 2 True 3 False 4 True 5 False

64.4

1 I'd really like to buy a new pair of shoes, **though I don't need to.**
2 I'm not sure if I can visit my aunt this weekend, **but I hope to.**
3 Jonas would really like to buy a car, **but he can't afford to.**
4 I'll watch a movie if all my friends want to, **but I wouldn't choose to.**
5 I don't insist on going to warm countries for vacations, **although I prefer to.**
6 I tried to get tickets for the concert, **but I wasn't able to.**

64.5

1 I am always really nervous before I go to the doctor's. It's difficult not **to be**.
2 It's not certain that I'll do well on my exams, but I **expect** to.
3 Marie wants me to go shopping with her, but I really don't **want** to.
4 I've never been to the US. I'd love the **chance**.
5 You can get a vaccination before your trip, but you don't **need** to.

64.6

1 I love listening to loud music, but my sister hates to.
2 You can leave work early this afternoon if you would like to.
3 Gigi asked me to go to her wedding and I said I'd be delighted to.
4 Don't agree to do the fun run if you really don't want to.

64.7

1 Yes, **I'd be delighted to.**
2 No, **I don't want to.**
3 No, **you don't need to.**
4 Yes, **she seemed to.**
5 No, **I can't afford to.**

65

65.1

1 Sorry, I had to take that call. So **as I was saying**, the gallery opened in 1903.
2 I've been to that museum, too. Hey, I love your shoes, **by the way**.
3 This gallery is beautiful. Oh, **by the way**, did you see there's a new café downstairs?
4 You think he's an expert? **Actually**, he doesn't really know anything about art.
5 **Anyway**, I'm afraid I will have to say goodbye now, but thank you for today.
6 No, **actually**, it was George who thought we should buy this painting, not me.
7 Mike's very happy because, **as I was saying**, he's getting married next September.
8 Yes, I'd like some coffee. So, **as I was saying**, we've got a lot of paintings at home.
9 **Anyway**, I'm sure you'll have a great time in Tokyo. See you when you get back!
10 So, **as I was saying**, Jenny and I have known each other for a long time.
11 Yes, **actually**, I've already been here a few times, so I know my way around.

65.2

1 Yes, but **as I was saying** before, I prefer Hockney.
2 No, it was sold out. **Anyway**, we should get moving!
3 I've already seen it, **actually**. I came here last month.
4 **Actually**, I've already been. But you go.

65.3

1 The fastest aircraft travel through the air at supersonic speeds.
2 Powerful computers can predict the outcomes of some experiments with amazing accuracy.
3 The first farms in human history were established in the Neolithic, or New Stone Age.
4 The postwar period, after the fighting had ended, saw an economic boom.

65.4

1 False 2 True 3 False 4 False 5 True

65.5

1 preview 2 superstructure
3 antibacterial 4 prolonged
5 neoclassical 6 postpone 7 antidote
8 superhuman 9 preassigned

65.6

1 He's interested in **neo**liberalism. I'm not sure what that is, but it's a new type of liberalism.
2 I've been enjoying the **pre**game buildup, but now I just can't wait for the game to start.
3 **Neo**classical architecture became popular when interest in ancient Greece rose again.
4 We've organized a **pre**-conference event so people can meet before the meetings start.
5 James must be **super**human! It's amazing how he manages to work and travel so much.
6 She specializes in **neo**natal care, so she looks after newborn babies.
7 **Post**modern art was a reaction by artists against the modernist art that came before it.
8 Instead of finishing her degree, she's decided to **post**pone her studies and go traveling.
9 You first go into the **ante**chamber of the tomb of Tutankhamun and then the main chamber.
10 If I could have any **super**power I wanted, I think it would be the ability to fly.
11 I've had enough of our neighbors' **anti**social behavior, they're always making noise!
12 We're celebrating the 50th anniversary of the introduction of **anti**discrimination laws.

66

66.1

1 I look so much better after having **my hair cut at the salon yesterday.**
2 Don't worry, we got the problem **with the internet sorted out in the end.**
3 Something's wrong with my back, so **I'm going to the doctor to get it checked.**
4 Ask the people at the restaurant if **we can get the food delivered to us.**
5 I'll call our landlord and ask him if **he can get the door fixed.**

66.2

1 My parents are having their house painted by a decorator.
2 He can't afford a new car, so he's getting it repaired.
3 Sally's getting her picture taken by a photographer.

66.3

1 False 2 True 3 False 4 False 5 False
6 True 7 False

66.4

1 Leah needs to go to the dentist as soon as possible **to have** her teeth fixed.
2 He's **getting** his birth certificate translated into English, so he can get married.
3 They **had** a marquee built in the grounds of the castle for their party last year.
4 She always **has** her essays checked by her mother before she hands them in.
5 My wedding ring **got** stolen when someone broke into our house last week.
6 We've been having problems with our website, but we're **getting** them sorted out.
7 Jessica can't come to the phone right now because she's **having** her nails done.
8 We've **had** a lot of changes made to the house since we moved in five years ago.
9 He's been **having** his hair cut at that barber's shop since he was five years old.

66.5

1 get 2 have 3 got 4 have
5 have 6 get 7 having
8 checked 9 check 10 had

66.6

1 I got a pizza delivered.
2 I got my car fixed.
3 We're having our house painted.
4 I'm getting my shirts dry-cleaned.
5 I got my picture taken.
6 I got the oven repaired.
7 I got my teeth checked.
8 They're having their garden landscaped.
9 I had my essay translated.
10 I got my eyesight tested.
11 I got my laundry done.

66.7

1 I'm having problems with my eyes, so I went to the optician to **get them checked**.
2 You won't believe it. I **had it stolen** when we were on vacation!
3 You can either pick the pizza up from the restaurant or you can **have it delivered**.
4 The business cards are here. Would you like me to **have them sent** to your home address?
5 No, but I can't believe how filthy it is. I need to **have it dry-cleaned** as soon as possible.
6 No, the internet at home still isn't working properly. We need to **get it sorted out** this week.
7 No, I'm going to the hairdresser's to **have it cut.**

67

67.1

1 The **audience** was so appreciative of our performance that they gave us three encores.
2 All the **staff** at the hotel where we stayed were extremely friendly and helpful.
3 My son's **orchestra** is doing a concert at the town hall on Saturday evening.
4 Jake's **family** is always arguing. His brother and sister are the worst.
5 Next week, all the **teams** in the office are going to do extra training.
6 The **government** is holding an emergency session to discuss foreign policy issues.
7 Our **department** is known for being the most environmentally friendly in the company.
8 My **company** is the market leader in the digital industry and has been for 10 years now.
9 Later this afternoon our **panel** is going to be discussing the issues you mentioned.

67.2

1 Spain has a very long border with Portugal. It's one of the longest in Europe.
2 The Netherlands is one of the best countries to go on vacation if you like cycling.
3 He's great at soccer, but athletics is the sport that he wants to focus on from now on.
4 Politics was my favorite subject at school, so I decided to study it in college.
5 The news about the celebrity couple was very hard to believe.

67.3

1 Either an essay or a report **is required by the end of this week.**
2 Neither my mom nor my dad **was there when I got home.**
3 Neither my cell phone nor my laptop **is connected to the internet.**
4 Media studies is a very popular **subject among the students.**
5 I think that either a dog or a cat **is the best pet to get.**
6 Neither my teacher nor my friends **know when our test will be.**
7 Either a box of chocolates or some perfume **is the best gift to give someone.**
8 Logistics is the area of the business world **that's the most interesting to me.**

67.4

1 All of the information about this **is** available to you on the college's website.
2 Neither my dad nor my mom **were** very happy when I got suspended from school.
3 **Is** *The Dragon Leader* a good book or do you not like fantasy novels?
4 Either pop music or rock music **is** what I like to listen to when I'm relaxing.
5 Physics **is** what Charlie studied in college, too.
6 Politics **is** slowly moving to the left in this country at the moment.
7 **Is** the mathematics you're doing in your class very difficult or can you do it easily?
8 Neither my presentation nor my essay **was** good enough to get me a passing grade.

9 The Bahamas **has** very warm weather at this time of year, so I'd recommend going there.
10 Either English or Spanish **is** the language that people most commonly learn at our school.

67.5

1 Not given
2 True
3 False
4 True
5 False
6 True
7 Not given

67.6

1 *Jungle Adventures* **is** the new television show that everyone is talking about.
2 The US **is** the largest country in North America when it comes to population.
3 This information **needs** to be shared with everyone else in the team right away.
4 Neither the adults nor the children **were** interested in the entertainment they provided.
5 I think politics **isn't** a topic that you should discuss when you're making small talk.
6 Neither my black suit nor my dark blue one **is** clean enough to wear.
7 Neither my phone nor Clark's phone **is** getting any signal at the moment.
8 Either the lemon or the lime **was** too strong in the sauce he made.
9 Everyone in Jack's family **is** interested in birdwatching, so he's going on a trip with them.
10 Neither history nor business **is** interesting to me.

68

68.1

1 Last night my mom called me to say that my grandma was very ill. It was **such** a shock.
2 Hong Kong is **such** a fascinating city. You should go there if you get the chance.
3 You've got **such** a difficult job. I don't think I'm patient enough to be a teacher.
4 He carried the baby **so** gently, as if he was scared she might break.
5 I can't believe I've got a job in Paris! It's **so** exciting!
6 That movie was **so** gripping. It was almost three hours long, but the time flew past!
7 You've got **such** a beautiful smile. Has anyone ever told you that?
8 It's always **such** a pleasure to spend time with Tom. He's a lovely man.
9 Keira is **so** generous. Did you know that she gave $250 to charity last month?
10 I'm not surprised the police stopped Mick. He drives **so** dangerously.
11 Thanks for responding **so** quickly. That was really efficient of you.
12 It was **such** a surprise when my cat turned up after being missing for six months!
13 You behaved **so** rudely in front of our guests. I felt quite embarrassed.
14 You learn languages **so** easily! Can you share your secret with me?
15 I think Martin is **so** brave. I couldn't do a bungee jump.
16 Your present job is **so** interesting. Is it also well paid, unlike the previous one?
17 *Back to City Life* was **such** a great book. I want to read it again!
18 It was **such** a relief when the doctor told me the good news. I've been celebrating.
19 I've had **such** a fun evening. Can I see you again tomorrow?

68.2

1 The medicine works so effectively **that we have a 98 percent cure rate.**
2 It was such a bad injury **that she was off work for months.**
3 It was such an unexpected result **that everyone was surprised.**
4 He recovered so quickly **that he was back at work within two weeks.**
5 Brian is so intelligent **that he's sure to go on to college.**
6 The doctor was so reassuring **that I didn't really feel worried.**

68.3

1 It's **such** a beautiful day. Why don't we go for a walk on the beach?
2 I am **so** grateful to the doctors that I'm going to send them a thank you card.
3 It was **such** a thrill to spend time with my grandchildren.
4 The movie was **so** boring that Pauline and I fell asleep.
5 It was **such** a surprise that I didn't know what to say.
6 Chantelle is **so** helpful. She's a lovely young woman.
7 Tom reacted **so** bravely when the doctor told him he had to go into the hospital.

68.4

1 **So** few people eat enough fruit and vegetables every day.
2 **So** little funding is available for research into age-related diseases.
3 There are so **many** medicines to choose from for your condition.
4 **So** many wonderful people work in our health service.
5 Charis feels so **much** better since she started doing more exercise.
6 **So** few students are bright enough to become doctors and engineers.
7 So **much** effort goes into making sure the patients are comfortable.
8 **So** little money is spent on healthcare services for the disabled.
9 **So** many people know someone who has been in the hospital.
10 There has been so **much** amazing progress in the field of medicine in the last decade.
11 So **much** time and money has been put into designing this new hospital.
12 It's so **much** easier to play sports since I lost a lot of weight.

68.5

1 Lyndsey is such an inspiration to me. I follow everything she posts on her blog.
2 Jamie made such an effort to find the right present for my birthday.
3 I have so much free time these days, I've started some new hobbies.
4 The exam was so easy that I wondered whether I had missed something.
5 You play the piano so beautifully! Can you play it again, please?
6 There are so few opportunities for people who can't read or write.

68.6

1 These stray cats are **such** a nuisance.
2 I feel **so** much calmer after a walk in the rain.
3 You opened the door **so** quietly last night.
4 *Color* was **so** amazing that I watched it again.
5 There are **so** many shirts to choose from.
6 It's **such** a lovely dress that I'm going to buy it.
7 My dog is always hungry. She eats **so** much.

69

69.1

1 My brother has **a** pet spider. I hate it!
2 I'd like a piece of cake and **an** orange juice, please.
3 **The** airplane was invented by the Wright brothers.
4 Can I ask you **a** question?
5 I can see **a** man over there with blond hair. But I'm not sure that it's Josh.
6 **The** bicycle is a very common form of transportation all over the world.
7 I have **an** arrangement with my colleague, where we share the commute to work.
8 There was **an** awkward silence when I asked Tami how her job was going.
9 **The** hummingbird is one of the smallest birds on the planet.

10 Would you like **a** cup of coffee?
11 **The** sandwich is named after the Earl of Sandwich, who supposedly invented it.

69.2

1 **An** apple a day keeps the doctor away.
2 **[-]** Women are still rarely paid as much as men.
3 **[-]** Human beings are the number-one predator on Earth.
4 There's **an** advertisement for a new smartwatch in today's paper.
5 **The** electric car is now a reality in many countries.
6 **[-]** Students usually don't have very much money.
7 **The** panda is in danger of becoming extinct.

69.3

1 I'm afraid there isn't a Mark Wilson in this office. Have you got the right name?
2 Are you saying you're good friends with John Smith?
3 This is my sister's best friend, Kristin Wyatt.
4 Let me introduce you to the manager of our company, Isaac Myers.
5 I don't know of a Lucy Armitage. Is there anyone else you'd like to speak to?
6 You don't mean the Cherry Baldwin, the famous actress, do you?

69.4

1 I can't find **a** Mikaela Zimmerman in the company directory. Are you sure she works here?
2 Did you manage to get yourself **a** ticket for the concert?
3 **The** cell phone has become a much smaller and lighter device in recent years.
4 Allow me to introduce you to my fiancé, **Brad** Livingstone.
5 I had **a** delicious meal at that new Italian restaurant last night.
6 There's no record of **a** Thomas Luckett ever having lived here.
7 **The** dog is often described as man's best friend. / **Dogs are** often described as man's best friend.
8 Can you believe I was sitting next to **the** Elizabeth Parker? She's such a huge star!
9 **The** dress is often the most important thing for a bride at her wedding.
10 This is my boss, **Francesco** Coppola.
11 We usually have **breakfast** at about 7:15am.
12 **The** internet has revolutionized our lives since its invention.

69.5

1 The company has captured **a significant share of the market.**
2 The tallest waterfalls in the world **are the famous Angel Falls in Venezuela.**
3 Izmir is the city with **the oldest working bridge.**
4 There isn't a Philip Fernandez here, **so you must have the wrong number.**
5 There was a good atmosphere in **the office until Jane started working here.**
6 We all know that the brain controls **everything that happens in our bodies.**
7 I couldn't believe that I was actually **sitting next to the Jo Halls. It was amazing!**

69.6

1 The Hawksbill turtle is a species that is critically endangered.
2 The Stephen Hawking told me I would become a scientist one day!
3 Televisions are now found in almost every home in the city.
4 I'm afraid that there isn't a Susie Fa on this list.

Agradecimientos

Los editores expresan su agradecimiento a: Jo Kent, Trish Burrow y Emma Watkins por la redacción de textos adicionales; Thomas Booth, Helen Fanthorpe, Helen Leech, Carrie Lewis y Vicky Richards por su asistencia editorial; Stephen Bere, Sarah Hilder, Amy Child, Fiona Macdonald y Simon Murrell por sus tareas de diseño; Simon Mumford por los mapas y banderas nacionales; Peter Chrisp por la comprobación de datos; Penny Hands, Amanda Learmonth y Carrie Lewis por la corrección de pruebas; Elizabeth Wise por el índice; Tatiana Boyko, Rory Farrell, Clare Joyce y Viola Wang por sus ilustraciones adicionales; Liz Hammond por la edición de los guiones de audio y la gestión de las grabaciones; Hannah Bowen y Scarlett O'Hara por compilar los guiones de audio; Richard Hughes y Jordan Killiard por la mezcla y el master de las grabaciones de audio; Heather Hughes, Tommy Callan, Tom Morse, Gillian Reid y Sonia Charbonnier por su apoyo técnico creativo; Priyanka Kharbanda, Suefa Lee, Shramana Purkayastha, Isha Sharma y Sheryl Sadana por su apoyo editorial; Yashashvi Choudhary, Jaileen Kaur, Bhavika Mathur, Richa Verma, Anita Yadav y Apurva Agarwal por su apoyo en diseño; Deepak Negi y Nishwan Rasool por la documentación iconográfica; y Rohan Sinha por sus tareas de gestión y su apoyo moral.
DK agradece su permiso para la reproduccion de sus fotografías a: 19 Peter Cook (c) **Dorling Kindersley**, cortesía del Pima Air and Space Museum, Tuscon, Arizona (centro). 146 **Dreamstime.com:** Smellme (arriba a la derecha).

Los derechos del resto de las imágenes son propiedad de DK.
Para más información visita: **www.dk.com/uk/information/contact-us**.